翻译名师
讲评系列

A CASEBOOK IN

UN DOCUMENT TRANSLATION

联合国文件翻译
译·注·评

清华大学出版社
北京

内 容 简 介

本书旨在培养译者通过宏观思维、逻辑思维、批判性思维和调查研究，发现和解决翻译中的理解、表达和变通问题的能力。本书的练习材料选自12份联合国文件，由青年译者翻译后，笔者按照联合国的标准精心修改，并详加解释。译文修改过程显示，即使译者没有任何专业背景，只要学会思考、学会查证，仍然可以接近甚至达到专业的翻译水平。本书传授的理念和方法，同样适用于其他体裁文件的翻译。

本书供打算从事或已经从事联合国文件翻译的读者学习参考，也可用作翻译专业的教材。

图书在版编目（CIP）数据

联合国文件翻译：译·注·评 / 李长栓，雷萌著. —北京：清华大学出版社，2020. 1（2024.11重印）
（翻译名师讲评系列）
ISBN 978-7-302-53702-1

Ⅰ. ①联… Ⅱ. ①李… ②雷… Ⅲ. ①联合国-文件-英语-翻译 Ⅳ. ①H315.9

中国版本图书馆CIP数据核字（2019）第184329号

责任编辑：刘 艳
封面设计：子 一
责任校对：王凤芝
责任印制：杨 艳

出版发行：清华大学出版社
  网 址：https://www.tup.com.cn，https://www.wqxuetang.com
  地 址：北京清华大学学研大厦A座   邮 编：100084
  社 总 机：010-83470000   邮 购：010-62786544
  投稿与读者服务：010-62776969, c-service@tup.tsinghua.edu.cn
  质量反馈：010-62772015, zhiliang@tup.tsinghua.edu.cn
印 装 者：涿州市般润文化传播有限公司
经 销：全国新华书店
开 本：185mm×260mm   印 张：13.25   字 数：301千字
版 次：2020年1月第1版   印 次：2024年11月第7次印刷
定 价：58.00元

产品编号：069946-01

面对目前翻译质量不尽如人意的局面,我们感到有工作可做。

应该说,沿学术体系写的教科书为数已相当可观,有些在翻译教学上也起到一些作用。但是总体看来,汗牛充栋的教程、津要、指南、技巧目不暇接,却并未对学生翻译水平的提高有多大影响。

沿学术体系展开的翻译教学是否必要? 当然必要;但这类翻译教学是否有效却值得怀疑。教科书把翻译纳入体系讲解,但是翻译的实际情况从来都是纷杂繁乱、有悖体系的。过于条陈缕析、逻辑严密的教学对于学术研究至关重要,但却并不是指导翻译实践的最佳途径。学生会把系统的课堂知识机械地应用到纷杂的翻译实践上,结果他们脑子里总想着那些成体系的知识,却拿不出解决实际问题的方案。

这套丛书就是提供具体解决方案的。系列中的每一本书都从翻译实践出发,从具体的文本中引出点评、注释、分析、讨论的话题,如需讲技巧就讲技巧,若该谈理论则谈理论,不凭空营造议题,不刻意强谈理论。具体而言,书以单元编排,大部分的书每单元都以一篇短小的原文和学生或新手的译文开始,辅以简明扼要的点评,再加上一篇或多篇参考译文,最后是短文一则,或借文中问题发挥,或择宏观题目议论,语言浅显易懂,力避故作高深的长篇大论。

本丛书循循教导,指点迷津,是一套适合自学的读物,但它也是一套与众不同的翻译教材。丛书抛弃了从技巧、议题、理论切入的编排方式,让学生开门见山,马上面对文本。传统教材中讲解的方方面面都自然地融汇在对文本的分析、点评和讲解中,所涉内容广泛,点评深入浅出,议论提纲挈领。为方便起见,有的分册书后另附原文数段,供布置作业之用。教师可将这套丛书作为主要教材,也可当成辅助材料。

我们有幸邀请到翻译界几位著名专家撰写这套丛书。他们都是各自领域的顶尖人物,都有多年的教学或实践经验。可以说,丛书是这几位作者多年教学与实践的结晶。

读者若能从这套书中有些收获,进而提高自己的翻译水平,那么我们的目的也就达到了。

叶子南

明德大学蒙特雷国际研究学院

本书旨在培养译者通过宏观思维、逻辑思维、批判性思维和调查研究，发现和解决翻译中理解（Comprehension）、表达（Expression）和变通（Adaptation）问题的能力。

翻译包括三个行为：理解、表达、变通。理解是表达的基础，译者对原文的理解要接近、达到，甚至超过作者的水平。理解包括了解写作背景和专业背景以及文本本身，如所有的概念、概念之间的关系、句子之间和段落之间的关系；理解还包括对翻译情景的了解。

表达是指用读者可以接受的方式，把原作的意思或作者的意图忠实传递出来，包括只能表达作者的意思或者原作中隐含的意思，不能添加译者自己的意思；还包括译文所使用的语言，如用词、搭配、句子结构、衔接方式等，要符合译文读者的习惯，语言的风格与原文接近。

变通是指在直译存在困难的情况下，译者通过省略、补充、变换说法等手段，有效传递原文的信息或者实现翻译的目的。

翻译中遇到的理解、表达、变通问题，主要通过宏观思维、逻辑思维、批判性思维和调查研究来解决。

宏观思维能力是指译者能够在每次翻译活动中，即使委托人没有告知，也去主动探寻6个W和1个H：Who is speaking to whom? About what? When, where and why? And how? 即原文的作者和读者是谁，主题是什么，写作的时间、地点、原因，以及原文的写作方式（指how, 即语言风格）。

凡是值得翻译的文章，都不是无病呻吟，而是有感而发。译者只有了解作者和写作背景，才能真正理解作者的观点和文章细节，仅仅从语言的角度分析原文是远远不能满足翻译需求的。当然，了解原文的写作风格并有意识地在译文中反映出来，也是翻译活动的要求之一。

同时，对原文写作背景的了解，还有助于译者作出变通取舍的决定。因为原文所处的交际情景（社会文化背景、读者的知识等）和译文所处的交际情景不同，往往迫使译者对原文进行一定程度的干预，以便读者更好理解原文的意图。

宏观思维还包括译者主动了解翻译的情景，包括委托人是谁、译文读者是谁、为什么要翻译、译文在什么时间和地点使用。这些信息同样服务于变通取舍的决定。

逻辑思维能力是指译者能够抓住作者的思路，理解原文的中心思想，包括发现文章与外部世界的联系，文章前后的关联，各种衔接关系、从属关系和同义关系；还包括能够在译文中以符合逻辑的方式再现原文的逻辑。

批判性思维能力是指译者能够通过逻辑思维和调查研究，发现原文的瑕疵，包括作者对事实描述的瑕疵和语言表述的瑕疵，并能够根据实际情况决定如何处理这些瑕疵，如保留瑕疵不变、自行纠正、请作者纠正，或者通过注释向读者作个交代。

批判性思维还包括对词典、网络、其他译本当中的译法持批判立场，重新审视原有译法的准确性，并通过思考和调查研究，给出符合情景或更加准确的译文。

查证能力是指针对宏观思维、逻辑思维、批判性思维中发现的理解、表达、变通问题，能够通过互联网（主要是谷歌）查找相关信息，通过分析论证作出知情决定。

本书节选了笔者参与翻译过的一些联合国文件作为练习材料，每个单元分为"学习要点""背景说明""练习和讲解"三大部分。

学习要点以清单形式列出，概括了练习中关注的思维方法、调查研究方法和理解、表达、变通问题，包含以下内容：

思维方法

★ **宏观思维**

★ **逻辑思维**

★ **批判性思维**

调查研究方法

★ **文本内**

★ **文本外**

理解

★ **补充知识**

1. 写作背景

2. 专业背景

3. 翻译背景

★ **理解语言**

1. 概念

2. 关系

3. 中心思想

表达

★ **意思准确**

★ **符合形式**

变通

★ **内容增删**

★ **形式变动**

背景说明介绍了文件出处、文件背景和联合国相关背景。练习和讲解部分包括原文、原译、改译和对改译的详细解释；每段解释之前，标注了这段解释的要点，并在单元开头的"学习要点"部分加以汇总。请注意：段落编号是原始文件中的编号，有些段落并不连续。这样做的目的，是迫使大家上网查找原始文件，通过上下文来理解，从而培养大家宏观思维的能力。

实际上，通过思考和调查研究解决的问题，都可以归入理解、表达或变通。但为了凸显思考和调查研究的重要性，把一些典型的例子归入了这两个类别。

各单元实际列出的要点，不一定全部体现在清单中，清单中的分类也不一定严密。读者出于研究需要，可以再作整理。

使用本书时，读者可以先找到原始文件*（注意：网上找到的文件与所选段落可能有细微差别，这是因为翻译之后原文又有编辑调整），通读或浏览文件全文，然后再翻译选定段落。在自己练习的基础上，参考"原译"和"改译"，以及对改译的解释说明。在看完第一篇的讲解之后，读者就会明白翻译一篇文章多么不易。在后续单元的练习中，可以按照前面掌握的方法，精雕细琢地进行翻译。

本书的共同作者北京外国语大学商学院的雷萌老师，是我的学生。她毕业后主动提出帮我做一些事情，于是我请她帮我整理以前修改过的文件，所以才有了这本书。雷萌老师从我众多的文件中精心挑选了12篇，做成了原文、原译、改译对照的格式，并初步提供了讲解。我在此基础上进行全面修改和补充，使讲解从关注语言表达改为侧重于意思的准确传达，包括提供背景信息、专业知识、辨析相关词语等。

编写本书的过程中，我最深刻的感触是译文永远难以做到尽善尽美。已经提交的译稿，今天看起来还有不少瑕疵，不得不做更多修改。所以，如果大家发现官方译本中有不当之处，也属于正常现象，因为每次翻译都受到时间和精力的限制，无法像编写教材那样，把每个地方都调查清楚。尽管如此，读者也不要降低对自己的要求；要通过对本书的学习，知道在条件允许的情况下，只要认真思考并做好调查研究，就有能力译出高质量译文。

最后，我要感谢参与译文制作和书稿审读的同学：费晨、冯怿之、李梦鸿、刘露、马尚、倪霓、彭春婷、祁琳、沈冠华、史金玉、王佳舜、王睿、王子慧、王子若、杨昉、杨西妮、喻凡、张湘龙、郑晨。

李长栓

2019年9月21日　北京

---

* 可以通过文号（如A/C.6/73/SR.13），在联合国正式文件系统（documents.un.org）中查找文件的原文和译文；也可以从清华大学出版社网站下载查阅：ftp://ftp.tup.tsinghua.edu.cn/；还可以截取原文的任意单词串，加双引号，通过谷歌检索获取。

目　录

第 **1** 单元 联合国大会和经社理事会会议简要记录(一)

📖 学习要点

思维方法

★ **宏观思维**

了解宏观背景

★ **逻辑思维**

根据上下文确定词义

★ **批判性思维**

批判看待他人译法

调查研究方法

1. 查作者名字

2. 查英文释义

理解

★ **补充知识**

1. decile

2. disposable income

3. domestic demand

4. economic cycle

5. fiscal management

6. Gini coefficient

7. interest group

8. intergenerational mobility

9. monetary policy

10. output

11. productive investment

12. spillover

13. supply-side reform

14. structural inequality

15. transfer policy

16. 挖掘文字背后的含义

★ **理解语言**

1. 辨析词义

2. 正确判断修饰关系

3. 在理解的基础上翻译

4. 理解每个单词

表达

★ **意思准确**

1. 根据英文解释确定译法

2. access的译法

3. 拘泥于原文形式导致意思扭曲

4. 注意表达的细微差异

5. 斟酌用词

★ **符合形式**

1. 注意搭配

2. 语言简洁

3. 注意语言节奏

4. 使用常见说法

5. 注意词义褒贬

变通

1. 尽量不增词

2. 增词使含义清晰

3. 概念尽量直译

4. 尊重约定译法

5. 适当变通

6. 以名词倒推动词译法

背景说明

联合国系统包括六大机构——大会（General Assembly）、安全理事会（Security Council）、经济及社会理事会（Economic and Social Council）、秘书处（The Secretariat）、国际法院（International Court of Justice）和托管理事会（The Trusteeship Council）。1994年，联合国最后一块托管领土（trust territory）帕劳独立后，联合国第六大机构托管理事会停止运行。

在联合国的六大机构中，有五个机构的总部设在联合国总部（United Nations Headquarters, UNHQ）纽约，只有国际法院位于荷兰海牙。联合国驻日内瓦办事处（United Nations Office at Geneva, UNOG）、驻维也纳办事处（United Nations Office at Vienna, UNOV）和驻内罗毕办事处（United Nations Office at Nairobi, UNON）设有联合国专门机构（specialized agencies）总部。其他联合国实体（entities）则分布在全球各地。联合国有六种官方语言，分别为阿拉伯文、中文、英文、法文、俄文和西班牙文。根据《联合国特权和豁免公约》，联合国及其机构在驻在国具有外交豁免权。

"大会"（不是指一般的大型会议，而是指"联合国大会"，国内媒体简称"联大"）下设众多委员会，如第一委员会（裁军与国际安全）、第二委员会（经济和金融）、第三委员会（社会、人道和文化）、第四委员会（特别政治和非殖民化）、第五委员会（行政和预算）、第六委员会（法务）、总务委员会（General Committee，审议大会及各委员会的工作进展并提出建议）、全权证书委员会（Credentials Committee，负责审查各会员国代表的证书并向大会汇报）。其中，第一委员会至第六委员会称为"主要委员会"（Main Committees）。本书附录1和附录2中有联合国系统的详细介绍。

联合国由全体会员国组成，每年9月至12月集中举行常会（即"大会"），并在之后视需要开会。根据1945年10月24日签署生效的《联合国宪章》（The United Nations Charter），大会有权讨论宪章范围内的任何问题或事项，并向会员国和安理会提出建议。大会接收并审议安理会及联合国其他机构的报告；选举安理会非常任理事国、经济及社会理事会和托管理事会的理事国；与安理会分别选举国际法院的法官；根据安理会的推荐，批准接纳新会员国和委任秘书长。联合国的预算和会费分摊（assessments）须经大会讨论决定。每一个会员国在大会有一个投票权。

本单元选自经济及社会理事会与联合国大会第二委员会于2013年在联合国总部纽约举行的关于"不平等、增长和全球经济展望"的联席会议的简要记录（文号: A/C.2/68/SR.17）。会议讨论了2008年全球金融危机爆发后世界经济发展的状况，分析了当下存在的挑战，并提出了解决方案。选段保留了原文的段落编号（注意: 编号不一定连续）。建议译者先浏览全文再来翻译。全文可在联合国正式文件系统中查找，具体来说，就是用文号进行检索。其中的A表示Assembly，C.2表示第二委员会，68表示第68届会议，SR表示Summary Record（简要记录），17表示第17次会议。文件系统中有六种语言的版本，包括中文，但练习之前请先不要查看。即使查看官方译文，也不要把官方译文看成是标准译文，因为这些译文大多是匆忙中完成的，也难免存在瑕疵。

练习和讲解

> **▷ 原文**

4. Ms. Akhtar (Department of Economic and Social Affairs) said that the primary economic risk had to do with possible *spillovers*[1] related to the exit from unconventional *monetary policies*[2].

> **✍ 原译**

4. 阿赫塔尔女士（经济和社会事务部）说，目前经济面临的首要风险是与终止非常规货币政策有关的副作用。

> **✍ 改译**

4. Akhtar女士（经济和社会事务部）说，目前主要的经济风险是非常规货币政策终止后的溢出效应。

> **★ 解 析**

1 【补充知识】spillovers 或 spillover effects（"溢出效应"）是一个经济学术语，需要翻译出来。spillover effects 是指 economic events in one context that occur because of something else in a seemingly unrelated context (Wikipedia: spillovers)，如 "The economic benefits of increased trade are the spillover effects anticipated in the formation of multilateral alliances of many of the regional nation states."，又如 "Orders from a rendering plant are negative spillover effects upon its neighbours."。溢出效应既有积极方面，也有消极方面，强调的是一件事情的外部效应（externality），而不是简单的"副作用"。

2 【补充知识】货币政策（monetary policy）指中央银行为实现既定的经济目标（如稳定物价、促进经济增长、实现充分就业和平衡国际收支），运用各种工具调节货币供应量和利率，进而影响宏观经济的方针和措施的总和。货币政策有常规性（conventional）与非常规性（unconventional）之分。常规性货币工具包括法定存款准备金率（statutory reserve requirement ratio）、再贴现率（re-discount rate）、公开市场业务（open market operation）等。而当经济衰退或经济危机十分严重时，常规性工具不足以调节经济，此时必须诉诸非常规性工具，包括前瞻指引（forward guidance）、量化宽松（quantitative easing）、收益率曲线控制（yield curve control）、负利率（negative interest rate），等等。请看相关英文资料：

The financial and economic crisis of 2007–2009 witnessed unprecedented policy responses from central banks. As the first responders, central banks acted aggressively, lowering policy interest rates and introducing extraordinary measures to provide liquidity to short-term funding markets. The intensification of the crisis in the autumn of 2008 and the collapse of real economic activity prompted many central banks to further lower policy rates, although their ability to continue to do so became constrained as short-term interest rates approached zero. Consequently, numerous unconventional monetary policy tools were introduced to provide additional monetary easing. These included new or expanded credit facilities, as well as large-scale purchases of government securities (often referred to as quantitative easing, QE). (investopedia.com)

再看什么是"量化宽松政策"（QE）：

量化宽松主要是指中央银行在实行零利率或近似零利率政策后，通过购买国债等中长期债券增加基础货币供给，向市场注入大量流动性资金的干预方式，以鼓励开支和借贷，也被简化地形容为间接增印钞票。

量化宽松政策所涉及的政府债券不仅金额庞大，而且周期也较长。一般来说，只有在利率等常规工具不再有效的情况下，货币当局才会采取这种极端做法。（百度百科：量化宽松）

【尊重约定译法】从这些解释来看，QE 应当翻译为"数量宽松"才便于理解。顾名思义，"量化"是把本来不易用数量表达的事物用数量来表达，放在此处比较费解。不过，既然已经约定俗成，译者可以沿用。

▶ 原文

8. Structural reforms were needed to *transform a cyclical recovery*[1] in advanced economies and *stimulate domestic demand*[2] in emerging markets. As the exit from the easy monetary policy *stance developed*[3], careful *fiscal management*[4] and *normalized private sector credit growth supported by structural reforms*[5] would be critical to sustainable growth.

✍ 原译

8. 需进行结构改革改善先进经济体的周期性复苏问题，和促进新兴市场的内需。随着各国正逐步撤销宽松的货币政策，建立审慎的财政管理制度，和通过结构改革增加对私营部门的借贷正常化，对可持续增长会起到至关重要的作用。

✍ 改译

8. 需通过结构性改革，转变先进经济体的周期性复苏，刺激新兴市场的内需。随着各国逐步表明将退出宽松的货币政策，如能实行审慎的财政管理，促进私营部门借贷增长正常化，辅之以结构调整，将对可持续增长起到关键作用。

★ 解 析

■1■ 【补充知识】经济周期（economic cycle）又称商业周期（business cycle），是指经济运行中周期性出现的经济扩张与经济紧缩交替更迭的一种现象，如下图所示：

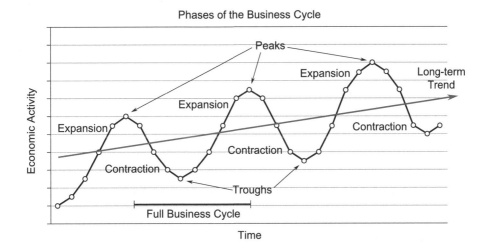

Economic cycle refers to the period of time during which an economy moves from a state of expansion to a state of contraction, before expanding again. In practice, a cycle should contain a phase of expansion or recovery (to a peak) and a phase of slowdown or recession (to a trough). If the rates of growth and contraction are very strong, an economy could be "booming" for a while at its peak, while the trough could see a phase of depression or stagnation. A trend governed by a business or economic cycle is termed cyclical. (lexicon.ft)

因此，cyclical recovery 指的就是在商业周期中，经济周期性复苏的过程。

【挖掘文字背后的含义】那么，什么叫 transform a cyclical recovery？我们可能会翻译成"改变周期性复苏"，但这又是什么意思？上网查这几个关键词，看到一篇演讲，题目叫 "Turn Cyclical Recovery into a Structural Recovery"（《把周期性复苏变为结构性复苏》），正好与本句话的意思相匹配。检索中文，也发现标题为《德拉基：结构性改革将会使周期性复苏转变为结构性复苏》的文章。由此可以推断，结构性改革（structural reforms）带来的结果叫作"结构性复苏"（structural recovery）。什么是结构性改革？看欧洲中央银行提供的解释：

What are structural reforms?

Structural reforms are essentially measures that change the fabric of an economy, the institutional and regulatory framework in which businesses and people operate. They are designed to ensure the economy is fit and better able to realise its growth potential in a balanced way.

Structural reforms work on the supply side of the economy. By tackling obstacles to the efficient—and fair—production of goods and services, they should help increase productivity, investment and employment. This can be done in many ways. For example, the overall business environment can be improved through regulations supporting more flexible labour markets, a simpler tax system or less red tape, making it easier for companies to conduct business and plan for the future. Households, in turn, may benefit from cheaper (and better) products, which also means more money to spend on other goods.

In addition, reforms can be targeted at specific sectors, such as those encouraging innovation in key industries. What is important, however, is that growth is balanced. This means that factors like social fairness and inclusion are also taken into account. Indeed, reforms which increase access to education or lower tax evasion and corruption would help support economic growth while promoting social fairness. (ecb.europa.eu)

其中的一句话"Structural reforms work on the supply side of the economy.",让我们想到中国的供给侧结构性改革（supply-side structural reforms）："供给侧结构性改革针对结构失衡、供需错配的经济现状，以改革为手段，推进经济结构调整，通过减少无效和低端供给，扩大有效和中高端供给，促进要素流动和优化配置，同时重视供给侧与需求侧的协同发力，实现更高水平的供需平衡"。（百度百科：供给侧结构性改革）

【补充知识】"供给侧"（supply-side）与"需求侧"（demand-side）是相对应的。需求侧有投资、消费、出口"三驾马车"，这三驾马车决定短期经济增长率；而供给侧则有劳动力、土地、资本、创新"四大要素"，这四大要素在充分配置条件下所实现的增长率即中长期潜在经济增长率。供给侧结构性改革旨在调整经济结构，使要素实现最优配置，提升经济增长的质量和数量。供给侧管理强调通过提高生产能力来促进经济增长，而需求侧管理则强调可以通过提高社会需求来促进经济增长，两者对于如何拉动经济增长有着截然不同的理念。（百度百科：供给侧结构性改革）

2 【补充知识】domestic demand 为"内需"，即国内的需求，包括投资需求和消费需求，即三驾马车中的前两驾。刺激内需就是通过扩大投资和消费来带动国民经济的增长。

3 【适当变通】develop a stance 就是形成一个立场，译文进行了灵活处理。这句也可以译为"随着各国逐步形成退出宽松货币政策的立场"。

4 【补充知识】财政管理（fiscal management）是指政府为了履行职能，对所需的物质资源进行的决策、计划、组织、协调和监督活动的总称；简言之，就是政府筹集、使用和管理资金的活动。它既是政府管理活动的重要组成部分，又是政府活动的物质保障。财政管理对于政府管理的重要性，是由财政的政治、经济双重属性决定的。（MBA 智库百科：财政管理）fiscal 的意思是 of or relating to taxation, public revenues, or public debt。（merriam-webster.com）

5 【正确判断修饰关系】supported by structural reforms 应该是修饰 fiscal management 和 normalized private sector credit growth。因为本段第一句谈的就是结构性改革；这句话是说，除了结构性改革，还需要采取另外两项政策。宏观调控有两大政策工具：财政政策和货币政策。财政政策主要是指政府支出、税收政策等，是由财政部门制定的；货币政策主要是指利率、货币发行量、存款准备金率等政策，是中央银行（人民银行）制定的。fiscal management 属于财政政策，而 normalized private sector credit growth 属于货币政策。翻译专业性内容需要具备一定的专业知识，否则即使翻译出来，也不敢确定是否正确。改译没有明确体现修饰关系，但可以理解为修饰两者。

▶原文

9. The crisis had left deep scars, including *output and financial losses and major job dislocation*[1]. Almost 600 million new jobs were needed. Social distress must be eased. While discussions of the MDGs referred to the need to lift some 1.2 billion people out of *extreme poverty*[2], evidence had not yet emerged regarding how that number might be affected by the crisis. In addition, inequality had *consequences that would linger and threaten sustained growth and development*[3].

原译

9. 此次危机留下了很深的伤痕，包括产量和金融方面的损失以及严重失业。差不多需要创造6亿个新工作岗位。社会问题亟待缓解。尽管在讨论千年发展目标时提到了需要使约12亿人摆脱极端贫困，但目前还没有迹象表明此次危机会对这些人造成怎样的影响。另外，不平等现象会造成放缓可持续增长和发展的后果。

改译

9. 此次危机留下了很深的伤痕：产出下降、金融行业受损、失业问题严重。现在需要创造近6亿个工作岗位，缓解社会压力。尽管在讨论千年发展目标时提到需要使大约12亿人摆脱极端贫困，但目前还没有证据表明此次危机可能对这些人造成怎样的影响。另外，不平等现象可能导致长期后果，威胁可持续增长和发展。

★解 析

1 【补充知识】Output in economics is the quantity of goods or services produced in a given time period, by a firm, industry, or country, whether consumed or used for further production. The concept of national output is essential in the field of macroeconomics. (Wikipedia: output) output 准确来讲应该是 national output，即"国民产出"。根据资料：

The Need to Understand the Impact of the Crisis on Potential Output

The crisis is already having a dramatic impact on Gross Domestic Product (GDP). In its economic forecast released on 4 May, the Commission estimated that GDP will contract by about 4% in 2009 and by 0.1% in 2010 in both the EU 27 and the euro area. The longer-term repercussions on potential output are however less clear. (ec.europa.eu)

国内生产总值（GDP）是计算国民产出最常用的方法，也是衡量国家（或地区）经济状况的指标。此处也可以译为"国民产出"。

【注意语言节奏】"产量和金融方面的损失以及严重失业"改为"产出下降、金融行业受损、失业问题严重"在节奏上更好一些。

2 【概念尽量直译】extreme poverty 在联合国有些文件中译为"极端贫困"，有些文件中译为"赤贫"。前者更切合字面意思，所以译文选用"极端贫困"。

3 【在理解的基础上翻译】原译对 linger 的理解不到位。linger 为不及物动词，意思是 to take a long time to leave or disappear。原文的结构是 consequences that would linger and [that would] threaten。

▶ 原文

10. In some economies, *growth was associated with reduced inequality*[1], while in others growth had had the opposite effect on income distribution. China and Brazil had *registered*[2] high growth rates from 1995 through 2005, but had very different outcomes with regard to inequality. The *Gini coefficient*[3] had increased in China from 0.35 to 0.42, while during the same period it had declined from 0.6 to 0.57 in Brazil.

✐ 原译

10. 在一些经济体中，增长通常与不平等现象减少有关，但在另一些经济体中，增长对收入分配的作用是相反的。中国和巴西从1995年到2005年双双录得了高增长率，但两国不平等现象方面的结果却截然不同。中国的基尼系数从0.35升到了0.42，而巴西同期的基尼系数却从0.6降到了0.57。

✐ 改译

10. 在一些经济体，增长减少了不平等现象，但在另一些经济体，增长对收入分配的作用则相反。中国和巴西从1995年到2005年都取得了高速增长，但增长对减少不平等的效果却截然不同。中国的基尼系数从0.35升到了0.42，而巴西同期的基尼系数却从0.6降到了0.57。

★ 解 析

1 【拘泥于原文形式导致意思扭曲】本段话讲的是，经济增长在不同国家带来的结果不同。有些国家（比如中国）经济增长导致贫富差距加大，有些国家（比如巴西）经济增长却缩小了贫富差距。本句话的字面意思是，不平等的减少伴随着经济增长，但实际上表示因果关系，即经济增长减少了不平等现象，这一点从下半句（while in others growth had had the opposite effect on income distribution）可以清楚推断出来。汉语的"与……有关"（"增长通常与不平等现象减少有关"）意思是"由……造成的"，后者是前者的原因，所以，原译的意思正好相反。出错的原因，不一定是译者的理解问题，可能是选词不当带来的意外后果。

2 【使用常见说法】Register means to indicate by a record, as instruments do; or to enroll in a school or course of study. (dictionary.com) 它既有"录取"之意，又可表示"记录到"。此处是后者的意思。原译"录得"即记录到，意思没有错，但显然不是汉语常见的用法，因此可灵活译为"取得""获得"等。

3 【补充知识】基尼系数（Gini coefficient）是衡量贫富差距的一个重要指标：

The Gini coefficient is a measure of inequality developed by the Italian statistician Corrado Gini and published in 1912. It is usually used to measure income inequality, but can be used to measure any form of uneven distribution. The Gini coefficient is a number between 0 and 1, where 0 corresponds with perfect equality (where everyone has the same income) and 1 corresponds with perfect inequality (where one person has all the income, and everyone else has zero income). The Gini index is the Gini coefficient expressed in percentage form, and is equal to the Gini coefficient multiplied by 100. (Wikipedia: Gini coefficient)

▶ 原文

12. *Greater inequality was associated with less sustained growth*[1], and a decrease in inequality increased the expected length of *a growth spell*[2] by 50 percent. In developing countries, concentration of assets *had been found*[3] to inhibit *productive investment*[4] and restrict growth potential. Growing levels of inequality in *access*[5], opportunities and income led to inadequate education, health care and social protection, *causing volatility, crises*[6] and *diminished productivity*[7]. *Rising inequalities had been associated with excessively debt-financed consumption and investment patterns that had contributed to financial and economic crises*[8].

✐ 原译

12. 不平等现象加剧往往与相对不可持续的增长有关，而不平等现象减轻会对预测增长期的准确率增加50%。有发现表明，在发展中国家，资产过度集中会抑制生产性投资和限制增长潜力。权利门槛、机会和收入方面的不平等现象加剧会导致教育、医疗保健和社会保障不足，从而使社会脆弱，危机频繁，生产力退化。现已发现不平等现象加剧与过度的负债消费和导致了金融和经济危机的投资模式有关。

✐ 改译

12. 不平等现象越严重，增长越不可持续；而不平等现象减轻，会使预期加速增长期延长50%。研究发现，在发展中国家，资产过度集中会抑制生产性投资，限制增长潜力。准入门槛、机会和收入方面的不平等加剧会导致教育、保健和社会保障不足，造成市场波动，触发危机，降低生产力。不平等现象加剧导致过度的负债消费和投资模式，而这样的消费和投资模式是引发金融和经济危机的因素之一。

⊛ 解　析

1 【在理解的基础上翻译】原译还是在不充分理解的前提下按字面翻译的，虽指出了不平等现象加剧与经济增长有关，但却未能具体表明是何种关系，即是正相关还是负相关；更未能指出何者为因，何者为果，与原文意思相去甚远。这一例子再次表明，忠实原文不等同于逐字对译。改译用最简单的形式表明了原文的意思。

2 【查英文释义】关于 growth spell 的解释，可参阅以下资料：

We define growth spells as periods of sustained growth episodes between growth accelerations and decelerations... (imf. org)

【根据英文解释确定译法】据此解释，可以把 growth spell 翻译为"加速增长期"或"高速增长期"。原译增加了"准确率"，想必是看到"预测"二字后，想象"预测"应该用"准确性"来形容。此句的意思是：社会越平等，人们预期经济加速增长的时间就越长。谈的是人们对未来的预期，而不是已经发生的事情。

spell 的意思是"一阵子"，见 merriam-webster.com：

> an indeterminate period of time
> *//* waited a *spell* before advancing
> *also*：a continuous period of time
> *//* did a *spell* in prison

【批判看待他人译法】有中国学者将 growth spell 翻译为"增长魔咒"：

纵观人类经济史，从来没有哪一个国家可以连续三四十年维持 9% 以上的增长。中国从 1978 年改革开放至今，已经有四十多年了。未来中国经济能否打破"增长魔咒"，在未来继续保持快速的增长，看好的人并不多。大多数人认为，中国经济从 2012 年开始，已经先于"刘易斯转折点"告别了快速增长周期，也就是说，1978 ~ 2012 年就是中国的 growth spell。（中国经营网）

从上文的英文解释可知，spell 并非"魔咒"的意思，把 growth spell 译为"增长魔咒"，等于把一个褒义词变成了贬义词，成了"打破"的对象。由此可见望文生义的危害。所谓"打破增长魔咒"，实为"保持加速增长"。

3 【以名词倒推动词译法】研究的结果叫作 findings，所以 had been found 是指"研究发现"。

4 【补充知识】productive investment 译为"生产性投资"没有错误，但译者最好顺便了解一下什么是生产性投资：

The main characteristic of a productive investment is to engender value, as the transformation of raw material into a product, planting seeds to grow agricultural products, investing shares in a company in order to increase its business, infrastructure construction so that the country develops and the international market increases. Anything that is not consumed and loses its value is considered a productive investment. As for governments, the investment in the people, their education, and development can also be considered productive investment.

5 【access 的译法】access 是一个需要"一事一议"的词，很难找到一个放之四海而皆准的译法。它的基本意思是 the state or quality of being approachable; the ability, right, or permission to approach, enter, or use (dictionary.com)，可以译为"接触""接近""获得""获取""进入""准入""访问""机会"，等等。原译中的"权利门槛"是一个很有创意的翻译，不排除在有些情况下可以使用。此处译为什么，要看作者的意思。这句话的后半句是 education, health care and social protection，与 access 搭配使用，就是"获得教育、保健和社会保障的机会"。但本句还有一个 opportunities，如果是一般文件，把 access 省掉也无妨，因为它的意思与 opportunities 几乎没有区别。但此处是联合国文件，通常不建议省掉任何有意义的词，所以，需要找一个与 opportunities 意思相近的词。译为"准入门槛"，也许能够表达"机会"的意思。"权利门槛"不常见，不进行解释有些突兀。

6 【查作者名字】Volatility refers to the trait of being unpredictably irresolute (thefreedictionary.com)，可以译为"易变性""波动性"。但此处是指什么的"波动"，恐怕不太清楚。我们在谷歌中搜索发言者的名字和这句话，找到了讲话原文，原话是这样的："Growing levels of inequality, not just in income, but also in access and opportunities—leading to inadequate education, health care and social protection—can create volatility, trigger crises and diminish productivity."。没有发现 volatility 的译法，却发现了 crisis 的含义：trigger crisis。所以，原译"危机频繁"就不准确，应该改为"触发危机"。

volatility 是什么意思？ 网上的这句话有个注释："See for example, Stiglitz, *The Price of Inequality*"。我们顺藤摸瓜，看看 Stiglitz 如何界定 volatility。这本书里共有 11 处出现 volatility (volatile)，意思都是"市场波动"，比如：

- This takes the form of capital controls, or limiting the volatile movement of capital across borders, especially during a crisis.

- Opening up a country can expose it to all kinds of risks, from the volatility of capital markets to that of commodity markets.

- The algorithmic traders claimed that they were making markets more liquid ("deeper"), but it was a liquidity that disappeared when it was needed, when a real disturbance occurred to which the market needed to adjust. The result was that the market began to exhibit unprecedented volatility.

- In fact, there are reasons to believe that flash trading actually makes markets not just more volatile but also less "informative". (resistir.info)

因此，此处应当改为"市场波动"。翻译过程中曾修改为"社会波动"，看来是错误的。

7　【查英文释义】Diminish means to reduce, lessen (dictionary.com)，意为"减少""削弱"，没有"退化"之意。再说，"退化"与"生产力"也无法搭配。

8　【正确判断修饰关系】原译对 be associated with 理解有误。本文谈的是金融危机，此处 that 从句应该修饰 debt-financed consumption 和 investment patterns 两个成分，不可能仅是其中一项与金融危机有关。原译理解为只修饰 investment patterns。

【注意表达的细微差异】contribute to 也不易翻译。如果后面跟的是积极行为，可以译为"有助于"，但此处是消极行为（"金融和经济危机"），因此换了个说法（"是引发……的因素之一"）。如果翻译为"这样的消费和投资模式会引发金融和经济危机"，意思就有些绝对。contribute 意味着仅仅是引发某种结果的因素之一。

▶ 原文

14. If appropriate *employment, corporate governance, competition, and wage and income distribution policies*[1] were in place, structural changes could reduce inequality. *The impacts of globalization and technological change on domestic income distribution depended on macroeconomic, financial and labour market policies*[2].

✐ 原译

14. 适当的就业、公司治理、竞争和收入分配的政策如能到位，不平等现象就可因为结构性改变得到减少。国内的收入分配最终能否得益于全球化和技术革新取决于宏观经济、金融和劳动力市场的政策。

✐ 改译

14. 如果就业、公司治理、竞争和收入分配政策到位，通过结构改革就可以减少不平等现象。全球化和技术革新对国内收入分配的影响取决于宏观经济、金融和劳动力市场政策。

★ 解析

1 【补充知识】employment, corporate governance, competition, and wage and income distribution policies 虽然可以翻译出来，但具体是指什么，译者恐怕不一定清楚。每次翻译，不妨认真查一下每个概念的含义，这样可以加深对原文的理解。比如，查一查 wage and income distribution policies，会看到有文章指出：

Many recent studies have shown a significant increase in income inequality since the 1980s. One of the proposed methods for fixing this trend is to increase the minimum wage, since this policy would help those at the low end of the income spectrum to see economic growth. (network.bepress.com)

这样，译者就知道工资政策（最低工资）和收入分配之间的具体关系。再查下一句的 labour market policies，看到其中也包含 minimum wages，这样就看到两句话之间存在联系。实际上，这两句话都在谈如何减少收入分配不平等的问题。

大家不妨再查一下其他概念的解释，借机学习一点其他专业的知识。

2 【了解宏观背景】这句话说白了，就是国内的低收入群体能否得益于全球化和技术革新，取决于宏观经济、金融和劳动力市场的政策。这句话是针对劳工阶层的反全球化浪潮而言的，很多人认为全球化没有给劳工阶层带来多大的好处。但既然贴近原文字面翻译可以充分表达原意，建议不改变原来的表达方式。

▶ 原文

16. In the past 30 years, *there had been a very significant increase in the income share earned by the top 1 percent*[1] in such countries as the United States and the United Kingdom, while in France, Germany, Japan and Sweden, that had been less noticeable. Diversity across countries was the result of different policies on *access to profits*[2]. In some countries, taxes and transfers attempted to eliminate *excess returns*[3] to certain economic participants. Even in industrial countries, the Gini coefficient varied widely depending on structures, economic characteristics and public policy. While the Gini coefficient had been rising in many countries, it was doing so at different rates. Not only had *disposable income*[4] in the top *decile*[5] increased dramatically, but there had been a widening of the gap across income classes, with higher income classes benefiting. Some countries had corrected the market or disposable income outcomes quite actively, while others had not.

原译

16. 过去30年里，在像美国和英国这样的国家，占全社会总人口1%的精英阶层收入份额迅猛增加，但在法国、德国、日本和瑞典，这种现象并不那么明显。国与国的差异源于有关利润门槛的不同政策。在一些国家，政府试图通过税收和转移支付消除某些经济活动参与者的过剩收入。甚至在工业国家中，基尼系数也依结构、经济特点和公共政策不尽相同。虽然许多国家的基尼系数一直在上升，但增速却各不相同。不仅最高等级的可支配收入大大增加，而且不同收入群体之间差距一直在扩大，获益的是较高的收入群体。一些国家对市场或可支配收入的分配进行了积极调整，但另一些则根本没有调整。

改译

16. 过去30年里，在美英等国家，占总人口1%的人在总收入中所占份额大幅增加，但在法国、德国、日本和瑞典，这种现象并不那么明显。国家之间的差异源于利润分配政策不同。在一些国家，政府试图通过税收和转移支付消除某些经济活动参与者的过度回报。甚至在工业化国家，基尼系数也依结构、经济特点和公共政策而不尽相同。虽然许多国家的基尼系数一直在上升，但增速却各不相同。不仅收入水平在前10%的人口可支配收入大大增加，而且不同收入群体之间的差距也一直在扩大；高收入群体获益更大。一些国家积极纠正市场化收入或可支配收入的不平等问题，但另一些国家则没有。

★ 解 析

1 【尽量不增词】原译"占全社会总人口 1% 的精英阶层收入份额迅猛增加"增加"精英阶层"可以，但无必要。

【斟酌用词】"迅猛"是指速度快，而 significant 是指数量大。

【增词使含义清晰】"收入份额"不是很清楚，可以具体说明"在总收入中所占份额／比例"。

2 【根据上下文确定词义】如前所述，access 的意思多样，每个翻译情景都需要动一番脑筋。access to profits 意思是获得企业盈利的机会，实际上就是指企业盈利的分配方案（给工人多少、给管理层多少）。与前文（第 14 段）income distribution 和 inequality 指向的内容相同。原译"利润门槛"显然意思错误，改为"利润分配"。

3 【根据上下文确定词义】excess returns 译为"过剩收入"，显然是没有理解原文的意思。收入差距拉大，就是少数企业高管工资太高、工人的工资太低造成的。

4 【补充知识】Disposable income is total personal income minus personal current taxes. (Wikipedia: disposable income) 可支配收入是指税后收入。

5 【补充知识】Decile means a tenth part of a distribution (thefreedictionary.com)，即 "（数据）分布中的十分之一"，也就是 10%。详见 en.oxforddictionaries.com 的解释和例子：

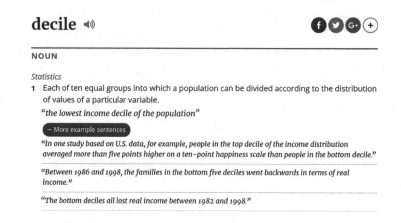

decile 还有一个意思——"十分位数"（collinsdictionary.com）：

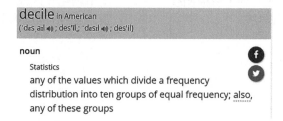

十分位数是将一组数据由小到大（或由大到小）排序后，用 9 个点将全部数据分为 10 等份，与这 9 个点位置上相对应的数值称为十分位数，分别记为 D1、D2……D9，表示 10% 的数据落在 D1 下，20% 的数据落在 D2 下……90% 的数据落在 D9 下。

与十分位数类似，四分位数（quartile）是指将一组数据由小到大（或由大到小）排序后，用 3 个点将全部数据分为 4 等份，与这 3 个点位置上相对应的数值称为四分位数，分别记为 Q1（第一四分位数）、Q2（第二四分位数，即中位数）、Q3（第三四分位数）。

同理，百分位数（percentile）是将一组数据由小到大（或由大到小）排序后分割为 100 等份，与 99 个分割点位置上相对应的数值称为百分位数，分别记为 P1、P2……P99，表示 1% 的数据落在 P1 下，2% 的数据落在 P2 下……99% 的数据落在 P99 下。

通过四分位数、十分位数和百分位数，可以大体看出总体数据在哪个区间内更为集中，也就是说，它们在一定程度上可以反映数据的分布情况。

分位数（或分位点）统称 quantile。其他分位数还有 quintile（五分位数）、sextile（六分位数）、septile（七分位数）、octile（八分位数）等，详见《SPSS 17 中文版统计分析典型实例精粹》一书。

▶ **原文**

17. A certain amount of inequality was probably essential to the effective functioning of a market economy, in order to provide *market signals and incentives for investment, growth and entrepreneurial activity*[1]. A tolerable *level*[2] should be distinguished from harmful, excessive inequality that could be damaging to long-term growth. Market outcomes could be controlled, and distribution, tax and *transfer policies*[3] applied. In some countries, excessive, persistent *structural inequalities interacted with market forces*[4a], significantly affecting the *human capital base*[4b]. Technical progress had raised returns to capital and skilled labour. The challenge was to enhance the skill set of the labour force so that it could participate in international competition. Over the past 30 years, unskilled labour had been hurt more than any other *sector*[5].

✎ **原译**

17. 某种程度上的不平等对于市场经济有效运行来说也许是必要的，因为可以将其作为市场信号，还可以激励投资、增长和创业。应把可忍受的不平等从过度并有可能伤及长期增长的水平区分开来。如果采取分配、税收和转移支付政策，市场结果是可以控制的。在一些国家，过度、长期存在的结构性不平等与市场的力量共存，严重影响了人力资本的基础。技术进步提高了资本金和熟练劳工的回报。目前的挑战是改善劳动力掌握的技能种类，使其有能力参与国际范围内的竞争。过去30年里，无技能劳工遭受到的伤害多于其他任何经济部门。

✎ **改译**

17. 一定程度上的不平等对于市场经济有效运行来说也许是必要的，因为它可以作为市场信号和激励机制，鼓励投资、增长和创业。应区分可忍受的不平等与可能伤及长期增长的有害和过度不平等。可以通过采取分配、税收和转移支付政策控制市场化结果。在一些国家，过度、长期的结构性不平等与市场的力量交互作用，严重削弱了人力资本的基础。技术进步提高了资本和技术工人的回报。目前的挑战是加强劳动力的技能，使其有能力参与国际竞争。过去30年里，非技术工人遭受到的伤害多于其他任何群体。

★ **解　析**

1【正确判断修饰关系】investment, growth and entrepreneurial activity 修饰的是 market signals and incentives，而不是仅修饰 incentives。因为如果仅修饰 incentives，读者会问：market signals for what? 这句话的意思是，如果干多干少一个样，吃大锅饭，就不会有那么多人去创业、去投资。所以，多干多得，拉大收入差距，也会激励人们去创业和投资。

2 【理解每个单词】这句话的意思是，应当区分有激励作用的不平等和过度不平等。level 是指 level of inequality。

3 【补充知识】transfer policy 是指 transfer payment policy。转移支付（可以译为 a transfer payment 或 government transfer）就是政府通过税收把有钱人的钱白白送给没有钱的人，是一种财富再分配的手段，俗称"劫富济贫"，参见以下信息：

One-way payment of money for which no money, good, or service is received in exchange. Governments use such payments as means of income redistribution by giving out money under social welfare programs such as social security, old age or disability pensions, student grants, unemployment compensation, etc. Subsidies paid to exporters, farmers, manufacturers, however, are not considered transfer payments. Transfer payments are excluded in computing gross national product. (businessdictionary.com)

4 【补充知识】Structural inequality is defined as a condition where one category of people are attributed an unequal status in relation to other categories of people. (Wikipedia: structural inequality) 比如，某个岗位只招收本地居民，外地人再优秀也进不来。Interact means to act one upon another，意为"互动""相互作用"。这句话的意思是，制度性的不平等加上市场力量（如教育产业化），影响了劳动力的素质。"人力资本的基础"（human capital base）就是指劳动力素质，参见以下信息：

Human capital, most ostensibly in the form of education, would be an inescapable input for ensuring competitive levels of productivity in various sectors, and for accelerating the overall pace of economic growth. The paper underscores that a poor human capital base is the Achilles' heel of our economy. The quality of workforce poses a frightening scenario in agriculture, mining-quarrying, and construction. (G.K. Chadha, *Human Capital Base of the Indian Labour Market: Identifying Worry Spots*)

5 【辨析词义】Sector means a distinct part, especially of society or of a nation's economy. (thefreedictionary.com) sector 最常见的意思是 a distinct part of a nation's economy，即"产业""部门""行业"，但用于此处显然不适合，因为无法说"非技术工人"是一个"产业"，此处的意思是 a distinct part of society，可译为"（社会）群体"。见 vocabulary.com 的更多解释：

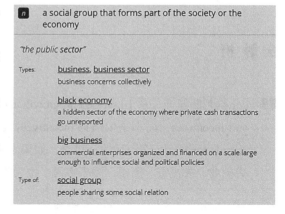

▶ **原文**

18. Economic *policy decisions*[1] had become increasingly politicized and influenced by *interest groups*[2]. Certain groups *had grown in importance and influence*[3] owing to redistribution of income to higher income brackets. Inequalities had a significant impact on *intergenerational mobility*[4]. Higher levels of inequality lowered intergenerational mobility, with subsequent generations finding it increasingly difficult *to move up the economic ladder*[5].

✎ **原译**

18. 经济政策的决策活动愈加政治化，而且受利益集团的影响。由于收入再分配使其能够升入更高的收入等级，某些群体在重要性和影响力上都有所壮大。不平等在很大程度上影响着代际流动力。较严重的不平等降低代际流动力，从而使下一代人感到在经济的阶梯上向上爬越来越难。

✎ **改译**

18. 经济决策越来越政治化，且受利益集团的影响。由于收入再分配使某些群体进入更高的收入等级，他们的重要性和影响力都在提高。不平等在很大程度上影响着代际流动。不平等程度越高，代际流动性越低，从而使下一代在经济阶梯上向上攀爬越来越难。

★ **解 析**

1 【语言简洁】policy decisions 译为"政策的决策"不如"决策"干净利落。

2 【补充知识】顺便了解一下"利益集团"：

Interest group, also called special interest group or pressure group, any association of individuals or organizations, usually formally organized, on the basis of one or more shared concerns, that, attempts to influence public policy in its favour. All interest groups share a desire to affect government policy to benefit themselves or their causes. Their goal could be a policy that exclusively benefits group members or one segment of society (e.g., government subsidies for farmers) or a policy that advances a broader public purpose (e.g., improving air quality). They attempt to achieve their goals by lobbying—that is, by attempting to bring pressure to bear on policy makers to gain policy outcomes in their favour. (britannica.com)

为了私利影响国家决策，这种行为在中国学者看来简直就是制度性腐败，在美国却是合法的。

❸ 【注意搭配】原译"重要性和影响力"与"壮大"搭配不当,改为"提高"均可搭配。

❹ 【补充知识】关于 intergenerational mobility 的解释,请参阅如下资料:

Intergenerational mobility means movement within or between social classes and occupations, the change occurring from one generation to the next. (collinsdictionary.com)

"代际流动"指同一家庭中上下两代人之间社会地位的变动。顺便了解一下 social mobility:

Social mobility is defined as the movement of individuals, families, households, or other categories of people within or between layers or tiers in an open system of social stratification. (Wikipedia: social mobility)

"社会流动性"有向上(upward)与向下(downward)两种方向之分,亦有同代流动性与代际流动性之分。"同代流动"(intragenerational mobility)指一个人社会地位的上下变动,比如从乞丐到富翁,或者相反;代际流动(intergenerational mobility)是指下一代比上一代过得好(或差)。

❺ 【注意词义褒贬】to move up the economic ladder 是指在经济上一步步向上攀爬。原译"向上爬"本意无错,但该词组在中文中有时表贬义,不妥。

第 **2** 单元　联合国大会和经社理事会会议简要记录（二）

📖 学习要点

思维方法

★ 宏观思维

　1. 注意发言者身份

　2. 关注上下文的联系

　3. 分析作者意图

★ 逻辑思维

　1. 根据上下文确定词义

　2. 抓住段落逻辑

调查研究方法

　1. 在文件内查找

　2. 查英文释义

理解

★ 补充知识

　1. agglomeration economies

　2. beggar-thy-neighbour

　3. business cycles

　4. capital inflow

　5. devaluation

　6. depreciation

　7. economies of scale

　8. interest rate liberalization

　9. job outsourcing

　10. jobs gap

　11. labour market segmentation

　12. leverage

　13. negative feedback

　14. network effect

　15. public sector

　16. quantitative easing

　17. risk premium

　18. 只有懂专业才能做到内心确信

　19. 利率不是汇率

　20. 译者的遗憾

★ 理解语言

　1. 辨析词义

　2. 正确判断修饰关系

　3. 会议记录的过去时视为现在时

表达

★ 意思准确

　1. 在理解的基础上翻译

　2. 不随意增译

　3. 再谈access的译法

　4. 注意表达的细微差异

　5. 译出同义词

　6. 旧信息在前，新信息在后

　7. 数字翻译须谨慎

★ 符合形式

　1. 注意搭配

　2. 语言简洁

　3. 补充逻辑主语

　4. 注意语言节奏

　5. 谈中国的事情，还原为中国说法

　6. 使用常见说法

　7. 尊重约定译法

变通

　1. 概念尽量直译

　2. 不增加原文没有的意思

　3. 修改约定译法

背景说明

本单元练习承接上一个单元，同样选自经济及社会理事会与联合国大会第二委员会联席会议的简要记录。会议于 2013 年在联合国总部纽约举行，主题是"不平等、增长和全球经济展望"。会议讨论了 2008 年全球金融危机爆发后世界经济发展的状况，分析了当下存在的挑战，并提出了解决方案。

练习和讲解

▶ 原文

19. As income *accrued*[1] more unequally, *access*[2] to knowledge, education and skills development became more limited. At the same time, *cluster*[3] of highly skilled workers formed in industrial and developing countries. Silicon Valley was an example. Knowledge, success and access to the benefits of one's work were thus *clustered*[4] as well. *Growth theorists*[5] saw *agglomeration*[6] as a way to increase technical innovation and information flows, but there was also a certain negative impact on economic growth. *Labour market segmentation*[7] and higher rewards for skills accompanied inequality. If such market outcomes were not corrected, a large part of the market was prevented from participating in market success. *Outsourcing of jobs*[8] affected low-skilled workers *more than anyone else*[9].

✎ 原译

19. 随着积累的收入愈加不等，获取知识、教育和技能培训的权利就愈加有限。同时，工业和发展中国家的高技术人员组成若干的群体。硅谷便是一个例子。知识、成功和获取工作所得的权利因而也被群分。聚集被增长论学者看成是一种提高技术创新和信息流通的方式，但对经济增长也有某种负面影响。劳动力市场的细分和对技能高回报的背后，随之而来的是不平等。这种市场结果如不加以纠正，市场的一大部分将分享不到市场的成功。低技术工人往往较易受到工作外包的影响。

✎ 改译

19. 随着收入不等加剧，一些人获取知识、教育和技能培训的机会就愈加有限。同时，在工业化和发展中国家高技术人员出现"扎堆"现象。硅谷便是一个例子。随之出现的是知识、成功和劳动收益向部分人聚集。"聚集"被增长理论视为提高技术创新和信息流通的方式，但它对经济增长也有某种负面影响。劳动力市场的分割和高技能高回报带来了不平等。这种市场结果如不加以纠正，市场中的一大部分人将分享不到市场的成功。低技术工人受外包的影响最为严重。

⊛ 解　析

1 【查英文释义】accrue 的意思确实是"积累"，见 merriam-webster.com：

Definition of *accrue*

intransitive verb

1 : to come into existence as a legally enforceable claim

2 **a** : to come about as a natural growth, increase, or advantage
// the wisdom that *accrues* with age

   b : to come as a direct result of some state or action
// rewards due to the feminine will *accrue* to me
— Germaine Greer

3 : to accumulate or be added periodically
// interest *accrues* on a daily basis

【会议记录的过去时视为现在时】但请注意：此处 accrued 是过去式，在联合国会议记录中，讲话时用的一般现在时要改为一般过去时，实际发言时说的是 as income accrues (more unequally)，"随着收入累积越来越不平等"，但译文没有必要亦步亦趋，可以简化为"随着收入不等加剧"。

2 【再谈 access 的译法】上一单元练习中讲过，access 是需要"一事一议"的词，很难找到放之四海而皆准的译法。此处再议一次。access 的基本含义可分为以下三类：

（1）access 的本意是指 the means to approach or enter a place (such as wheelchair access)，即指做某事的"方式"。

（2）access 也指 the right or opportunity to use or benefit from something (for example, help people gain access to training) or see someone (for example, we were denied access to our grandson)，即指做某事的"权利"或"机会"。

（3）access 还指 the process of obtaining or retrieving information stored in a computer's memory (for example, this prevents authorized access or inadvertent deletion of the file)，有"获得"或"查阅"之意。（en.oxforddictionaries.com）

【根据上下文确定词义】access 取何含义由语境决定。当 access 同 knowledge, education and skills development 搭配使用时，应取第二种含义，指的是获取知识的机会而非权利（如法律上每个人都有权利读书，但没有必要条件无法实现）。

【补充逻辑主语】另外，"获取"的主语补充出来意思就比较连贯。既然是收入不平等，一定意味着一些人多，一些人少。所以，增加"一些人"作主语，也在情理之中。

3 【查英文释义】Cluster as a noun means a number of similar things that occur together (merriam-webster.com)，即同类事物同时出现。原译为"组成若干的群体"，似乎是说工人们有意识组成团体，但从上下文看，是指一类人聚集在一起，即"扎堆"，与下文的 agglomeration 意思相同。

4 【辨析词义】Cluster as a verb means to grow, assemble, or occur in a cluster (merriam-webster.com)，译为"集聚"或"聚集"。原译"群分"虽然可以解释为"划分为不同的群体"（"物以类聚，人以群分"），但这种用法很少见，改译为"知识、成功和劳动收益向部分人聚集"，增加"向部分人"也是为了使意思清晰明了。

5 【语言简洁】经济增长理论（growth theory）是研究解释经济增长规律和影响制约因素的理论。growth theorists 可以译为"经济增长理论家""增长学派"，或者更简单一些："增长理论"。如果意思不变，可以用最简单的说法。

6 【补充知识】Agglomeration economies (or economies of agglomeration) first considered in a systematic manner by Weber (1909) refers to the cost savings that come when firms and people locate near one another together in cities and industrial clusters. This concept relates to the idea of economics of scale and network effects. (John B. Parr, *Agglomeration Economies: Ambiguities and Confusions*, 2002)

【补充知识】Economies of scale refers to the cost advantages that enterprises obtain due to their scale of operation (typically measured by the amount of output produced), with cost per unit of output decreasing with increasing scale. (Wikipedia: economies of scale)

【补充知识】Network effect (also called network externality or demand-side economies of scale) is the positive effect described in economies and business that an additional user of a good or service has on the value of that product to others. (Wikipedia: network effect)

这三个概念虽有相似之处，却各有侧重。

查阅 Wikipedia 的中文词条"规模经济效应"，找到如下资料：

规模经济效应，简称聚集经济，又称为聚集经济效应、集聚效应、群聚效应等，是一个建立在规模经济和网络外部性之间的学说。这个词是用来形容在一个地区之上，许多相同抑或不同类型的产业聚集后，会因为空间上的集中而获得好处。

例如，工业区设立后，各种产业共用公共设施，节省成本；汽车生产工厂设于某地后，相关零部件厂商设于该工厂旁，以降低运输成本，节约时间。类似的例子还有硅谷的电脑产业，底特律的汽车产业，香港的波鞋街、旺角花墟，等等。

【概念尽量直译】从前面的英文解释来看，三个概念之间有区别。尽管 Wikipedia 的中文词条称，三个概念可以互换，我们建议还是用"聚集"或"聚集效应"，即尽量按字面翻译。本段中的 cluster 和 agglomerate 表示同样的意思，翻译时不一定要一个萝卜一个坑。

7 【补充知识】关于"劳动力市场分割理论"（labour market segmentation theory），参见以下信息：

与其他要素市场相比，劳动力市场具有较明显的非竞争性。西方劳动力市场分割理论正是以区别于传统劳动力市场理论的新范式来解释这种非竞争性的。该理论认为传统劳动力市场理论无法很好地解释劳动者收入差距的不断扩大和劳动力市场中存在的各种歧视现象，而劳动力市场分割理论强调劳动力市场的分割属性、强调制度和社会性因素对劳动报酬和就业的重要影响，因而具有较强的现实解释能力。（MBA 智库百科：劳动力市场分割理论）

【查英文释义】Labour market segmentation is the division of the labour market according to a principle such as occupation, geography and industry (Wikipedia: labour market)，意思是行业之间、职业之间、地区之间的工人无法自由流动，因此不具有竞争性。

劳动力市场分割理论是相对于新古典经济理论而言的，后者认为劳动力市场是统一和充分竞争的。

【修改约定译法】market segmentation 通常翻译为"市场细分"，意思是企业按照某种标准将市场上的顾客划分成若干个顾客群。每一个顾客群构成一个子市场，不同子市场之间的需求存在着明显差别。但"劳动力市场细分"无法表达行业和地域之间劳动力的隔绝，因此，在谈劳动力市场的时候，改用"分割"而不是"细分"。

8 【补充知识】关于"工作外包"（outsourcing of jobs），请看下面的资料：

Job outsourcing is when U.S. companies hire foreign workers instead of Americans. In 2013, U.S. overseas affiliates employed 14 million workers. The four industries most affected are technology, call centers, human resources, and manufacturing.

How does it affect the economy?

Job outsourcing helps U.S. companies be more competitive in the global marketplace. It allows them to sell to foreign markets with overseas branches. They keep labour costs low by hiring in emerging markets with lower standards of living. That lowers prices on the goods they ship back to the United States.

The main negative effect of outsourcing is that it increases U.S. unemployment. The 14 million outsourced jobs are almost double the 7.5 million unemployed Americans. If all those jobs returned, it would be enough to also hire the 5.7 million who are working part-time but would prefer full-time positions.

That assumes the jobs could, in fact, return to the United States. Many foreign employees are hired to help with local marketing, contacts, and language. It also assumes the unemployed here have the skills needed for those positions. Would American workers be willing to accept the low wages paid to foreign employees? If not, American consumers would be forced to pay higher prices.

Donald Trump said he would bring jobs back during the 2016 presidential campaign. To do this, he renegotiated NAFTA. He imposed tariffs on imports from Mexico and China. That started a trade war and raised the prices of imports from those countries. That benefits companies that make all their products in America. Without tariffs, it can be difficult for American-made goods to compete with cheaper foreign goods.

Imposing laws to artificially restrict job outsourcing could make U.S. companies less competitive. If they are forced to hire expensive U.S. workers, they would raise prices and increase costs for consumers.

The pressure to outsource might lead some companies to even move their whole operation, including headquarters, overseas. Others might not be able to compete with higher costs and would be forced out of business. (thebalance.com)

9 【辨析词义】more than anyone else 意为"比其他任何人都更加……",形式虽为比较级,但语义上却相当于最高级。原译处理成了比较级"较易受到……的影响",不符合原文,语气也不够强烈。

▶ **原文**

22. There was *strong evidence*[1] that less inequality was associated with more *durable, sustainable*[2] growth. Determining factors included economic openness, political and *institutional*[3a] stability, well-developed *institutions*[3b], and, most important, relatively fair income distribution. Inequality increased the frequency and amplitude of *business cycles*[4]. While there might be a short-term *trade-off between equity and efficiency*[5], that disappeared in the long run.

📝 **原译**

22. 确凿证据表明，不平等现象越轻，增长越是可持续的。决定因素包括开放的经济环境、稳定的政治和制度、完善的机构，以及最重要的一点，相对公平的收入分配模式。不平等会增加商业循环的频率和振幅。尽管短期内有公平和效率中和的效应存在，但长远来看这种效应终会消失。

📝 **改译**

22. 有力的证据表明，不平等现象越轻，越有可能取得持久和持续增长。经济的持久持续增长要求经济开放、政治和制度稳定、机构健全，以及最重要的一点，收入分配模式相对公平。不平等会增加商业周期的发生频率和波动幅度。尽管公平优先短期内会导致效率降低，但长远来看这种现象会消失。

1 【注意表达的细微差异】strong evidence 意思是"有力的证据"或"强有力的证据"。如果是 irrefutable、solid 或 unequivocal，或许可以译为"确凿的证据"。两个概念不同，不能因为某个搭配更常见就选用哪个。

2 【译出同义词】durable 和 sustainable 为同义词。既然汉语中存在这样两个同义词（"持久"和"持续"），那就不妨都翻译出来。改译的表述方式略有调整，这样语言显得较为正式。

3 【查英文释义】The term "institution" commonly applies to both informal institutions such as customs, or behavior patterns important to a society, and to particular formal institutions created by entities such as the government and public services. (Wikipedia: institution) 所以，institution 既可以表示"制度"，也可以表示"机构"，有时候两者都包括。这就给翻译带来了挑战。本段有两处用到了 institution，它们都可能表示两个意思，但译者只能选用一个。为避免重复，第一个用了"制度"，第二个用了"机构"。这么翻译不一定完全符合作者本意，但也不能因为这一点小事去麻烦作者，所以只能如此。

4 【尊重约定译法】原译将 business cycles 译为"商业循环"，也未尝不可，但更常用的说法是"经济周期"。经济周期也称商业周期、商业循环、景气循环，它是指经济运行中周期性出现的经济扩张与经济紧缩交替更迭、循环往复的一种现象，是国民总产出、总收入和总就业的波动。

【补充知识】什么是 business cycle？

The business cycle describes the rise and fall in production output of goods and services in an economy. Business cycles are generally measured using rise and fall in real or inflation-adjusted gross domestic product (GDP), which includes output from the household and nonprofit sector and the government sector, as well as business output. "Output cycle" is therefore a better description of what is measured. The business or output cycle should not be confused with market cycles, measured using broad stock market indices; or the debt cycle, referring to the rise and fall in household and government debt. (investopedia.com)

5 【查英文释义】A trade-off (or tradeoff) is a situational decision that involves diminishing or losing one quality, quantity or property of a set or design in return for gains in other aspects. In simple terms, a trade-off is where one thing increases and another must decrease. (Wikipedia: tradeoff) trade-off 的概念在诸多领域均有应用，总体而言，trade-off 描述的是一种此消彼长的过程，即提高一种特征的优势的时候，另一种特征的优势将降低。

本文 trade-off between equity and efficiency 指的是在公平和效率之间顾此失彼，即照顾分配公平（吃大锅饭），就会降低效率。因为干多干少一个样，大家自然就失去了工作的积极性。改革开放初期，我们提出"效率优先，兼顾公平"，极大地提高了经济效率，但也导致收入差距拉大。本段认为，公平优先的政策短期内会降低效率，但长远来看并不影响效率。

▶ 原文

24. *Profits*[1] had been generated through *regulatory failures*[2] over the last 30 years that were very hard to correct. *Combined*[3] with generous tax policies, *income inequality*[4] became *wealth inequality*[5]. In some *industrial countries*[6], the ratio of private wealth to national income had more than doubled over the past three or four decades.

✎ 原译

24. 过去30年里，有相当一部分利润都是在监管不力的情况下产生的，局面时至今日已难以纠正。在慷慨的税收政策推动下，收入不等的问题已演变成了财富不等的问题。在一些工业国家，私有财富对国民收入的比例在过去三四十年里增加了一倍多。

✎ 改译

24. 过去30年，有些利润是在监管失败的情况下产生的，而这种失败很难补救。加上慷慨的税收政策，收入不平等问题已演变成财富不平等问题。在一些工业化国家，私有财富与国民收入的比例在过去三四十年间增加了一倍多。

1 【不随意增译】profits 处理为"相当一部分利润"，增添了原文没有的意思，所以改为"有些利润"。

2 【在文件内查找】什么是 regulatory failures？如果译者不确定，可以先搜一下原文看有无解释。搜索 regulatory，发现第 28 段有这样的话：

In addition, regulatory policies in some countries, particularly deregulation of financial markets, had allowed the creation and collection of profits in ways that had shifted economic activity to redistribution and accumulation of wealth, as opposed to production.

同一发言者在第 85 段也表达了同样的意思：

Professor Pauly (University of Toronto) said that incentives and regulatory environments in many industrial countries favoured wealth redistribution over wealth creation, directing resources to activities that did not generate output. Policy decisions designed to free up economic activity had led to serious misallocations of resources. Underlying legitimate short-term concerns about lack of demand, jobs and real investment was a long-term structural problem. The regulatory and policy environment must favour real wealth creation over financial wealth creation.

金融企业不创造财富，只是重新分配财富，应该鼓励发展实体经济，这样才能解决结构性问题。看来监管失败，就是放松对金融企业的监管，导致过多资源进入金融行业，而非实体经济。

【注意表达的细微差异】"监管不力"程度上低于"监管失败"，故修改。

3　【在理解的基础上翻译】combined 意思是"加上"，所以 tax policies 起辅助作用。原译"推动"似乎是起主导作用，不够准确。

4　【查英文释义】Income includes the revenue streams from wages, salaries, interest on a savings account, dividends from shares of stock, rent, and profits from selling something for more than you paid for it. Income inequality refers to the extent to which income is distributed in an uneven manner among a population. (inequality.org) 所以，income inequality 就是收入不平等。原译"收入不等"含义模糊。

5　【注意表达的细微差异】Wealth equals to "net worth", the sum total of the assets minus liabilities. In the United States, wealth inequality runs even more pronounced than income inequality. (inequality.org) 收入不平等与财富不平等有内在联系，但也有所区别，两者不可混淆。另外，"不平等"不能简化为"不等"。

6　【查英文释义】industrial countries 即使在英文中也不常见，常见的是 developed countries 或 industrialized countries。请看 Wikipedia 的解释：

> Developed country, industrialized country, more developed country, or more economically developed country (MEDC), is a sovereign state that has a developed economy and advanced technological infrastructure relative to other less industrialized nations. Most commonly, the criteria for evaluating the degree of economic development are gross domestic product (GDP), gross national product (GNP), the per capita income, level of industrialization, amount of widespread infrastructure and general standard of living. Which criteria are to be used and which countries can be classified as being developed are subjects of debate.

▶ 原文

25. Societies with greater intergenerational mobility were more equal. The United States had once been a country of unlimited opportunities, *but there were other countries where it was currently far easier for people with low incomes to rise into higher income brackets in the next generation*[1]. The *new persistence*[2] in inequality was very worrisome. In the short run, policy could correct it through taxes and transfers. In the long run, there was no easy resolution. Solutions must increase education, skills and innovative capacities and pay close attention to the regulatory framework in order to *capture certain profits*[3].

✎ 原译

25. 代际流动力高的社会更公平。美国曾是一个拥有无限机遇的国度，但现在有些国家的环境在让低收入人群的下一代跃升至更高收入等级方面，容易程度远超美国。不平等问题回潮而且挥之不去令人忧心。短期内，可通过税收和转移支付政策加以矫正。长期内如要根除并不容易。唯有提高教育、技能和创新能力并重视有关追缴某些利润的监管制度。

✎ 改译

25. 代际流动性高的社会更加公平。美国曾是一个拥有无限机遇的国度，但现在在有些国家，低收入人群的子女跃升至更高收入等级远比美国容易。新出现的不平等问题长期化，令人担忧。短期内，可通过税收和转移支付政策加以矫正。长期来看如要根除并不容易。唯有提高教育、技能和创新能力，并重视监管制度，才能截获某些利润。

★ 解 析

1 【注意语言节奏】原译意思正确，但句子有些欧化。改译调整了句子结构，更容易阅读。

2 【注意表达的细微差异】If an unpleasant feeling or situation persists, it continues to exist (dictionary.cambridge.org)，即持续存在。原译"挥之不去"可以表达这个词的含义，但改为"长期化"简单明了。原译"回潮"一词暗示 persistence 这一情况之前就已出现过，不准确。

3 【注意表达的细微差异】根据上下文，capture certain profits 是指通过有效监管，避免利润流到个人腰包，而是上缴国库，用于再分配（转移支付）。原译"追缴"隐含利润已经到了个人手中，再收回去，所以不准确。

▶ 原文

55. Premature *unwinding*[1] of quantitative easing could also lead to a *sell-off*[2] in global equity markets, *a sharp reversal of capital inflows*[3] to emerging economies and a spike in *risk premiums*[4] for external financing in emerging countries. Such *shocks*[5] to financial markets could move quickly to the real economy in developed and emerging economies and *derail*[6] world economic growth. If, on the other hand, the central banks kept quantitative easing measures in effect for too long, they would heighten the risk of asset bubbles and inflation, making the future exit even more difficult to manage.

✎ 原译

55. 过早撤销量化宽松也会导致全球证券市场恐慌性抛售，资本骤然逆流至新兴经济体并且新兴经济体外部融资需求的风险溢价急升。金融市场受到的刺激可能会很快传导至发达国家和新兴经济体的实体经济，进而使全球经济增长陷入停滞。另一方面，如果央行不撤销量化宽松，久而久之就会使资产泡沫和通胀风险上升，日后量宽一旦退出局面将会更难把握。

✎ 改译

55. 过早退出量化宽松也会导致全球股票市场低价抛售、新兴经济体资本流入骤然逆转、外部融资风险溢价急升。金融市场受到的此等冲击，可能会很快传导至发达国家和新兴经济体的实体经济，进而使全球经济增长希望落空。另一方面，如果央行不退出量化宽松，久而久之就会使资产泡沫和通胀风险上升，日后量化宽松一旦退出，局面将会更难把控。

★ 解 析

1　【使用常见说法】unwind 在 merriam-webster.com 中的解释为：

> **3** ： to undo (a financial arrangement or position) through the necessary legal or financial steps
> *// unwound* most of its natural gas hedges
> — *The New York Times*

所以，unwind 翻译为"撤销"也未尝不可，但"退出"似乎是更常见的说法。本段最后一句中的 kept 与 unwind 构成一对反义词。

2　【查英文释义】关于 sell-off，参见以下资料：

A sell-off is the rapid and sustained selling of securities at high volumes that causes a sharp drop in the value of the traded securities.

A sell-off may occur for many reasons, such as the sell-off of a company's stock after a disappointing earnings report, the departure of an important executive or the failure of an important product. Markets and stock indexes can also sell-off when interest rates rise or oil prices surge, causing increased fear about the energy costs that companies will face. Sell-offs can also be caused by political events, or terrorist acts. (investopedia.com)

从以上的定义可以看出，sell-off 这一行为本身不包括恐慌性，只是客观陈述抛售的行为。"恐慌性抛售"在英文中对应的是 panic selling。

此外，当 sell 与 off 连写时，selloff 或 sell-off 是一个名词，指抛售的行为；当两者分开写时，sell off 是一个动词短语，指抛售的动作。

3 【查英文释义】Capital inflow means a net flow of capital, real and/or financial, into a country, in the form of increased purchases of domestic assets by foreigners and/or reduced holdings of foreign assets by domestic residents. Recorded as positive, or a credit, in the balance on capital account. (investorguide.com)

【判断修饰关系】结合原文第 47 段的内容 "quantitative easing...triggering a reversal in capital inflows to emerging economies. It was estimated that capital inflows would register a decline of 12 percent from the previous year..." 可看出，量化宽松导致流入新兴市场的资金减少，因此，sharp reversal 修饰的是整个 capital inflows to emerging economies，即逆转了资金流入新兴经济体的现象；原译误以为 sharp reversal 修饰的仅仅是 capital inflows，导致意思相反。如果不敢确定一个词的意思，可以用这个词搜索全文，也许能找到线索。

4 【补充知识】risk premiums 翻译为"风险溢价"没有问题，但这究竟是什么意思呢？查找资料发现："A risk premium is the return in excess of the risk-free rate of return an investment is expected to yield; an asset's risk premium is a form of compensation for investors who tolerate the extra risk, compared to that of a risk-free asset, in a given investment." (investopedia.com)，也就是高风险，高收益。

这句话到底是什么意思？下面这段话可能有帮助：

美联储扩张资产负债表，不断释放美元时，这些流动性就如洪水猛兽般冲向新兴经济体，导致国际资本流入，本币升值，国内信贷扩张，以及通货膨胀的加剧；而当美联储进入加息周期时，新兴经济体又面临着资本外流，本币汇率急跌，国内流动性紧张，资产价格大幅缩水，引发金融市场的剧烈波动，直至爆发危机。20 世纪 80 年代的拉美危机，1994 年的墨西哥危机，1997 年的亚洲金融风暴及 2000 年的阿根廷危机等有着相同的逻辑。（soc.gov.cn）

5 【注意表达的细微差异】shock 的力度远比"刺激"大，所以改为"冲击"。

6 【查英文释义】Derail means to cause to fail or become deflected from a purpose; to reduce or delay the chances for success or development. (dictionary.com) 因此，to derail world economic growth equals to reduce the chances for world economic growth，即减少世界经济增长的可能性，而不是使经济增长停滞。

▷ 原文

58. Economic challenges facing developing countries and economies in transition had caused some to institute institutional reforms. In response to a slowdown in GDP growth, China had undertaken measures to *cut paperwork*[1], reduce administrative intervention in business operations and *liberalize interest rates*[2].

✎ 原译

58. 摆在发展中国家和转型经济体面前的经济难题已经迫使有些国家展开了制度改革。为应对GDP增长放缓，中国已采取措施减少行政审批程序，降低行政对企业经营的干预，并放松了对汇率的控制。

✎ 改译

58. 摆在发展中国家和转型经济体面前的经济难题已经迫使有些国家展开了体制改革。为应对GDP增长放缓，中国已采取措施，简化办事程序，减少政府对企业经营活动的干预，实现利率自由化。

✦ 解 析

1 【查英文释义】paperwork 是指文书工作，见 collinsdictionary.com：

> uncountable noun
>
> **Paperwork** is the routine part of a job which involves writing or dealing with letters, reports, and records.
>
> *A pile of paperwork demanded my attention.*

【谈中国的事情，还原为中国说法】但"减少文书工作"在汉语中不常用。我们常用的是"减少繁文缛节""简化办事程序""减少审批环节"。此处既然在谈中国的事情，信息来源很可能就是用的这些说法。相关英文报道也是用的 cut paperwork：

- China will cut paperwork by sharing the basic information of citizens, enterprises and social organizations... (*China Daily*)

- An administrative reform aimed at cutting paperwork for startup businesses will be launched across China soon... (*China Daily*)

下面这段中文报道也可以很好阐释什么叫 paperwork：

首先，要发挥"互联网+"的优势，信息共享，简化办事程序。取消可有可无的证明，减少办事过程中的繁文缛节，这是改革要遵循的基本原则。因此，客观存在的，所在单位或基层社区能证实的，就不一定要求非得"执法机关"盖章敲定；鉴于集体办事机关的权限比普通群众要高，如果能主动关联相关管理信息源查得到的，就不要让当事人自己去跑去找；当然，形成更多电子化资料库，方便办事人、经办人查询，也是相关部门有待努力的方向。（dy.163.com）

美国有一部法律，就叫 Paperwork Reduction Act（《减少书面工作法》）。The Paperwork Reduction Act of 1980 is designed to reduce the total amount of paperwork burden the federal government imposes on private businesses and citizens. (Wikipedia: Paperwork Reduction Act) 发言者提到中国，可能与其华人身份有关（Mr. Hong, Department of Economic and Social Affairs）。

2 【利率不是汇率】liberalize interest rate 意为"利率自由化"，是指国家放松对利率的管制，由金融市场上的资金供求双方根据市场资金供求状况和自身资金需求等因素自行决定利率的行为。这种不受政府控制，由市场决定利率的行为就是利率自由化。又或者说是政府放松了利率管制，由商业银行根据市场上的资金需求和贷款项目的风险程度自行决定利率，通过利率差别来区分不同风险的贷款人，又称利率市场化。（百度百科：利率市场化）原译把"利率"译为"汇率"（exchange rate），是个重大失误。In finance, an exchange rate is the rate at which one currency will be exchanged for another. (Wikipedia: exchange rate)

▶ **原文**

59. *International policy coordination should be enhanced, with major central banks improving communication regarding timing and targets of policy actions to mitigate shocks and spillover effects*[1] *from the quantitative easing exit.*[2] Such dialogue had often been held *in the context of the Group of 20 (G20)*[3]. It should also occur in more broadly representative forums, such as the *Economic and Social Council*[4] and the Second Committee.

✍ 原译

59. 应该加强国际政策协调，主要央行之间改善有关推出政策措施的时间点和目标的沟通，减小因撤销量化宽松政策引起的波动和副作用。这样的对话通常都是在20国集团（G20）会议期间举行，但还应该在代表性更广的机构进行，例如经济及社会理事会和第二委员会。

✍ 改译

59. 应该加强国际政策协调，主要央行之间应改善沟通，协调政策措施推出的时间点和目标，减小因退出量化宽松政策引起的冲击和溢出效应。这样的沟通通常都是在20国集团（G20）框架下进行，但还应该在代表性更广的机构进行，例如经济及社会理事会和第二委员会。

★ 解　析

1　【查英文释义】spillover effects 在第 1 单元的练习中已经讲解过，这里不再重复。

需要明确的是，溢出效应既然有积极的一面，也就有消极的一面，消极的一面就是"副作用"。此处从上下文看，就是指"副作用"，这样说也没问题。不过，既然经济学家喜欢用一个新的说法，译者不妨也采用。

2　【注意语言节奏】这句话原译意思可以看懂，但句子较长，断开更便于阅读。

3　【查英文释义】Context 意思是 the set of circumstances or facts that surround a particular event, situation, etc. (thefreedictionary.com)。in the context of the Group of 20 指的是在 20 国集团的背景下，原译译为"在 20 国集团会议期间"，过于具体，说不定很多工作都是在开会之前完成的。

4　【注意发言者身份】发言者是 Mr. Hong，所以他会提到经社理事会。

▶ 原文

65. The *negative feedback loops*[1] were unfavourable to *the labour market*[2]: *if the private sector was not spending, the only way to renewed growth was through competitiveness and export growth*[3]. The fixed exchange rate in the eurozone and the fact that there could be no *international devaluation*[4] led to wage reductions or freezes in many advanced economies.

✏️ 原译

65. 消极的反馈环路对劳动力市场不利：如果私营部门不打算投资的话，重回增长轨道的唯一办法就是提高竞争力和增加出口。欧元区实行固定利率，各国货币不可能都贬值，这些情况导致许多先进经济体的工资减少或冻结。

✏️ 改译

65. 这些负反馈循环对劳动力市场不利：如果私营部门不愿支出，恢复增长的唯一办法就是提高竞争力、增加出口。欧元区的固定利率制，以及不可能出现国际贬值，导致许多先进经济体的工资减少或冻结。

★ 解析

1 【补充知识】什么是 negative feedback（负反馈或消极反馈）？ Negative feedback involves a response that is the reverse of the change detected (it functions to reduce the change). (Wikipedia: negative feedback) 比如：体温升高，身体出汗，出汗过后，体温降低，这就是负反馈。Positive feedback involves a response that reinforces the change detected (it functions to amplify the change). (Wikipedia: positive feedback) 我们平时所说的良性循环或恶性循环都属于正反馈。比如：孩子不喜欢某一门课，不努力学习，成绩越来越差，结果更加不喜欢这门课，这是"恶性循环"；孩子喜欢某一门课，努力学习，结果越学越喜欢，这是"良性循环"。从这些例子来看，negative (positive) feedback loop 翻译为"负（正）反馈循环"可能比"消极（积极）反馈回路"更便于理解。

【关注上下文的联系】回到本段内容，该句所述 the negative feedback loop 就是发言人在第 63 段最后一句提出、第 64 段举例说明的经济现象：

63. ....However, there were many negative feedback loops in the global economy.

64. Households were recovering from asset and wage income loss and were therefore not spending. Despite unconventional monetary policies, such as the reduction of interest rates to nearly zero and quantitative easing on both sides of the Atlantic, firms were not investing sufficiently. Banks were not lending enough because their portfolios were still infected...

【分析作者意图】但从严格意义上来讲，这段（第 64 段）所述两种现象：第一，家庭财富缩水，收入减少，无法消费，增长乏力；第二，尽管利率很低，又有大量资金注入（"量化宽松"），但企业投资还是疲软，增长乏力——是前面所说的负反馈循环吗？还是仅仅表示"恶性循环"（一种正反馈循环）？因为"负反馈循环"确实有被误解的用例：

这就形成了东北营商环境的一种负反馈循环，因为经济不景气，财政收入下滑，只好去向企业"揩油"，投资环境进一步恶化，财政收入进一步下滑，地方政府继续采取"杀鸡取卵"的短视行为，而不是着力培育企业，壮大税基，在长期实现财政收入和企业发展的共赢。（即"断粮"导致去"杀鸡"，"杀鸡"导致更大规模的"断粮"。）（ baijiahao. baidu.com）

上面这段中文报道，明显符合前文所说"正反馈循环"的定义，属于其中的"恶性循环"。作者为了追求时髦，用了一个新词，但却没有用对。本篇摘要记录，会不会也是这种情况呢？译者并不是经济学专家，无法作出准确判断，暂且按照作者的说法翻译。

【只有懂专业才能做到内心确信】说到这里，也要顺便发一点感慨：译者经常处于一知半解的状态。虽然能够按字面翻译出来，但到底是什么意思，译者心里并不明白。比如，还是第 64 段："The transfer of debt to the public sector meant that the cost of borrowing had increased."（债务向公共部门的转移意味着借贷的成本增加。），这句话估计大家都能翻译出来，也可能是正确的。但为什么是这样，恐怕不懂经济学的译者说不清楚。所以，要想做好翻译，译者必须具备相关专业的知识，语言知识仅仅是辅助。

2　【注意发言者身份】发言者是国际劳工组织的代表，所以他会提到劳动力市场。Act local, think global.

3　【关注上下文的联系】上一段讲家庭不花钱、私人部门不投资（也是花钱），所以，经济增长的三驾马车中就剩下了一驾，就是本段所说的出口。competitiveness 一定是指国际竞争力。只有在国际上有竞争力，才能出口。但译者心里清楚即可，不必在译文中增加"国际"。

4　【补充知识】什么是 international devaluation？在网上查不到。但仔细看看什么是 devaluation（货币贬值）：

What is devaluation?

Devaluation is a deliberate downward adjustment of the value of a country's currency relative to another currency, group of currencies or standard. Countries that have a fixed exchange rate or semi-fixed exchange rate use this monetary policy tool. It is often confused with depreciation and is the opposite of revaluation. (investopedia.com)

How to break down devaluation?

The government issuing the currency makes the decision to devalue a currency and, unlike depreciation, it is not the result of non-governmental activities. One reason a country may devalue its currency is to combat a trade imbalance. Devaluation reduces the cost of a country's exports, rendering them more competitive in the global market. This, in turn, increases the cost of imports so that domestic consumers are less likely to purchase them, further strengthening domestic businesses. (investopedia.com)

可见货币贬值是固定或半固定汇率制国家主动调低本国货币与他国货币的比值。比如，本来1美元兑换6元人民币，但我们调整为7元。但贬值是相对的，不可能所有国家一起贬（"国际贬值"），一起贬等于没有贬。这就是 there could be no international devaluation 的意思。

【抓住段落逻辑】无法通过货币贬值提高国际竞争力，只有降低或冻结工人工资（从而降低成本）。这就是本段话的逻辑。

【补充知识】顺便再研究一下 depreciation。depreciation 和 devaluation 都是货币价值降低，前者是实行浮动汇率的国家，货币价值随行就市向下波动；后者是实行固定汇率制的国家，官方（中央银行）突然调低货币价值。共同之处都是货币价值降低，所以中文都翻译为"贬值"。汉译英时，就要注意区分属于哪种贬值，然后选用适当的词语。英译汉时，如有必要区分，可把 devaluation 译为"调低货币价值"，depreciation 译为"贬值"。再看看与 devaluation 相对的 revaluation：

Revaluation is a calculated upward adjustment to a country's official exchange rate relative to a chosen baseline. The baseline can include wage rates, the price of gold or a foreign currency. In a fixed exchange rate regime, only a decision by a country's government, such as its central bank, can alter the official value of the currency. Revaluation is contrasted by devaluation, which is a downward adjustment. (investopedia.com)

可见，revaluation 是"调高"货币价值，而不是货币价值"调整"，后者隐含双向调整。

▶ 原文

66. *Fiscal balancing[1] was taking place through a reduction in the public sector wage bill[2]. That was what was causing the 32.2 million jobs gap[3]. The drop in aggregate demand that had resulted from private sector deleveraging[4a]* and *rebalancing in the public sector[4b]* and *improved growth through exports or competitiveness[4c]* was based not on improving the common good but on *beggar-thy-neighbour[5]* policies. More balanced drivers of growth and recovery were needed. *Until export demand was balanced by domestic demand[6]*, growth would remain weak and the jobs gap would increase.

✎ 原译

66. 目前，财政平衡是通过削减公营部门的工资达到的。这就是为什么损失了3220万个工作岗位。由于私营部门去杠杆化和公营部门的再平衡导致的总需求下滑，以及通过出口或提高竞争力使

✎ 改译

66. 财政平衡是通过削减公共部门的工资总额实现的，这就导致公共部门少雇佣3220万人。私营部门去杠杆化、公共部门再平衡、通过提高出口或竞争力促进增长的方式，导致总需求下降，无

原译

增长得到改善的做法，并不是想改善共同福祉，而是在以邻为壑。需要更能平衡各方利益的增长和复苏推动力。除非外需和内需实现平衡，否则增长会依然疲软，岗位损失也会扩大。

改译

法增进各国共同利益，属于以邻为壑，所以需要更平衡的增长和复苏动力。除非外需和内需实现平衡，否则增长会继续疲软，岗位损失也会增加。

★ 解 析

1 【旧信息在前，新信息在后】fiscal balancing 就是第 64 段提及的 fiscal rebalancing，即重新实现政府收支平衡。这一概念前文已经提过，作为已知信息，置于句首是合适的。如果翻译为"正在通过削减公共部门的工资实现财政平衡"，即将新信息前置，会破坏与下一句的连贯性。

2 【在理解的基础上翻译】经济危机爆发后政府税收减少，如何实现收支平衡？只能通过减少工资支出总额（wage bill）来实现。wage bill 的定义是：the total amount that an organization pays its employees during a particular period (idoceonline.com)。用 fiscal rebalancing、job gaps、reduction in the public sector wage bill 等关键词查找，发现减少公共部门工资支出总额有两种方式：一是降低或冻结工资；二是削减公共部门雇员人数。注意：32.2 million 是公共部门的员工人数，不是所有经济部门。

【补充知识】Wikipedia 对"公共部门"和"私营部门"的定义是：

The public sector (also called the state sector) is the part of the economy composed of both public services and public enterprises.

Public services include public goods and governmental services such as the military, police, infrastructure (public roads, bridges, tunnels, water supply, sewers, electrical grids, telecommunications, etc.), public transit, public education, along with health care and those working for the government itself, such as elected officials. The public sector might provide services that a non-payer cannot be excluded from (such as street lighting), services which benefit all of society rather than just the individual who uses the service. Public enterprises, or state-owned enterprises, are self-financing commercial enterprises that are under public ownership which provide various private goods and services for sale and usually operate on a commercial basis.

Organizations that are not part of the public sector are either a part of the private sector or voluntary sector. The private sector is composed of the economic sectors that are intended to earn a profit for the owners of the enterprise. The voluntary, civic or social sector concerns a diverse array of non-profit organizations emphasizing civil society.

3 【补充知识】什么是 jobs gap？参考如下资料：

We also continue to explore the nation's "jobs gap", or the number of jobs that the U.S. economy needs to create in order to return to pre-recession employment levels. (brookings.edu)

另见图片说明：

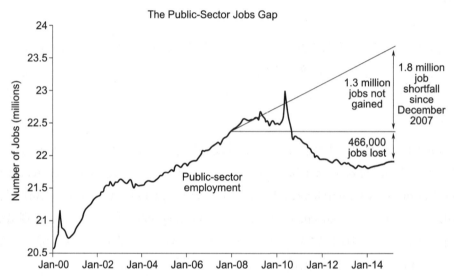

The Public-Sector Jobs Gap

Note: The spikes in public-sector employment in 2000 and 2010 are temporary workers hired to conduct the decennial Census. Population data are from FRED (Federal Reserve Economic Data). Total population: All ages including armed forces overseas.

如有必要翻译出来的话，可以译为"工作缺口"或"岗位缺口"。

【数字翻译须谨慎】另外请注意，数字的翻译要慎之又慎，一不小心就会出错，通常需要专门检查一遍数字。不过，机器辅助翻译的出现，可以减少数字错误。

4 【补充知识】什么是 leverage（杠杆）?

Leverage results from using borrowed capital as a funding source when investing to expand the firm's asset base and generate returns on risk capital. Leverage is an investment strategy of using borrowed money—specifically, the use of various financial instruments or borrowed capital—to increase the potential return of an investment. Leverage can also refer to the amount of debt a firm uses to finance assets. When one refers to a company, property or investment as "highly leveraged", it means that item has more debt than equity. (investopedia.com)

什么是 deleverage（去杠杆）？

Deleveraging is when a company or individual attempts to decrease its total financial leverage. The most direct way for an entity to deleverage is to immediately pay off any existing debt on its balance sheet. If unable to do this, the company or individual may be in a position of an increased risk of default. (investopedia.com)

【译者的遗憾】所以，去杠杆化就是偿还债务。但了解了这个词，也不一定清楚 The drop in aggregate demand that had resulted from private sector deleveraging 是什么意思：为什么私营部门减少负债，会引起总需求减少？仅就翻译而言，译为"私营部门去杠杆导致的总需求减少"应该没问题，但其中的经济学原理，译者恐怕还需要深入研究。不过译者总是受到时间和资源的制约，有时难以为了好奇心而刨根问底。

【正确判断修饰关系】另外，4a、4b、4c 是 resulted from 的并列宾语。句子结构是 the drop was based...。如果主语是多个成分并列，was 应当改为 were。

【正确判断修饰关系】关于提高出口竞争力如何导致总需求减少，国际劳工组织同一时期的报告指出：

A decrease in the labour share not only affects perceptions of what is fair—particularly given the growing concerns about excessive pay among CEOs and in the financial sector—it also hurts household consumption and can thus create shortfalls in the aggregate demand. These shortfalls in some countries have been compensated by increasing their net exports, but not all countries can run a current account surplus at the same time. Hence, a strategy of cutting unit labour costs, a frequent policy recommendation for crisis countries with current account deficits, may run the risk of depressing domestic consumption more than it increases exports. If competitive wage cuts are pursued simultaneously in a large number of countries, this may lead to a "race to the bottom" in labour shares, shrinking aggregate demand.

5 【补充知识】关于 beggar-thy-neighbour，详见下述解释：

Beggar-thy-neighbour is a type of strategy that is designed to enhance the financial stability and prosperity of one nation at the expense of other nations that currently do business with that country. Essentially, this trading strategy will make use of the devaluation of currency as well as changes in import and export policies and other economic measures to move the internal economy of the nation in a desired direction. Depending on the severity of the changes, a beggar-thy-neighbour situation may temporarily alleviate some of the economic issues faced by the nation, but can in the long run create new difficulties as the measures negatively impact the nation's trading partners. (wisegeek.com)

即一国采取的政策行动虽然对本国经济有利，但却损害了别国经济。任何一个经济体为实现内外均衡而实施的宏观经济政策，都不可避免地具有外部性，其中，负的外部性就是以邻为壑效应。

6 【关注上下文的联系】前文说国内需求疲软，只能靠出口，而出口是以邻为壑，长期来看对本国经济也没有好处。所以，要想真正复苏，还是要平衡国内国外两个需求。

▶原文10

77. *Increasing unemployment and inequality were outcomes of a particular consumption model more closely tied to the whims of the rich than to the needs of the poor*[1]. The production of *items that were not a priority*[2] was linked to environmental deterioration. Unsustainable consumption led to growth that did not benefit humanity as a whole.

✑原译

77. 不断加剧的失业和不平等是一个与富人冲动而非与穷人需求挂钩的消费模式关系更密切的产物。环境恶化与生产次要商品有关。不可持续的消费模式导致增长无法惠及全人类。

✑改译

77. 失业和不平等不断加剧，是特定消费模式的结果；这种消费模式更多地产生于富人的兴致，而非穷人的需求。非必需品的生产与环境恶化有关。不可持续的消费模式导致增长无法惠及全人类。

★解析

1 【注意发言者身份】要理解这段话，还是要看发言者是谁。发言者来自委内瑞拉，该国长期受到美国制裁，政局不稳，人民生活艰难，因此发言者关心贫困人口。这段话背后的含义十分丰富。如果想了解失业增加、不平等加剧与消费模式、环境恶化之间的关系，可以用这些关键词查找。

这是笔者在 newint.org 找到的一幅图：

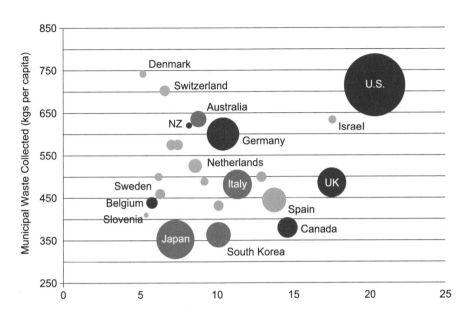

该图的纵坐标是各个国家的城市垃圾生产量，横坐标是这些国家的不平等程度，圆圈大小表示人口多少。可以看到，美国这个最不平等的国家，城市垃圾生产量最大。

【注意语言节奏】这句话原译前置定语过长，需要断开才便于阅读。

2 【根据上下文确定词义】结合上一句对富人的指责，items that were not a priority 很可能是指奢侈品：

Luxury purchases were once status symbols above all else. For decades the luxury world seemed to be one of superyachts, diamond-encrusted watches, "it" bags and big brand logos. As news of hellish sweatshop conditions, devastating pollution, animal cruelty and blood diamonds became more and more prevalent, luxury purchases became intrinsically linked with guilt. (creamuk. com)

【注意表达的细微差异】这些商品不是生活必需品，不需要优先生产。翻译为"次要商品"虽然不违背 priority 的本义，但意思不够明确，所以改为"非必需品"，也可以改成"非优先需求品"或其他能够清楚表达原文意思的说法。

第 ③ 单元　联合国大会第三委员会会议简要记录

📖 学习要点

思维方法

★ 宏观思维

1. 关注上下文的联系
2. 关注发言者身份

★ 逻辑思维

1. abuse和maltreatment: 通盘考虑相近术语的翻译
2. and不一定翻译出来
3. children and youth: 注意逻辑严密
4. 指代关系

★ 批判性思维

1. 理解结构瑕疵
2. 淡化原文瑕疵

调查研究方法

1. 查阅背景材料
2. 查找原始文件

理解

★ 补充知识

1. perpetrator
2. reservation
3. hear和listen辨析
4. "来文"和"调查程序"
5. 任择议定书
6. 决议的组成部分
7. 缔约行为术语

★ 理解语言

1. party和signatory
2. reservation
3. inform: 词义的发展
4. informed participation: 透彻理解
5. 修饰关系: with短语
6. 并列还是偏正

表达

★ 意思准确

1. member: "成员国"还是"会员国"
2. child labour 与 "童工": 咬文嚼字
3. children、youth、adolescent、teenagers、young adults: 通盘考虑系列概念的翻译
4. 斟酌用词: "平等参与"还是"平等代表"
5. violence in schools: "学校暴力"还是"校园暴力"
6. human trafficking: "人口贩运"还是"人口贩卖"
7. human smuggling: 走私人口
8. well-being: "福祉"还是"幸福"
9. right to be heard: 表达意见权
10. 衔接和连贯: 明确指代关系
11. 避免无意中造成歧义
12. 注意表达的细微差异: 重心后置

★ 符合形式

1. 注意搭配
2. governments: 有时需要翻译复数
3. 警惕便装术语
4. 逻辑主语一致
5. voiceless: 避免造词
6. 被动句的处理
7. 顿号用法探讨
8. 改用流水句
9. 注意语言节奏
10. 确保语气连贯

变通

1. 补充句子成分
2. 中国代表发言尽量回译
3. 译为上义词
4. 变通翻译
5. 不添加显著标点
6. 避免另起炉灶

背景说明

本篇练习选自联合国大会第三委员会于 2012 年 10 月 18 日在纽约总部举行的第 14 次会议的简要记录，全文可在网上查找，文号为 A/C.3/67/SR.14。

此次会议的议题为"促进和保护儿童权利"，会议讨论了儿童权利遭受侵害的状况、各国保护儿童权益的有关立法进程及措施等。开会之前，会议代表都会拿到相关文件（如记录开头提到的 A/67/291），翻译过程中如果有不清楚的地方，可以先查看这些文件。

练习和讲解

▶ 原文

3. To overcome those obstacles, child participation *should be considered*[1] a core component of a rights-based child protection system. *Such participation*[2] included *information, hearing/listening, consultation*[3], taking children's opinions into consideration, and support for children's initiatives. Participation should be institutionalized, with appropriate legislative changes and resources to provide children with access to information without discrimination and involve them in producing *materials*[4]. *Participation should be voluntary and informed, and encouraged through awareness-raising*[5]. The protection of child victims and witnesses should be guaranteed and *equal representation*[6] of girls and vulnerable children ensured. *Child-led initiatives*[7] should be supported. *Monitoring and evaluation was needed, with systematic child participation*[8], *and children should be informed of the use to be made of their contribution*[9].

✎ 原译

3. 为了扫除这些障碍，儿童的参与应当被视为一个以儿童权利为基础的儿童保护体系的核心部分。这样的参与包括信息、听到/倾听、征询意见、考虑儿童的想法以及支持儿童的行动。这种参与应当制度化，而且应适当调整相关法律并提供相关资源，以无歧视地为儿童提供信息，并让他们参与材料编制。这种参与应当是自愿的，并让当事人了解情况，还应通过提高意识鼓励参与。应保证儿童受害者和证人的安全，并保证女童和易受害儿童的平等参与。应支持儿童领导的行动。需要监督和评估，儿童的参与也应是系统化的，而且需要告知儿童他们的贡献将被如何使用。

✎ 改译

3. 为了扫除这些障碍，应当把儿童参与视为基于权利的儿童保护体系的核心部分，包括向儿童提供信息，听取、征求、考虑儿童意见，支持儿童提出的倡议。应当把儿童参与制度化，适当调整立法并提供资源，确保儿童不受歧视地获得信息，并参与编写相关材料。应当确保儿童自愿、知情参与，还应扩大宣传力度，鼓励儿童参与。应保证儿童受害者和证人的安全，并保证女童和易受伤害儿童得到平等代表。应支持儿童牵头开展的行动。需要加强监督和评估，并让儿童系统参与其中。应当告知儿童他们的贡献将发挥什么作用。

✦ 解析

1 【被动句的处理】本段话几乎全部都是被动句或抽象名词作主语。以抽象名词作主语的句子（以及被动句）直接翻译为汉语被动句往往比较拗口。本段都改为隐含主语为人（"我们"）的无主句，读起来通顺许多。

2 【改用流水句】根据逻辑，第二句的 such participation 回指上一句中的 child participation。既然汉语可以用流水句，不如省略 such participation，两句一气呵成。

3 【hear 和 listen 辨析】hearing 和 listening 均有"听"的含义，但意思有诸多不同：

Basis for Comparison	Hearing	Listening
Meaning	Hearing refers to one's ability to perceive sounds, by receiving vibrations through ears.	Listening is something done consciously, which involves the analysis and understanding of the sounds you hear.
What is it?	An ability.	A skill.
Nature	Primary and continuous.	Secondary and temporary.
Act	Physiological.	Psychological.
Involves	Receipt of message through ears.	Interpretation of the message received by ears.
Process	Passive bodily process.	Active mental process.
Occurs at	Subconscious level.	Conscious level.
Use of senses	Only one.	More than one.
Reason	We are neither aware nor have any control over the sounds we hear.	We listen to acquire knowledge and receive information.
Concentration	Not required.	Required.

(keydifferences.com)

简而言之，hearing 是指通过听觉系统捕捉声音的一种与生俱来的能力；listening 则更为复杂，该过程不仅涉及听，还包括听到后对声音信号的思考和解读，除听觉系统外，还涉及人类的大脑活动。正因如此，我们的听觉能力称为 hearing ability，而课堂上的听力训练叫作 listening practice。查阅文件 A/67/291，里面多处用到 hearing/listening 的表达方式，目的是强调不仅要听到儿童的声音，而且要听进去。鉴于两个词分别翻译不太可行，故选用"听取"一言以蔽之。

【补充句子成分】另外，从上下文看，information 是指让儿童获得信息或向儿童提供信息，hear/listen 是指听取儿童呼声，consult 是指征求儿童意见。如果只翻译动词，不添加宾语"儿童"，在汉语中意思不完整，因此改译作了适当补充。

4 【查阅背景材料】如果不敢肯定 materials 是指什么，可以在文件 A/67/291 中搜索。查看后发现，materials 是指读物、宣传材料等。

5 【informed participation：透彻理解】informed participation 即知情参与。所谓知情参与，就不是被大人拉过去做做样子，而是事先了解情况，能够发表自己的意见和看法。awareness-raising 通常翻译为"提高意识"，但此处翻译为"宣传"更加通顺达意。

6 【斟酌用词："平等参与"还是"平等代表"】representation 是指代表。检索文件 A/67/291，看到 avoid the participation and representation of children from only privileged backgrounds 这样的说法，所以，此处"参与"和"代表"还是有区别的。因为有些活动可以全体参与，有些活动只能派代表参与。所以，改译把"平等参与"改为"得到平等代表"。

7 【避免无意中造成歧义】Child-led initiatives 译为"儿童领导的行动"，可能会把"儿童领导"误读为名词短语，即领导儿童的人，因此改为"儿童牵头开展的行动"。

8 【注意语言节奏】"需要监督和评估"改为"需要加强监督和评估"，主要是为了照顾句子节奏。增加"加强"这个词，没有改变原文的意思。

【修饰关系：with 短语】with 短语用来说明儿童系统参与监测评估，与前句不是并列关系。

9 【注意搭配】make use of 有"使用""利用"之意，但此处将 make use of contribution 直译为"使用……贡献"搭配不当。因此，需要灵活处理，如改译为"应当告知儿童他们的贡献将发挥什么作用"，也可译为"需要告知儿童其贡献的用途"。contribution 在英文里用得很多，可以是捐款捐物，也可以是贡献智慧。这篇报告是指后者，参见如下资料：

Children and young people have shown that, as informed and voluntary participants, they can contribute as active advocates for change and bring innovative ideas to legislation, analysis, research, the drafting of laws, programmes and petitions, among other things. (A/67/291)

▶ **原文**

8. Mr. El Mkhantar (Morocco) asked what measures were taken by *Governments*[1] to involve civil society in the *mapping*[2] of child participation, and how receptive they were to such mapping.

✍ 原译

8. 埃·姆坎塔先生（摩洛哥）问，政府采取了哪些措施让民间社会参与到推广儿童参与的行动中，民间社会是否愿意接受这样的推广。

✍ 改译

8. El Mkhantar先生（摩洛哥）问，各国政府采取了哪些措施，让民间社会参与评估儿童参与情况，以及各国政府对这种评估的接受程度。

★ 解 析

1【governments：有时需要翻译复数】英语的单复数有时在中文里不需要体现出来，有时候有实际意义，要视情况而定。此处不是指哪个国家的政府，而是指联合国会员国的政府。这一点从第 12 段的回答中，可以清楚得知（见画线的 Many States，本段也有助于理解 mapping）：

12. <u>Many States</u> had action plans for the implementation of <mark>mapping</mark> but suffered from coordination and resource problems. The feedback from <u>her country visits</u> had indicated that the concept of <mark>mapping</mark> had been well received. Its implementation required time, support and the mobilization of United Nations agencies such as the United Nations Children's Fund (UNICEF) and the country and regional offices of the Office of the United Nations High Commissioner for Human Rights (OHCHR). <mark>Mapping</mark> should be in place by 2015 in order to build a world fit for children and achieve the Millennium Development Goals (MDGs).

2【译为上义词】Map means to represent or delineate on or as if on a map; to sketch or plan (dictionary.com)，对应的中文为"测绘""计划""绘图"等。mapping child participation 就是通过调查统计，以图表形式展示各类儿童在各个领域的参与情况。但要把 mapping 直译出来，在这个句子中很难，可以考虑使用上义词（即一个上位概念）来表达这个意思，比如"调查""评估"。从文件 A/67/291 中可以查出来，mapping 就是为了评估：

A mapping and assessment of child participation must be carried out, in accordance with the relevant principles and standards, with a view to identifying the *remaining achievements and gaps*. (斜体部分似应改为 achievements and remaining gaps)

【关注上下文的联系】第 12 段的回答还告诉我们，receptive 的逻辑主语是"各国政府"，不是"民间社会"；receptive 的对象是 the concept of mapping，不是 mapping 的结果。

▶ 原文

19. At their thirty-third regular meeting in July 2012, the CARICOM Heads of Government had called for a holistic approach to *child abuse*[1], including parenting education, awareness-raising and legislative reform to protect children and deal with *perpetrators*[2] and *those who supported abuse through silence*[3]. The most critical issue discussed at the twenty-third meeting of the Council for Human and Social Development in July 2012 had been violence against *children and youth*[4]. The Council had called for studies to *inform*[5] policy and interventions against *violence in schools*[6], had reaffirmed members' commitment to the recommendations of the United Nations study on *violence against children*[7], and had agreed *to bring the investigation of child sexual abuse cases into line with the Convention on the Rights of the Child*[8].

✎ 原译

19. 在于2012年7月召开的第33次常会上，加共体成员国的政府首脑呼吁采取全方位手段解决虐待儿童的问题，包括教育家长、提高意识及改革立法，以保护儿童并处置犯罪分子及默许支持虐待的人。在2012年7月召开的加共体人类和社会发展理事会第23次会议上，讨论的最重要的问题就是对儿童和青少年的暴力行为。理事会呼吁相关的研究能够引导政策和对学校暴力的干预中，重新确定了成员国对联合国关于对儿童的暴力行为的研究建议的支持，并同意按照《儿童权利公约》调查儿童性虐待案件。

✎ 改译

19. 在2012年7月召开的第33次常会上，加共体政府首脑呼吁采取全方位手段解决虐待儿童问题，包括育儿教育、提高认识及改革立法，从而保护儿童、处理虐待者和纵容虐待的人。在2012年7月召开的加共体人类与社会发展理事会第23次会议上，讨论的最重要问题就是针对儿童和青少年的暴力行为。理事会呼吁开展研究，为制定应对和干预校园暴力的政策提供参考；理事会重申成员国致力于执行联合国暴力侵害儿童问题研究报告提出的建议，同意提升儿童性虐待案件的调查标准，使之符合《儿童权利公约》的要求。

★ 解 析

1 【通盘考虑相近术语的翻译】关于 child abuse，请参阅下列资料：

The World Health Organization (WHO) defines child abuse and child maltreatment as "all forms of physical and/or emotional ill-treatment, sexual abuse, neglect or negligent treatment or commercial or other exploitation, resulting in actual or potential harm to the child's health, survival, development or dignity in the context of a relationship of responsibility, trust or power". (Wikipedia: child abuse) child abuse 具体可分为以下几种类型（见 mayoclinicorg）：

Physical abuse（身体虐待）: Physical child abuse occurs when a child is purposely physically injured or put at risk of harm by another person.

Sexual abuse（性虐待）: Sexual child abuse is any sexual activity with a child, such as fondling, oral-genital contact, intercourse, exploitation or exposure to child pornography.

Emotional abuse（精神虐待）: Emotional child abuse means injuring a child's self-esteem or emotional well-being. It includes verbal and emotional assault—such as continually belittling or berating a child—as well as isolating, ignoring or rejecting a child.

Medical abuse（医疗虐待）: Medical child abuse occurs when someone gives false information about illness in a child that requires medical attention, putting the child at risk of injury and unnecessary medical care.

Neglect（疏于照管）: Child neglect is failure to provide adequate food, shelter, affection, supervision, education, or dental or medical care.

abuse 针对人的时候，通常翻译为"虐待"，比如"虐待儿童""虐待老人""虐待妇女"，等等。如果是 abuse of power，则译为"滥用职权"。网上资料和联合国词汇表基本都是这样处理的。但英语中还有一个词——maltreatment，在英汉词典中也是翻译为"虐待"。这两个词是一对近义词，可能正是因为不易区分，世界卫生组织才把 child abuse and child maltreatment 放在一起定义。但有些国家还是作了区分，比如美国纽约州 Office of Children and Family Services (ocfs.ny.gov) 提供如下定义：

Definitions of Child Abuse and Maltreatment

Child Abuse   (En Español)

Generally, the term *abuse* encompasses the most serious harms committed against children. An abused child is a child whose parent or other person legally responsible for his/her care inflicts upon the child serious physical injury, creates a substantial risk of serious physical injury, or commits an act of sex abuse against the child. A person who perpetrates any of these actions against a child in their care can be abusive, and so can a person who allows someone else to do these things to a child. *Child abuse* is defined in Section 412 of the Social Services Law and at Section 1012 of the Family Court Act.

Child Maltreatment

Maltreatment refers to the quality of care a child is receiving from those responsible for the child. Maltreatment occurs when a parent or other person legally responsible for the care of a child harms a child, or places a child in imminent danger of harm by failing to exercise the minimum degree of care in providing the child with any of the following: food, clothing, shelter, education or medical care when financially able to do so. Maltreatment can also result from abandonment of a child or from not providing adequate supervision for the child. A child may be maltreated if a parent engages in excessive use of drugs or alcohol such that it interferes with their ability to adequately supervise the child.

从以上定义中可见，abuse 包括最严重的伤害；maltreatment 是指照管的质量不高，没有善待。这样看来，还是有必要在汉语中加以区分。如果用"虐待"来对译 maltreatment（mal-意思是"不好""坏"，treatment 是"待遇"），就需要修改 abuse 的译法。实际上，一些词典已经给出了除"虐待"以外的另一个译法，即"伤害"（比如，陆谷孙主编的《英汉大词典》）。世界卫生组织列出的各种形式的 abuse，都可归结为"伤害"，包括身体伤害和精神伤害，以及作为（如打骂）和不作为（如疏于照管）造成的伤害。为了更准确"捕捉"精神层面的 abuse，还可以选用"侵害"（侵犯＋伤害）一词。使用"侵害"还可以解决 sexual abuse 译为"性虐待"造成的名不符实问题。世界卫生组织给 sexual abuse 下的定义是：

7.1 Definition of child sexual abuse

These guidelines adopt the definition of child sexual abuse formulated by the 1999 WHO Consultation on Child Abuse Prevention (62) which stated that:

"Child sexual abuse is the involvement of a child in sexual activity that he or she does not fully comprehend, is unable to give informed consent to, or for which the child is not developmentally prepared and cannot give consent, or that violates the laws or social taboos of society. Child sexual abuse is evidenced by this activity between a child and an adult or another child who by age or development is in a relationship of responsibility, trust or power, the activity being intended to gratify or satisfy the needs of the other person. This may include but is not limited to:

— the inducement or coercion of a child to engage in any unlawful sexual activity;
— the exploitative use of a child in prostitution or other unlawful sexual practices;
— the exploitative use of children in pornographic performance and materials".

由此可以看出，sexual abuse 不仅包括"暴力"侵害儿童的行为，还包括利用儿童年幼无知而对儿童产生的性侵害以及对儿童的性剥削，后者可能没有使用暴力，而只是"引诱"（inducement）。

然而，child abuse 翻译为"虐待儿童"由来已久，几乎约定俗成，要想变更十分不易。建议大家至少在翻译联合国文件时继续使用"虐待儿童"的说法，毕竟 child abuse 和 child maltreatment 意思相近，且同时出现的情况也不多。在其他情境下，如果译者有自主权，可以译为"侵害儿童"。

2 【补充知识】Perpetrator refers to one who perpetrates, especially one who commits an offence or crime. (Wikipedia: perpetrator) 其中的 offence 是指"违法行为"，crime 是指"犯罪行为"。违法不一定犯罪。违反《治安管理处罚法》会受到行政处分，公安机关就能处理。只有违反《刑法》的行为才是犯罪。犯罪需要公安机关侦查、检察机关起诉、法院判决。治安处罚不计入犯罪记录，被法院定罪才计入犯罪记录。填表的时候要注意这一点。因此，perpetrator 视情况可以译为"违法者"或"犯罪者"。但虐待儿童的行为在很多国家既不是违法行为，也不是犯罪，所以，此处的 perpetrator 可以具体化为"施虐者""虐待者"。如果在谈家庭暴力问题，可以译为"施暴者"。一个中性的译法是"行为人"。该词在拉丁语中就是一个中性词。请看 en.oxforddictionaries.com 的解释：

Origin

Mid 16th century from Latin perpetrat-"performed", from the verb perpetrare, from per- "to completion" + patrare "bring about". In Latin the act perpetrated might be good or bad; in English the verb was first used in the statutes referring to crime, hence the negative association.

3 【注意搭配】those who supported abuse through silence 译为"默许支持虐待的人"搭配不太好，可以改为"默许虐待的人"。笔者曾一度改为"通过沉默来支持虐待的人"和"以沉默方式支持虐待的人"，但比较啰嗦。"默许 / 纵容虐待的人"就可以清楚表达这个含义。

4 【通盘考虑系列概念的翻译】children and youth 翻译为"儿童和青少年"是正确的说法。children、youth、adolescent、teenagers、young adults 在联合国的统计中有明确区分：

▲ What does the UN mean by "youth" and how does this definition differ from that given to children?

The United Nations, for statistical purposes, defines "youth", as those persons between the ages of 15 and 24 years, without prejudice to other definitions by Member States. This definition was made during preparations for the International Youth Year (1985), and endorsed by the General Assembly (see A/36/215 and resolution 36/28, 1981). All United Nations statistics on youth are based on this definition, as illustrated by the annual yearbooks of statistics published by the United Nations system on demography, education, employment and health.

By that definition, therefore, children are those persons under the age of 14. It is, however, worth noting that Article 1 of the United Nations Convention on the Rights of the Child defines "children" as persons up to the age of 18. This was intentional, as it was hoped that the Convention would provide protection and rights to as large an age-group as possible and because there was no similar United Nations Convention on the Rights of Youth.

Many countries also draw a line on youth at the age at which a person is given equal treatment under the law — often referred to as the "age of majority". This age is often 18 in many countries, and once a person passes this age, they are considered to be an adult. However, the operational definition and nuances of the term "youth" often vary from country to country, depending on the specific socio-cultural, institutional, economic and political factors.

Within the category of "youth", it is also important to distinguish between teenagers (13–19) and young adults (20–24), since the sociological, psychological and health problems they face may differ.

联合国对 adolescent 的定义如下：

ADOLESCENT AND YOUTH DEMOGRAPHICS: A BRIEF OVERVIEW

Definitions. While there are no universally accepted definitions of adolescence and youth, the United Nations understands adolescents to include persons aged 10–19 years and youth as those between 15–24 years for statistical purposes without prejudice to other definitions by Member States. Together, adolescents and youth are referred to as young people, encompassing the ages of 10–24 years. Due to data limitations, these terms can refer to varying age groups that are separately defined as required.

梳理一下上述定义：children——14 岁以下；youth——15 ~ 24 岁；adolescents——10 ~ 19 岁；young people——10 ~ 24 岁；teenagers——13 ~ 19 岁；young adults——20 ~ 24 岁。从联合国词汇表和翻译实践看，children 一般翻译为"儿童"，youth 翻译为"青年"，adolescents 翻译为"青少年"，young people 翻译为"年轻人"，teenagers 翻译为"少年"，young adults 译法不确定，包括"青年""青少年""年轻人"。

为这组复杂的词找到确切的译法确实是一件难事。比如，按此划分，把十五六岁的孩子归为"青年"（youth）似乎早了一些；但把 youth 翻译为"青少年"，adolescents 就找不到译法。所以，只能把 youth 翻译为"青年"，理解为联合国重新定义。

根据定义，young adults（年轻的成年人）是 20 ~ 24 岁，显然不包括少年，所以译为"青少年"不合适（但有时也指"青少年"），译为"青年"和"年轻人"又与 youth 和 young people 冲突。好在汉语中还有"年青"的说法，不妨重新定义，把刚刚步入成年的年轻人称为"年青人"。当然，必要时直译为"年轻的成年人"也是一个选择。

不过，话又说回来，除非是在翻译统计表格中，实际翻译中还是有灵活性的，不一定一个萝卜一个坑。比如，children, young adults, disabled people, migrants, refugees and people from other vulnerable groups 可以翻译为"儿童、年青人、残疾人、移民、难民和其他弱势群体"。但根据联合国的定义，儿童是 14 岁以下，年青人是 20 ~ 24 岁，这中间还有一个 15 ~ 19 岁的群体，难道不包括在内？所以，此处把 young adults 理解为"青少年"，反倒更加合理。这是因为汉语中年龄段的划分是儿童—少年—青年，"儿童"和"青少年"构成一个完整的群体。

【children and youth：注意逻辑严密】同样，本篇练习中的 children and youth 也是指"儿童和青少年"。再比如，develop youth and young adult collectives 可以合并译为"发展青少年团体"，逐字翻译为"青年和年青人团体"会让人困惑。infants, children, adolescents, and young adults 译为"婴幼儿、儿童、青少年和年轻成年人"，构成一个年龄组的连续体，可以接受。infants 平时译为"婴儿"，但"婴儿"和"儿童"之间还有"幼儿"，所以译为"婴幼儿"逻辑更加严密。

5 【inform：词义的发展】inform 最近这些年又发展出一个新的意思：to provide information for。例如，to inform policy decisions 意为"为决策提供信息"；conducting national studies that inform Goals-related processes 意为"开展国内研究，为可持续发展目标相关进程提供参考"。这个意思还没有被一些词典收录，比如 en.oxforddictionaries.com：

inform 🔊

VERB

1 *[reporting verb]* Give (someone) facts or information; tell.
  [with object] "*He wrote to her, informing her of the situation.*"
  [with object and direct speech] "'*That's nothing new,' she informed him.*"
  [with object and clause] "*They were informed that no risk was involved.*"
  (+ More example sentences) (+ Synonyms)

  1.1 *[no object]* Give incriminating information about someone to the police or other authority.
  "*He had been recruited by the KGB to inform on his fellow students.*"
  (+ More example sentences) (+ Synonyms)

2 *[with object]* Give an essential or formative principle or quality to.
  "*Religion informs every aspect of their lives.*"

有些词典中收录了相关的意思，如《朗文当代高级英语词典》，但不完全一样：

in·form /ɪnˈfɔːm $ -ɔːrm/ ●●○ S3 W3 verb [transitive] *formal* 🔊 🔊

  1 to officially tell someone about something or give them information
    🔊 They decided to inform the police.
  inform somebody about/of something
    🔊 Please inform us of any change of address as soon as possible.
  inform somebody (that)
    🔊 We regret to inform you that your application has been rejected.
  ▶ see thesaurus at **tell**

  2 *formal* to influence someone's attitude or opinion
    🔊 Her experience as a refugee informs the content of her latest novel.

原译的理解错误，改译予以纠正。

6 【violence in schools："学校暴力"还是"校园暴力"】violence in schools 译为"学校暴力"，不如"校园暴力"常见。校园暴力的表现形式就是 school bullying（校园欺凌）（Wikipedia：school bullying）：

School bullying is a type of bullying that occurs in any educational setting.

For an act to be considered bullying it must meet certain criteria. This includes hostile intent, imbalance of power, repetition, distress, and provocation. Bullying can have a wide spectrum of effects on a student including anger, depression, stress and suicide. Additionally, the bully can develop different social disorders or have a higher chance of engaging in criminal activity.

If there is suspicion that a child is being bullied or is a bully, there are warning signs in their behavior. There are many programs and organizations worldwide which provide bullying prevention services or information on how children can cope if they have been bullied.

7　【警惕便装术语】violence against children 翻译为"对儿童的暴力"意思正确，很多情况下确实这么翻译。但 the United Nations study on violence against children 实际上是一份报告的名称，尽管没有大写单词的首字母。这份报告的中文版叫作《联合国关于暴力侵害儿童问题的研究》。翻译中应当警惕便装术语。

【violence against children：变通翻译】violence against children/women 如何翻译，也经过很多讨论。过去倾向于统一为"针对儿童 / 妇女的暴力"，但有时修饰成分过长会导致语流不畅，于是改为"暴力侵害儿童 / 妇女"。比如，Message on the International Day to End Violence Against Women 译为"制止暴力侵害妇女行为国际日致辞"就优于"制止对妇女暴力的国际日致辞"。

8　【注意表达的细微差异：重心后置】bring...into line with 强调以前不符合规定，现在符合规定，原译意思不错，但没有体现这个细微差别。改译将重要的信息（"使之符合《儿童权利公约》的要求"）后置，突出了这一含义。

▶ 原文

31. *It*[1a] had launched a campaign for the ratification of the *Optional Protocols*[2] to the Convention on the Rights of the Child and of International Labour Organization Convention No. 182 on the worst forms of *child labour*[3]. *It*[1b] reiterated its call to States parties to withdraw any *reservations*[4] to the Convention[5] and Protocols, and underlined the importance of the *Optional Protocol on a communications procedure*[6]. The European Union Charter of Fundamental Rights required *it*[1c] to take children's views into consideration, *and*[7] it would collect data on its *members'*[8] legislation, policy and practice in order to uphold *the right of children to be heard*[9].

✍ 原译

31. 欧盟已经开展了一项运动，旨在批准《儿童权利公约的任择议定书》和关于最恶劣形式的童工劳动问题的《国际劳工组织第182号公约》。欧盟重申，呼吁缔约国收回对公约和议定书的一切保留意见，并强调《任择议定书》在来文程序方面的重要性。《欧洲联盟基本权利宪章》要求欧盟考虑儿童的观点，而且欧盟将收集成员国在立法、政策和实践方面的数据，以维护儿童的声音被听到的权利。

✍ 改译

31. 欧盟已经开展了一项运动，推动批准《儿童权利公约的任择议定书》和关于最恶劣形式的童工劳动问题的《国际劳工组织第182号公约》。欧盟重申，呼吁缔约国收回对《儿童权利公约》及其议定书的一切保留意见，并强调《关于来文程序的任择议定书》的重要性。《欧洲联盟基本权利宪章》要求欧盟考虑儿童的观点。欧盟将收集成员国在立法、政策和实践方面的数据，以维护儿童表达意见的权利。

★ 解 析

1 【衔接和连贯：明确指代关系】翻译时，必须弄清楚所有代词的指代对象，并根据汉语习惯决定是否翻译、是否还原。本段的 it(1a/1b/1c) 是指欧盟，查看上一段最后一句话可知："The European Union had adopted a four-year Action Plan on Unaccompanied Minors in 2010, and had contributed €70 million to UNICEF in 2011."。

2 【补充知识】关于"任择议定书"，请参阅以下资料：

Very often, human rights treaties are followed by "Optional Protocols" which may either provide for procedures with regard to the treaty or address a substantive area related to the treaty. Optional Protocols to human rights treaties are treaties in their own right, and are open to signature, accession or ratification by countries who are party to the main treaty. (un.org)

optional 的意思是，国家可以选择加入，也可以选择不加入。

【补充知识】凡是涉及来文程序（communications procedure）和调查程序（inquiry procedure）的公约条款和议定书，中国都没有接受。前者允许公民个人到相关公约的监测机构（monitoring body）去投诉政府，后者允许监测机构到国内进行调查。

3 【child labour 与"童工"：咬文嚼字】child labour 在国内都翻译为"童工"，但 child labour 是一个抽象概念，即雇佣儿童的现象，可以翻译为"儿童劳动"；而"童工"则是指具体的人，即被雇佣的儿童。请看 Wikipedia 给 child labour 的定义：

Child labour refers to the employment of children in any work that deprives children of their childhood, interferes with their ability to attend regular school, and that is mentally, physically, socially or morally dangerous and harmful. This practice is considered exploitative by many international organizations. Legislations across the world prohibit child labour. These laws do not consider all work by children as child labour; exceptions include work by child artists, family duties, supervised training, certain categories of work such as those by Amish children, some forms of child work common among indigenous American children, and others. (Wikipedia: child labour).

再看 MBA 智库百科对"童工"的定义：

童工是指未满 16 周岁，与单位或者个人发生劳动关系从事有经济收入的劳动或者从事个体劳动的少年、儿童。

可见，两个概念不同。"童工"在英文中是 child labourer。如下列两个例句：

- ILO says global number of **child labourers** had been down by a third since 2000.

- A new ILO report shows that the fight against **child labour** is on the right track, but the goal of eliminating its worst forms by 2016 will not be met at the current pace.

实际上，国际劳工组织反对的是"最恶劣形式的儿童劳动"，并非一切儿童劳动；用更常见的中文表达，是"消灭最恶劣形式的童工现象"。但既然第 182 号公约的中译本已经使用"童工劳动"的译法，引用时还是严格照搬，叙述中可以灵活翻译。

4　【补充知识】关于"保留"（reservations），意思如下：一个国家在加入公约时，如果不喜欢某个条款，可以对这个条款提出保留意见，不受这一条约束。但被保留的条款不能是公约的核心条款。

5　【指代关系】此处的大写 Convention，是指《儿童权利公约》。因为第一句话说呼吁各国加入《国际劳工组织 182 号公约》，说明各国还未加入；没有加入，就无所谓保留。因此，只能是对《儿童权利公约》的保留。

6　【理解背景】The Optional Protocol to the Convention on the Rights of the Child on a communications procedure was adopted and opened for signature, ratification and accession by General Assembly Resolution A/RES/66/138 of 19 December 2011. 本次练习涉及的会议是 2012 年 10 月 18 日召开的，也就是《任择议定书》刚开放签署不久，因此他强调该议定书的重要性。

7　【and 不一定翻译出来】and 是否翻译，要看它和上文的关系。take children's views into consideration 和 the right of children to be heard 存在呼应关系。可见，and 之前是因，and 之后是果。and 可以翻译为"因此"，或者省略不译，把逗号改为句号或分号，形成"意合"。and 的此种用法，参见 en.oxforddictionaries.com：

1.2 Used to connect two clauses, the second of which refers to something that results from the first.

"There was a flash flood and by the next morning the town was under water."

— More example sentences

"Early successes in some areas were dramatic, and by the early 1960s malaria was reduced to very low levels in certain countries."

"Don't take the movie too seriously, and you might enjoy it too."

"Catch all the rust spots before they spread—do that and a car will last forever."

"But the fun had gone out of it and the next day we did not travel."

8 【member："成员国"还是"会员国"】此处 members 指的是 members of the European Union，即欧盟的成员国。值得注意的是，members 并非在任何情况下皆可译为"成员国"。在新华社发布的《新华社新闻信息报道中的禁用词和慎用词（2016 年 7 月修订）》中提到：

在涉及国际关系时，若一些国际组织的成员既包括国家也包括地区，则在谈及此类国际组织时，不得使用"成员国"，而应使用"成员"或"成员方"，例如，不可称"世界贸易组织成员国"和"亚太经合组织成员国"，而应称"世界贸易组织成员"或"世界贸易组织成员方"与"亚太经合组织成员（members）"或"亚太经合组织成员经济体（member economies）"。联合国的成员，称为"会员国"。

9 【right to be heard：表达意见权】the right to be heard 有不同的译法，比如"倾诉权""陈情权"，在一定情境下也许可以使用，但在《儿童权利公约》中，有专门的定义：

The right to be heard (also children's participation) is a child rights principle as defined by the UN Convention on the Rights of the Child. According to Article 12 of the Convention, children have the right to express their views in all matters affecting them and their views have to be given due weight in accordance with the age and maturity of the child. This right applies equally to children's participation in social and political matters as well as in judicial and administrative proceedings. As a general principle, the child's right to be heard reflects the concept of children's "agency", viewing children not only as vulnerable persons in need of special protection, but also as informed decision makers, rights holders and active members of society.

由此看来，翻译为"表达意见权"可能比较中性，也更准确。"倾诉"（一股脑把心里话全说出来）和"陈情"（述说自己的情况或衷情）似乎都有些感情色彩，直译为"被听到的权利"又不太符合中文习惯。

▶ 原文

46. As part of efforts to reform the Nicaraguan social model and eradicate poverty progressively *with a special focus on early childhood*[1], *an early childhood policy had been developed that illustrated the shift in both focus and actions—families were being*[2] shown that it was possible to raise children with love and respect. The Government had restructured the entire social welfare system, *with*[3] each institution carrying out its proper role. Through the early childhood intervention programme, the Government would *reach*[4] some 900,000 families nationwide in 2013.

✍ 原译

46. 作为改革尼加拉瓜社会模式以及逐步消除贫困工作（特别关注早期童年）的一部分，政府出台了一个早期童年政策，阐明了关注重点和行动方面的变化——向家庭展示，能够用爱和尊重抚养孩子成长。政府已经重组了整个社会福利体系，每个机构各司其职。通过早期童年干预计划，在2013年，政府的影响将遍及全国90万个家庭。

✍ 改译

46. 作为尼加拉瓜社会模式改革及逐步消除贫困工作的一部分，政府特别关注幼童，制定了幼童政策，调整了工作重点和行动方案，以此向家庭表明，可以用关爱和尊重儿童的方式抚育儿童成长。政府改组了整个社会福利体系，确保每个机构各司其职。通过幼童干预方案，2013年全国约90万个家庭将得到政府帮助。

⊛ 解 析

1 【不添加显著标点】原译加了个括号（而且加的地方不对），这是联合国文件翻译不鼓励的。除非搭建句子结构特别困难，否则不添加显著的标点符号（如括号、破折号、引号）。

2 【确保语气连贯】原译破折号之前已经很长，"向家庭表明"的主语不明确；改译打乱重组，省略破折号，一气呵成。

3 【逻辑主语一致】改译在"每个机构各司其职"之前增加了一个无实质意义的"确保"，使两个句子主语一致，读起来更加连贯。

4 【变通翻译】reach 无论是作为动词或是名词，均有众多词义，需要根据情况变通翻译。此处笔者调整了句子结构，避开了 reach 一词。

▶ 原文

51. Thailand was the first country in the world *to become a party to*[1] the Optional Protocol to the Convention on the Rights of the Child on a communications procedure, reflecting its willingness to listen and *to give voice to the voiceless*[2], *particularly*[3] children themselves.

✍ 原译

51. 泰国是《儿童权利公约关于来文程序的任择议定书》的第一个签约国，这表明泰国愿意倾听并为无声者尤其是儿童本身赋声。

✍ 改译

51. 泰国是《儿童权利公约关于设定来文程序的任择议定书》的第一个缔约国，这表明泰国愿意倾听并让那些无法表达意见的人、尤其是儿童表达自己的意见。

★ 解 析

[1]【party 和 signatory】party 通常翻译为"缔约国""缔约方"（取决于相关实体是否为主权国家）。一个国家签署条约后，还需要经过批准才能成为缔约方。"签字国"和"缔约方"的区别如下：

A country may become a party to a treaty through more than one path. One path is to sign the treaty during the period in which the treaty is open for signature and then to ratify the treaty. However, a country may also become a party by acceding to or by accepting the treaty.

When a country becomes a signatory to a treaty, it declares its intention to make the terms of the treaty legally binding on itself, but the act itself does not make that act binding. When a country ratifies a treaty, it makes the terms of the treaty legally binding, once the treaty's requirements for entry into force are met.

For example, the U.S. has signed the Kyoto Protocol, but not ratified it. The Kyoto Protocol is not binding on the U.S.

Members of the European Union have both signed and ratified the Kyoto Protocol; when the Kyoto Protocol meets the minimum requirements for entry into force, the protocol will be binding on them. Kyoto has not yet met those requirements, however, so Kyoto is not legally binding on any country. (sedac.uservoice.com)

【缔约行为术语】涉及缔约行为的一些术语，请搜索联合国的词汇表"Glossary of Terms

Relating to Treaty Actions"，其中包括以下词条（译文来自联合国文件）：

- Acceptance or Approval（接受或核准）
- Accession（加入）
- Act of Formal Confirmation（正式确认行为）
- Adoption（通过）
- Amendment（修正）
- Authentication（［条约文本的］认证）
- Correction of Errors（错误更正）
- Declarations（声明）
- Definitive Signature（确定签署）
- Deposit（交存）
- Entry into Force（生效）
- Exchange of Letters/Notes（换函/换文）
- Full Powers（全权证书）
- Modification（（个别缔约国之间对条约的）修改）
- Notification（通知）
- Objection（（对保留的）反对）
- Provisional Application（暂时适用）
- Ratification（批准）
- Registration and Publication（登记和公布）
- Reservation（保留）
- Revision（变更）
- Signature ad Referendum（暂签/签署后须经确认）
- Signature Subject to Ratification, Acceptance or Approval（签署后须经批准、接受或核准）

2　【voiceless：避免造词】Voiceless means without the power or right to express an opinion (collins dictionary.com)，是个比喻的说法，表示无法为自己的权利发声，但简化为"无声者"，还不曾见到。译者尽量不造新词。"赋声"也是一个新造的词，我相信来自"赋权"（empower）。除非有媒体大力宣扬，否则新词很难生存下来。"赋权"（empower）是联合国中文处成功创造的少量词语之一，把 support 翻译为"支助"，就不成功。

3　【顿号用法探讨】"让那些无法表达意见的人、尤其是儿童表达自己的意见"，此句中的顿号用法是否规范？中华人民共和国国家标准《标点符号用法》（GB/T 15834-2011）中规定，顿号表示并列词语之间的停顿。"无法表达意见的人"和"尤其是儿童"不是并列关系，按照国标，不能使用顿号，只能改用逗号。但改为逗号明显感觉停顿太长。搜索汉语语料库发现，类似情况下使用顿号的"实践"（practice）广泛存在，只是国标没有能够反映这一实践。比如：

- 如果把这一观念的变化比作一座缓慢移动的冰山，那么在激流中与惊涛骇浪殊死搏斗的漂流勇士，是露出海面的冰山之顶；而**千百万人、尤其是青年们**的关注，则是没于海面之下的巨大座基。（《振奋中华民族的探险开拓精神》，陈小川，《红旗》杂志，1986-12-16）

- 四年多来，电影创作解放思想，冲破禁区，把爱情内容**作为人们、尤其是广大青年**的一个重要侧面来表现，让人耳目一新，这是一大进步。（《当前电影创作中的二三问题》，依英，《文汇》月刊，1981-5-1）

在联合国的翻译语料库中，遇到 especially 短语，有以下各种译法，包括使用顿号：

（1）不用标点，例如：

- 这对**加沙地带平民尤其是妇女和儿童生活**的方方面面产生了不利影响。

- 再次强烈谴责**贩运人口特别是贩运妇女和儿童**的行为。

（2）用顿号，例如：

- 进一步加强**联合国与区域和次区域组织、尤其是非洲联盟**的关系。

- 我们再次强烈谴责**贩运人口、特别是贩运妇女和儿童**的行为。

（3）用逗号，例如：

- 并应按照**国际法，尤其是国际人权法、难民法和人道主义法**采取这种措施。

- Progression 的专长是为穷人和**被边缘化者，尤其是妇女**提供支持。

（4）用括号（原文无括号），例如：

- 委员会对依然有大量的厄瓜多尔**妇女（尤其是土著妇女和非裔妇女）**陷于贫穷和受到社会排斥感到关切。

- 最近的全球性事件（比如冲突和金融危机）在很多方面构成了**实现（特别是帮助女童实现）**目标 2 的障碍。

由此看来，实践中有人使用顿号表示并列之外的较短停顿。但为了慎重起见，译者最好问一下委托人关于标点使用的具体规定。如果没有，译者可以自行决定。

▶ 原文

53. The Chinese Government had implemented a development strategy that made children a *priority*[1a] and had a *complete legal system*[1b] on the protection of the rights of the child. Plans for child development in China included specific requirements for implementing *nutrition and health programs for preschool children*[2a] in poor areas, special care to vulnerable groups, including orphans, children with disabilities and *street children*[2b] and bans on *foetal sex identification*[2c] and *illegal abortion*[2d].

✐ 原译

53. 中国政府已实施一项以儿童为重点的发展策略，并且拥有保护儿童权利的完备法律体系。中国儿童发展计划包括：贫困地区学前儿童营养和保健项目实施的具体要求；包含孤儿、残疾儿童、街头儿童在内的弱势群体特殊照顾；禁止产前性别识别和非法堕胎。

✐ 改译

53. 中国政府实施了儿童优先的发展战略，完善了保护儿童权利的法律体系。中国儿童发展纲要的具体要求包括：实施贫困地区学龄前儿童营养和健康干预项目；特别关注孤儿、残疾儿童、流浪儿童等弱势儿童群体；禁止胎儿性别鉴定和非法堕胎行为。

★ 解 析

1 【中国代表发言尽量回译】这是中国代表的发言，翻译的时候尽量向委托人获取原始的中文发言材料，按照中文回译。如果找不到，就在网上查找相关资料。《中国儿童发展纲要（2011—2020 年）》包括相关内容（1a/1b），可以借鉴，比如："在经济和社会发展总体规划中体现儿童优先原则""十年来，国家加快完善保护儿童权利的法律体系"。

2 【查找原始文件】与这一句（2a/2b/2c/2d）相关的表述包括："实施贫困地区学龄前儿童营养与健康干预项目""孤儿、贫困家庭儿童、残疾儿童、流浪儿童、受艾滋病影响儿童等弱势儿童群体得到更多的关怀和救助""加大对利用 B 超等进行非医学需要的胎儿性别鉴定和选择性别人工终止妊娠行为的打击力度"。原译"学前儿童""街头儿童"都是正确的说法，但既然中国政府用"学龄前儿童""流浪儿童"，译者不妨沿用。illegal abortion 是否要翻译为"选择性别人工终止妊娠"？由于字面差别太大，建议不更改。

▶ 原文

83. The increasingly frequent removal of *Russian-Finnish children*¹ from their families by Finnish authorities was grounds for concern. Such actions had negative consequences for the development and well-being of the children involved, and ran counter to the Convention on the Rights of the Child, whose *preamble*² stated, *in part*³, that *"the family, as the fundamental group of society and the natural environment for the growth and well-being*⁴ *of all its members and particularly children, should be afforded the necessary protection and assistance so that it can fully assume its responsibilities within the community"*⁵.

✍ 原译

83. 芬兰当局日益频繁地把俄裔芬兰儿童从家中带走的行为令人担忧。这种行为对相关儿童的发展和福祉有负面影响，与《儿童权利公约》背道而驰。《公约》前言中写道：（部分引用）"家庭是所有家庭成员尤其是儿童成长和福祉的基本社会群体和自然环境，应该被提供必要的保护和援助，才能充分承担其社区责任。"

✍ 改译

83. 芬兰当局日益频繁地把俄裔芬兰儿童带离家庭的行为令人关切。这种行为对这些儿童的发展和幸福有负面影响，与《儿童权利公约》背道而驰。《公约》序言指出："家庭作为社会的基本单元，作为家庭所有成员、特别是儿童的成长和幸福的自然环境，应获得必要的保护和协助，以充分负起它在社会上的责任。"

★ 解 析

1 【关注发言者身份】为什么要提"俄裔芬兰儿童"？因为发言者来自俄罗斯联邦，亲情使然。

2 【决议的组成部分】preamble 统一译为"序言"，不用"前言"。所有的公约和决议都有序言部分（preambular part）和执行部分（operative part）。关于这两部分的语言特点，读者可以通过英文关键词检索。

3 【淡化原文瑕疵】in part 在原文中是插入语，在原译中被放入括号里，还置于句子开头，很突兀。此处"部分引用"其实很多余。引用默认是部分引用，全文引用的很少。所以，译文要淡化这个意思。改译干脆省略这个词。

4 【well-being："福祉"还是"幸福"】Well-being refers to a good or satisfactory condition of existence; a state characterized by health, happiness, and prosperity. (dictionary.com) 联合国的很多文件都翻译为"福祉"，很书面化。《儿童权利公约》中将其译为"幸福"，比较接地气，此处沿用。

5 【避免另起炉灶】这段话引自《儿童权利公约》，译者需要找到公约的中译本，直接抄录相关中文。除非有重大错误，否则译者不要改动公约的原译，也不要另起炉灶。

▶ 原文

88. Under *an agreement signed by the Government of Nigeria*[1a], *the International Labour Organization and the International Programme on the Elimination of Child Labour*[1b], shelters were being established to *rehabilitate and reintegrate rescued trafficked children with their families*[2]. *Human trafficking*[3] must be addressed not only through law enforcement actions, but also through policies aimed at prevention and, most important, protection of the victim.

✎ 原译

88. 根据尼日利亚政府同国际劳工组织签订的《消除童工国际项目协议》的要求，该国正建立收容所，同已救出的被贩卖儿童的家人一道，帮助这些儿童恢复正常生活并重新融入社会。人口贩卖问题不仅仅必须靠执法行动解决，还要靠以预防、更重要的是保护受害者为目标的政策解决。

✎ 改译

88. 根据尼日利亚政府同国际劳工组织和废除童工国际计划签署的一项协议，尼日利亚正在建立一些收容所，帮助获救的被贩运儿童恢复正常生活、重新融入家庭。人口贩运问题不仅必须通过执法行动解决，还必须通过旨在预防、特别是保护受害者的政策加以解决。

★ 解 析

1 【并列还是偏正】an agreement signed by the Government of Nigeria（1a）与 the International Labour Organization and the International Programme on the Elimination of Child Labour（1b）是并列成分，即协议是由尼日利亚政府与两者共同签订，原译理解有误。the International Labour Organization and the International Programme on the Elimination of Child Labour 简称为 the ILO-IPEC。笔者在网上找到如下资料：

It commits to help in reducing the cases of child labour. This ILO programme assumes responsibility of giving direct services of 9,350 children involved in child labour in the Philippines. (ilo.org)

2 【理解结构瑕疵】rehabilitate 可以视情况翻译为"恢复""改造""平反"等，参见 en.oxforddictionaries.com：

VERB

[WITH OBJECT]

1 Restore (someone) to health or normal life by training and therapy after imprisonment, addiction, or illness.

"helping to rehabilitate former criminals"

(+ More example sentences) (+ Synonyms)

    1.1 Restore (someone) to former privileges or reputation after a period of disfavour.

    "With the fall of the government many former dissidents were rehabilitated."

    (+ More example sentences)

    1.2 Return (something, especially a building or environmental feature) to its former condition.

    "The campaign aims to rehabilitate the river's flood plain."

    (+ More example sentences) (+ Synonyms)

Origin
Late 16th century (earlier (late 15th century) as rehabilitation) (in the sense "restore to former privileges"): from medieval Latin rehabilitat-, from the verb rehabilitare (see re-, habilitate).

原译对 rehabilitate and reintegrate rescued trafficked children with their families 的理解有误。该短语的结构有瑕疵，需要分解为 rehabilitate rescued trafficked children and reintegrate rescued trafficked children with their families。

3 【human trafficking："人口贩运"还是"人口贩卖"】Human trafficking is the trade of humans for the purpose of forced labour, sexual slavery, or commercial sexual exploitation for the trafficker or others. Human trafficking is the trade in people, especially women and children, and does not necessarily involve the movement of the person from one place to another. (Wikipedia: human trafficking)

human trafficking 翻译为"人口贩运"还是"人口贩卖"，联合国中文处也是争论不休，最后定为"人口贩运"，不再改了。所以，即使中文读者不太习惯，也需要沿用。国内更多使用"贩卖人口"的说法。因为 traffic 的本意就是 trade，只不过是非法交易，参见 en.oxforddictionaries.com：

VERB

[NO OBJECT]

Deal or trade in something illegal.

"The government will vigorously pursue individuals who traffic in drugs."

(+ More example sentences) (+ Synonyms)

Origin

Early 16th century (denoting commercial transportation of merchandise or passengers): from French traffique, Spanish tráfico, or Italian traffico, of unknown origin. Sense 1 dates from the early 19th century.

从词源也可看到，这个词确实隐含着货物或乘客的运输。我想这也是最终确定为"贩运"的原因。"贩卖"当中的"贩"，已经隐含了买卖，"贩运"就是为了贩卖而进行的运输，符合这个词的本义。当然，如果确定为"贩卖"，也有道理，甚至更有道理，因为如前所述，human trafficking...does not necessarily involve the movement of the person from one place to another，即 trafficking 不一定涉及"运输"。

【human smuggling：走私人口】一个相关的概念是 people smuggling，Wikipedia 的解释如下：

People smuggling (also called human smuggling), under U.S. law, is "the facilitation, transportation, attempted transportation or illegal entry of a person or persons across an international border, in violation of one or more countries' laws, either clandestinely or through deception, such as the use of fraudulent documents".

可见，smuggle 是帮助他人偷渡或自行偷渡，在联合国文件中有多种译法，包括"偷渡""偷运人口""人口走私"。people smuggler 译为"蛇头"。

第 ④ 单元　联合国大会第六委员会会议简要记录

背景说明

　　本单元选自联合国大会第六十八届会议的正式记录, 内容为第六委员会开会的简要记录。全文见文件 A/C.6/68/SR.26, 可在联合国正式文件系统中找到。

　　遇到比较难的文件, 需要进行更多背景调查, 才能较好理解原文。

　　从文件上的目录和简要记录可以看到, 在这次会议上, 第六委员会听取了国际法委员会主席就该委员会前两届(第六十三届和第六十五届)会议所做工作的介绍。进一步调查发现，第六十五届会议所做工作的报告内容如下：

Summary of Contents

其中的第七章和第八章，就是本单元涉及的内容。如果事先查看相关内容，就可以更好理解会议的讨论。注意：该报告在会前已经发到第六委员会委员手中，所以，主席不是宣读报告，而是在作简要介绍后，听取第六委员会的意见（即简要记录的内容）。

关于第六委员会和国际法委员会，请参阅以下资料：

The United Nations General Assembly Sixth Committee (the Legal Committee) is the last of the six main committees of the United Nations General Assembly. The Sixth Committee is the primary forum for the consideration of legal questions in the General Assembly.

The Sixth Committee meets every year from late September to late November, in parallel with the General Assembly's annual session. At the beginning of the session, the General Assembly assigns to the Sixth Committee a list of agenda items to be discussed. Those items usually include the annual reports of the International Law Commission, the United Nations Commission on International Trade Law, the Ad Hoc Committee established by Resolution 51/210 of 17 December 1996 on Terrorism, the Special Committee on the Charter of the United Nations and on the Strengthening of the Role of the Organization and the Host Country Committee, as well as the item Measures to Eliminate International terrorism.

The International Law Commission was established by the General Assembly at its second session, in 1947, with a view to giving effect to Article 13, Paragraph 1 (a), of the Charter and with the objective of promoting the progressive development of international law and its codification (Resolution 174 (II)). It holds an annual session at the United Nations Office at Geneva. (Wikipedia: United Nations General Assembly Sixth Committee)

练习和讲解

▷ 原文

1. Mr. Misonne (Belgium) said, in response to the Commission's request for information on State practice concerning the *provisional application of treaties*[1], that article 167 of the Belgian Constitution as revised in 1994 set out the basic principle that all treaties must be submitted for approval to the Parliament or to the *competent assembly or assemblies*[2], and that approval was necessary for treaties *to have effect in Belgian law*[3]. Neither article 167 nor the Cooperation Agreement of 8 March 1994 among the Federal State, the Communities and the Regions of the Kingdom of Belgium in relation to the modalities of concluding *mixed treaties*[4] (in the Belgian constitutional sense) contemplated the provisional application of treaties. While the provisional application of treaties could be agreed between the parties and produce effects in international law, it was therefore limited with respect to the domestic law of Belgium as a result of the constitutional requirement of approval. *If the provisional effect sought pertained to domestic law, the agreement for provisional application and the treaty provisions concerned were subject to the approval process*[5].

✎ 原译

1. Misonne先生（比利时）在回应委员会请求各国提供资料、说明其关于暂时适用条约的惯例时说，1994年修订的《比利时宪法》第167条规定的基本原则是：所有条约必须提交议会、主管的一个或多个会议批准，并且条约必须获得批准才能具备比利时法律效力。《宪法》第167条及比利时王国联邦、各大区和各语区间于1994年3月8日达成的、关于缔结（《比利时宪法》所称的）混合条约方式的《合作协议》，均未详细考虑暂时适用条约的问题。各方可就暂时适用条约达成协议，并产生国际法效

✎ 改译

1. Misonne先生（比利时）在回应委员会请各国提供资料说明暂时适用条约的国家实践时表示，1994年修订的《比利时宪法》第167条规定的基本原则是，所有条约必须提交联邦议会或一个或多个主管地方议会审议，获得批准后才能在比利时法律中发生效力。《宪法》第167条和1994年3月8日比利时王国联邦、各族群和各地区关于（《比利时宪法》所谓）混合条约缔结方式的《合作协议》，均未述及条约暂时适用的问题。虽然条约的暂时适用由各方商定并由此产生国际法效力，但因为《宪法》规定条约须经批准，

⊡ **原译**

力；由于《宪法》规定暂时适用条约必须得到批准，因而这一问题在比利时国内法上受到了限制。条约若要在国内法上产生想要的暂时效力，暂时适用协议和相关的条约条款须通过批准程序。

⊡ **改译**

所以条约的暂时适用在涉及比利时国内法时受到限制。如果暂时适用的效果涉及国内法，有关暂时适用的协议及相关条约条款就必须通过批准程序。

⊛ **解 析**

1 【补充知识】条约的暂时适用（provisional application of treaties）问题属于国际法的前沿问题，译者不一定清楚，需要查阅相关资料。这份记录的内容为"Agenda Item 81: Report of the International Law Commission on the work of its sixty-third and sixty-fifth sessions (continued)"，其中有个"续"字，可知会议记录还有前半部分。本文件的编号是 A/C.6/68/SR.26，其中的 26，是指第 26 次会议，不妨查查第 25 次会议的记录，以了解更多背景。在谷歌中搜索 A/C.6/68/SR.25，就可以找到（此处从略）。

也可以直接查找 provisional application of treaties：

The provisional application of treaties is a relatively recent development in international treaty law designed to address some of the shortcomings of the traditional practice of concluding treaties. Generally, the process of concluding a treaty has taken place under a three-step process of signature（签署）, ratification（批准）, and entry into force（生效）. Parties to a treaty must express their consent to be bound, a process most commonly achieved through a simple signature that expresses a party's consent to be bound subject to domestic ratification of the treaty. Signatories then must ratify the treaty under their respective domestic procedures. Once the required number of signatories has ratified the treaty, the treaty will definitively enter into force. It is only at this point that positive legal obligations arise under the treaty. Prior to entry into force, a treaty does not impose positive legal duties and obligations on signatory parties; and as a result of each state's varying process of ratification, there is often a substantial gap in time between treaty signature and entry into force. By contrast, provisional application imposes duties and obligations on signatories during this gap period and can be best understood as an attempt to solve collective action problems created by this gap. Under the provisional application of a treaty, signatory states undertake to give effect to treaty obligations prior to the completion of the domestic ratification procedures, with the intention of acceding to the treaty once domestic ratification has been completed. However, the extent to which these obligations are binding, affirmative legal obligations has not been firmly established in international law. (harriman.columbia.edu)

概括起来就是，条约必须在国内立法机关批准之后才对该国有约束力，但"条约的暂时适用"要求国家在没有批准之前就接受条约的约束。提出这个概念是因为条约正式生效可能需要很长时间，而在这期间需要采取集体行动。所谓 positive obligation（积极义务），就是国家必须采取行动才能履行的义务；negative obligation（消极义务）是指国家只要不干预，就算完成了义务。与此相对的是 positive rights（积极权利），即需要国家采取行动公民才能享受的权利，比如健康权需要国家建立医疗保险制度；negative rights（消极权利）是指只要国家不干预，公民就能实现的权利，比如言论自由。

【顿号可能引起的误解】原译当中的顿号应当去掉，否则，顿号前后可能被误解为两项并列的内容。按说可以分为两个句子："委员会请各国提供资料，说明关于条约暂时适用的国家实践。Misonne 先生（比利时）对此作出回应时表示……"，但鉴于简要记录英文版把所有发言者的名字和国别都放在段落开头，让读者对发言者的变化一目了然，中文版也要求遵循这一格式，尽管这样做可能导致句子冗长。

2 【查英文释义】A competent authority is any person or organization that has the legally delegated or invested authority, capacity, or power to perform a designated function (Wikipedia: competent authority)，中文通常译为"主管当局"或"主管部门"。此处的 competent assembly 可参照这种译法。

【理解文字背后的含义】但更为重要的问题是此处的 assembly 指什么？首先从 Wikipedia 查到比利时的行政区划情况：

federal state	1	Kingdom of Belgium										
language areas	4	Dutch				bilingual	French					German
communities	3	Flemish Community					French Community					German-speaking Community
regions	3	Flemish Region					Brussels Capital Region	Walloon Region				
provinces	10	West Flanders	East Flanders	Antwerp	Limburg	Flemish Brabant	Brussels Capital Region	Walloon Brabant	Hainaut	Luxem-bourg	Namur	Liège
arrondissements	43	8	6	3	3	2	1	1	7	5	3	4
municipalities	589	64	65	70	44	65	19	27	69	44	38	75	9
judicial areas	5	Ghent		Antwerp			Brussels		Mons		Liège	
judicial arrondissements	12	1	1	1	1	1	1 (2)	1	1	1	1	1	1

（Wikipedia: communities, regions and language areas of Belgium）

从最左边一栏，可以看到基于不同标准划分的区域：language areas、communities、regions、provinces，等等。

综合考虑，language areas 可以译为"语言区"。"语言区"共有4个，包括3个单语区和1个双语区（荷、法）。communities 共有3个：佛莱芒语（一种荷兰语）族群、法语族群、德语族群，是按照语言划分的群体。communities（族群）尽管以语言为区分，但不能译为"语言区"，否则与 language areas 无法区分。regions 分为3个，是地理概念，因此可以译为"地区"。根据另一份资料：

Federal Belgium as we now know it today is the result of a peaceful and gradual political development seeking to give the country's various Communities and Regions wide-ranging self-rule. This enables them to run their own policies in a way that is closely geared to the needs and wishes of their own citizens. In amongst other elements, the diversity and self-rule of the Regions and Communities manifest themselves in their own Parliaments and Governments. Same as the Federal Parliament, each of these Regional Parliamentary assemblies has its own powers, is able to autonomously adopt laws and regulations for its territory and population and ratify international treaties in respect of its own powers. (docs.vlaamsparlement.be)

由此可知，简要记录中的 parliament 应该是指联邦议会；assembly 应该是指"地方议会"（包括地区和族群的议会），可以在译文中体现出来。至于"地区""族群"的概念，因为这是会议记录，不便解释。读者不懂的话，只能自己去查资料。

3 【正确理解修饰关系】原译"具备比利时法律效力"说法很奇怪，原文 in Belgian law 限定 to have effect。Belgian law 不是一部法律，而是指比利时法律体系。条约批准之后，等于纳入了国内法律体系，所以产生效力。

4 【补充知识】关于 mixed treaties，比利时外交部网站提供的信息为：

Depending on the distribution of authority between the federal authorities and the federated entities, a distinction is made between exclusively federal treaties, treaties which exclusively concern the Communities and Regions, and mixed treaties...The mixed treaties must be approved by all legislative authorities concerned.

其中的 federated entities 就是指 Communities and Regions。所以，翻译为"混合条约"没有错。此处尽管不查资料也能翻译正确，但不查资料无法增长见识。同时，通过这些资料也加深了对前文的理解：我们可能以为 the competent assembly or assemblies 仅仅是为了表示语法上的严谨性，笼统翻译为"地方议会"即可，但了解到有些条约一个议会批准即可，有些需要多个议会批准，就知道最好还是译为"一个或多个地方议会"。

5 【在理解的基础上翻译】此处原译理解不到位。该句的意思是，如果条约的暂时适用影响到国内法，相关协议和条款就要得到议会批准。这样规定是可以理解的，因为条约的签署是国家首脑、外交部部长等行政机关代表完成的，但立法权由议会行使，所以涉及法律修改时，应该交给议会完成。条约的暂时适用实际上是行政权力越权，因此是有争议的，仅限于紧急和特殊情况下使用。比如，某条约规定要建立一个秘书处，负责条约的实施，如果等到条约生效再来建立，不知道要等多久。这时如果签署国同意暂时适用，就可以马上建立。

▶ **原文**

2. *Prior to the revision of the Constitution, Belgium had provisionally applied some agreements, including agreements on air transport and on raw materials, without the prior approval of the competent assemblies*[1]. With regard to the legal effects of provisional application, his delegation considered that, in most cases, if the parties agreed to the provisional application of a treaty, *its provisions would apply just as if it had entered into force*[2].

✐ **原译**

2. 在修宪之前，比利时在没有获得主管会议事前批准的情况下暂时适用了一些协议，包括关于空运和原材料的协议。关于暂时适用的法律效力问题，比利时代表团认为，在多数情况下，如果各方就某个条约的暂时适用达成一致，该条约条款将产生与该条约已经生效同样的效力。

✐ **改译**

2. 在修宪之前，比利时曾经未经主管地方议会事先批准而暂时适用过一些协定，包括关于航空运输和原材料的协定。关于暂时适用的效力，比利时代表团认为，在多数情况下，如果各方就某个条约的暂时适用达成一致，则条约条款的适用将视同该条约已经生效。

★ **解 析**

1 【揣测言外之意】从上一段看，《比利时宪法》规定暂时适用须经议会批准。本段说宪法修订前，曾经未经批准暂时适用过某些协定。合理的推断是宪法修订后，未经批准不再允许暂时适用；或者之前未经批准而暂时适用发生在不影响国内法的情况下，今后遇到这种情况还可以暂时适用。如有兴趣，可以进一步查阅《比利时宪法》当年修订的相关资料。注意：本次会议是 2013 年 11 月 5 日召开的，要查的是在此之前的修订内容。

原译意思没有问题，但似乎存在一点责备的口气，改译缓和一下。

2 【语言简洁】原文说得过去，改译更加简洁。

> ▶ **原文**
>
> 4. Mr. Momtaz (*Islamic Republic of Iran*[1]), speaking on the topic, "*Formation and evidence of customary international law*[2]", said that his delegation welcomed the decision to change the title of the topic to "Identification of customary international law" and did not consider that it would affect the scope of the topic or the mandate given to the Commission. The question of the source of *peremptory norms (jus cogens)*[3] should be excluded from the topic for several reasons: the concept was more closely related to the *hierarchy of norms*[4], and the formation of *jus cogens* followed a different path from that of customary international law. Some of the rules that applied to the latter, such as *the notion of the "persistent objector*[5]" had no place in the formation of *jus cogens*. Nevertheless, the interest in peremptory norms and the lack of generally accepted criteria for identifying them was a subject that merited *consideration*[6] by the Commission, which might attempt to determine under what conditions an ordinary rule reached the *status of jus cogens*[7].

✏ **原译**

4. Momtaz先生（伊朗伊斯兰共和国）就"习惯国际法的形成和证据"专题发表意见时说，伊朗代表团欢迎将本专题的名称变更为"习惯国际法的识别"的决定，不认为这会改变本议题的范围或本委员会的任务授权。强制法（jus cogens）的来源这一问题应该被排除在这个专题之外，有如下几条原因：这一概念与法律规范的层级联系更密切，强制法的形成遵循的是一条与习惯国际法不同的路径。适用于后者的一些规则，例如"一贯反对者"这一概念在强制法的形成中并未发挥任何作用。然而，人们对强制法的兴趣犹存，而又没有用于识别强制法的普遍接受的标准；这一问题值得本委员会考虑，可以试图确定在何种条件下普通规则达到了强制法的状态。

✏ **改译**

4. Momtaz先生（伊朗伊斯兰共和国）就"习惯国际法的形成与证据"专题发表意见时说，伊朗代表团欢迎将本专题的名称变更为"习惯国际法的识别"的决定，不认为这会影响本专题的范围或国际法委员会的职责。强制性规范（强行法）的来源这一问题应该排除在这个专题之外，因为这一概念与规范的层级性联系密切，其形成遵循的是一条与习惯国际法不同的路径。适用于习惯国际法的一些规则，例如"一贯反对者"的概念在强行法的形成中没有任何位置。但强制性规范令人关注，又缺乏公认的识别标准，是一个值得国际法委员会审议的问题。委员会不妨尝试确定在何种条件下普通规则可提升至强行法地位。

⊛ 解 析

1 【国名翻译紧贴原文】伊朗的名字要用全称，原译正确。在联合国文件翻译中，要遵守一条规则：原文用全称，译文也用全称；原文用简称，译文也用简称。The United States of America 译为"美利坚合众国"，U.S.、U.S.A.、America 都译为"美国"。The United Kindom of Great Britain and Northern Ireland 译为"大不列颠及北爱尔兰联合王国"，the United Kingdom 译为"联合王国"，the U.K. 译为英国。重要的术语，可以利用联合国术语库查找，但要注意鉴别。

2 【议题参照已有译法】议题的名称，在开会之前都已经翻译好，会议记录中要采用已有的译法。如果无处查找，可以猜测一个译法，然后在网上检验。比如，此处猜测为"国际习惯法的形成和证据"，一查，看到以前的文件用"习惯国际法的形成与证据"。由此可知：不用"国际习惯法"，而用"习惯国际法"；不用"和"，而用"与"。上网查《联合国日刊》，可看到每天召开的各种会议和相关议题。

3 【补充知识】peremptory norms，拉丁文为 *jus cogens*，分别译为"强制性规范"和"强行法"，意思相同，指必须绝对服从和执行的法律规范，原本为国内法上的概念，是同国内法上的任意法（*jus dispositivum*）相对而言的。把强行法概念引入国际法的是奥地利学者菲德罗斯。1969 年的《维也纳条约法公约》第一次正式使用了强行法概念。强行法是为了整个国际社会的利益而存在的，是国际社会公认为不能违背且以后只能以同等性质的规则才能变更的规则，它不能因个别国家的条约排除适用。（chinalawedu.com）

"强行法"的英文解释请看如下资料：

A peremptory norm (also called *jus cogens*, Latin for "compelling law") is a fundamental principle of international law that is accepted by the international community of states as a norm from which no derogation（减损）is permitted. Unlike ordinary customary law（普通习惯法）, which has traditionally required consent and allows the alteration of its obligations between states through treaties, peremptory norms cannot be violated by any state "through international treaties or local or special customs or even general customary rules not endowed with the same normative force". (Wikipedia: peremptory norm)

4 【补充知识】规范的层级（性）是指法律规范层次的高低。在中国，从高到低的法律规范是：宪法（constitution）、法律（law）、法规（regulations）、行政规章（administrative rules）。关于国际法的层级和强行法，下面一段文字会有启发：

In international law there is no hierarchy of sources or rules, at least as between the two primary law-creating processes, that is, custom and treaty. Both these processes and the sets of rules created through them possessed equal rank and status. The reason for this state of affairs is that States did not intend to place limitations on their sovereign powers that they had not expressly or implicitly accepted. However, a special class of general rules made by custom has been endowed with a special legal force: they are peremptory in nature and make up the so-called *jus cogens*, in that they may not be derogated from by treaty (or by ordinary customary process); if they are, the derogating rules may be declared null and void. Thus, these peremptory norms have a rank and status superior to those of all the other rules of the international community. This chapter discusses the emergence of *jus cogens*; establishment and the scope of *jus cogens*; instances of peremptory norms; the limitations of *jus cogens* as envisaged in the Vienna Convention; partial remedies to those limitations, provided by customary international law; the legal effects of *jus cogens*; the limited reliance on *jus cogens* in international dealings; and national cases using *jus cogens* as a *ratio decidendi* and national legislation relying upon the same notion. (Antonio Cassese. International Law (2nd ed.), Chapter II: The Hierarchy of Rules in International Law— The Role of *Jus Cogens*)

5 【补充知识】Wikipedia 对 "一贯反对者"（persistent objector）的解释是：

In international law, a persistent objector is a sovereign state which has consistently and clearly objected to a norm of customary international law since the norm's emergence, and considers itself not bound to observe the norm. The concept is an example of the positivist doctrine that a state can only be bound by norms to which it has consented.

由此可知，对于一个习惯国际法规则，如果一个国家长期表示反对，就可以不遵守；但对于强行法，长期反对也没用（have no place）。原译译为过去时 "未发挥作用" 不正确，意思是 "不发挥作用"（改译换了个说法，意思不变）。原文之所以用过去时，是因为简要记录采用转述的方式，把现在时改成了过去时，翻译为汉语时，要恢复现在时。同样，过去完成时要理解为现在完成时或过去时。依此类推。

6 【根据上下文确定词义】Consideration refers to the act of considering, meditation, deliberation (dictionary.com)，在此语境下应为 deliberation，即 "审议" "商议" 的意思。原译为 "考虑"，但后文说 which might attempt to determine under what conditions an ordinary rule reached the status of *jus cogens*，表明在 consideration 之后应是 determination，而委员会仅靠 "考虑" 是无法作出决定的，因此必然是 "审议"。

7 【根据上下文确定词义】the status of *jus cogens* 中的 status 被译为"状态"不准确。前面谈到规范的层级，所以，此处是指"地位"。reached 表面看是过去时，但应理解为现在时。

▶ 原文

5. In order to preserve the unity of the rules of customary international law, the Special Rapporteur should avoid *approaching each branch of international law differently*[1]. The tendency to give priority to *opinio juris*[2] at the expense of State practice in certain fields, such as international criminal law, *endangered*[3] the unity of international law. In all cases, a customary rule of international law did not emerge unless both those elements were firmly established. The Special Rapporteur rightly stressed the need to consider *State practice*[4] in all legal systems and all regions of the world, an approach that would ensure the *universality*[5] of international law. To that end, the Commission should not rely heavily on the jurisprudence of tribunals *mandated*[6] to settle specific disputes. Unfortunately, access to State practice was not always easy: it was rare that all States systematically compiled and published their practice of international law in *one of the official languages of the United Nations*[7], and some States did not have the expertise and capacity to make their practice known.

✍ 原译

5．为了保持习惯国际法规则的统一，特别报告员应该避免对国际法的每个分支采用不同的方法区别对待。在诸如国际刑法等领域，为了一味强调法律确念而不顾国家惯例的倾向使国际法的统一性处于危险之中。所有的情况下，只有这两个因素确立起来，国家法的习惯规则才会出现。特别报告员正确地强调了需要考虑世界上所有法律体系和所有地区的国家惯例，这一方法可以确保国际法的普适性。为此，委员会不应严重依赖解决具体争端的特设法庭的判例。不幸的是，获取国家惯例往往并非易事：各国很少以联合国一种官方语文编撰和出版其国际法方面的惯例，一些国家也不具备宣传其实践的专门知识和能力。

✍ 改译

5．为了保持习惯国际法规则的统一，特别报告员应该避免区别对待国际法的每个分支。在诸如国际刑法等领域，过于强调确信为法、不顾国家实践的倾向威胁到国际法的统一。在所有的情况下，只有这两个要件都牢固确立，国际法的习惯规则才会出现。特别报告员强调了需要考虑世界上所有法律体系和所有地区的国家实践，这是正确的想法，可以确保国际法的普遍性。为此，委员会不应过于依赖奉命解决具体争端的特别法庭的判例。遗憾的是，获取国家实践往往并非易事，因为各国很少用联合国官方语文系统编纂和出版国际法实践，一些国家也不具备宣传其国家实践的专才和能力。

⊛ 解 析

1 【语言简洁：少用"把"和"对"】原译"对国际法的每个分支采用不同的方法区别对待"，可以简化为"区别对待国际法的每个分支"。翻译时尽可能少用"把"字和"对"字结构，直接用动词＋宾语。

2 【补充知识】关于习惯国际法规则形成的两个要素——"法律确念"（译为"确信为法""信守为法"或"信以为法"可能更恰当）（*opinio juris*）和"国家实践"（state practice），见Wikipedia 的解释：

Opinio juris sive necessitatis ("an opinion of law or necessity") or simply *opinio juris* ("an opinion of law") is the belief that an action was carried out as a legal obligation. This is in contrast to an action resulting from cognitive reaction or behaviors habitual to an individual. This term is frequently used in legal proceedings such as a defense for a case.

Opinio juris is the subjective element of custom as a source of law, both domestic and international, as it refers to beliefs. The other element is state practice, which is more objective as it is readily discernible. To qualify as state practice, the acts must be consistent and general international practice.

3 【斟酌用词】endangered 译为"处于危险之中"虽然意思没错，但感觉有些过头，译为"威胁到"可能更好。

4 【使用常用说法】state practice 可能有人翻译为"国家惯例"，但"国家实践"应该更常用，也更准确。中国代表、外交部条法司司长徐宏在第七十一届联合国大会第六委员会关于"国际法委员会第六十八届会议工作报告"议题的发言中有这样一段话：

国家实践是习惯国际法规则形成的最重要证据，国家实践应是全面的、一贯的和具有充分代表性的，不仅要看以往的国家实践，也要看当前的国家实践。特别是在联合国成立后，发展中国家在国际舞台上愈发活跃，在国际规则和国际秩序发展中的作用更加明显，发展中国家的国家实践应受到足够重视，应被视为习惯国际法规则形成的重要证据。

5 【补充知识】universality 被译为"普适性"，是就法律适用而言，但此处并未涉及其适用性，而是讲其来源的普遍性。国际法的来源主要有四个方面：国际条约、国际习惯、一般法律原则、国际组织决议。本段探讨的就是其中的第二方面。

国际习惯是指各国在其实践中通过重复类似的行为而形成的具有法律拘束力的行为规则，其形成须具备两个要件：一个是物质要件，即必须有"惯例"的存在（惯例是指各国重复的类似行为）；另一个是心理要件，即确信为法，也就是存在的惯例已被各国普遍接

受为法律（也就是普遍性）。（参见李广民等主编的《国际法》第16页，清华大学出版社2006年出版）

6 【根据上下文确定词义】原译漏译了mandated。Mandate means to authorize or decree a particular action (dictionary.com)，通常译为"授权"。站在被授权人的角度，可译为"受权"。名词mandate视情况译为"职责""任务"等。一些联合国文件译为四个字"任务授权"，但其中的"任务"和"权"（"权力"）意思上有冲突。

7 【避免表达歧义】one of the official languages of the United Nations译成"联合国一种官方语文"可能会产生歧义：很少有国家用"一种"联合国语文编撰文件，是否意味着大多数国家都用两种或多种语言编写？此处的one没有强调的意思，可以不译。"很少用联合国官方语文"既包括用一种，也包括用多种。注意：联合国惯用"语文"，而不是"语言"。

▶ 原文

7. With regard to the topic, "Provisional application of treaties", *his delegation had doubts about the assessment that provisional application was consistent with the definitive commitment of States pursuant to their constitutional procedures*[1]. The commitment to provisionally apply the treaty must be based on the agreement of the States parties and *was justified*[2] by the intention of the parties to achieve its purpose quickly. Some treaties, particularly those including rights and obligations for individuals, could not be applied provisionally. Similarly, provisions creating monitoring mechanisms could not be subject to provisional application. On an exceptional basis only, States might utilize provisional application as a measure of confidence-building and good will. *To the extent that*[3] provisional application produced obligations identical to those resulting from the entry into force of the treaty, the decision to put an end to its application could create complex situations. In sum, from many points of view *the topic was not ripe for consideration by the Commission*[4].

✍ 原译

7. 关于"条约暂时适用"这一专题，伊朗代表团对暂时适用符合各国按照宪法程序作出的确定承诺的评估表示怀疑。暂时适用条约的承诺必须基于国家缔约方的同意，并以缔约方有意快速实现条约为基础。有些条约，尤其是包含了个人权利和义务的条约，无法暂时

✍ 改译

7. 关于"条约的暂时适用"这一专题，伊朗代表团质疑报告的评估意见，即暂时适用符合各国依各自宪法程序作出的明确承诺。对暂时适用条约的承诺必须基于缔约国的同意，承诺的正当性在于缔约国希望尽快实现条约目的。有些条约，尤其是包含个人权利和义务的条约，不能暂

📝 原译

适用。类似地，设立监测机制的条款也无法实行暂时适用。只有基于极个别的理由，国家才能用暂时适用作为建立信任和表达善意的工具。如果暂时适用产生了与因条约生效而产生的义务完全相同的义务，终止暂时生效的决定可能会造成复杂的局面。总之，从多个视角来看，本委员会考虑这一主题并不成熟。

📝 改译

时适用。与此类似，设立监测机制的条款也不能暂时适用。只有在例外情况下，国家可以将暂时适用作为建立信任和表达善意的工具。鉴于暂时适用产生了与条约生效完全相同的义务，终止暂时适用的决定可能造成复杂的局面。总之，从多个视角看，国际法委员会审议这一专题的条件并不成熟。

★ 解 析

1【查找历史资料】这句话比较抽象，需要结合国际法委员会的报告来理解。不妨找到这份报告，通过关键词（如 procedure）查到相关内容。在报告中有一句话（第119段）：

A further concern was expressed that the provisional application of treaties raised serious questions about the circumvention of established domestic procedures, including constitutional requirements, for participation in treaties. Other members did not share such concerns.

这句话可能与本段有关。但这句话当中的 A further concern 用的是单数，说明只有一个代表团表示关注，说不定就是伊朗代表团。Other members did not share such concerns 的言外之意是，表示关切的国家很少，大家都认为暂时适用不违反国内程序。原句中的 assessment 是指国际法委员会在报告中的情况评估。为了便于表达，可以加上"报告"或"国际法委员会"。弄清楚英文每个抽象名词的逻辑主语对于灵活翻译很重要。原译没有错，只是定语长了一点。

2【灵活翻译】be justified 不容易翻译，有时译为"理由是"或"是有道理的"，此处灵活处理为"正当性"（也可以说"合理性"）。本句中的 its 应当理解为 the treaty's，尽管距离遥远。

3【查英文释义】To the extent that is used for saying that because one thing is happening, something else happens (collinsdictionary.com)，即表示原因，所以改译为"鉴于"。

4【为搭配增译】"本委员会考虑这一主题并不成熟"意思不清楚。改为"审议这一问题/主题的时机/条件……"，意思就明确了。即使在联合国文件中，也可以增加个别没有实质意义的词，让句子更加通顺。

第 ⑤ 单元 《残疾人权利公约》缔约国会议简要记录

学习要点

思维方法

★ **宏观思维**
1. 关注部分在整体中的位置
2. 关注上下文的联系
3. 关注文件形成的年代
4. 用宏观思维解决微观问题

★ **逻辑思维**
　区分and表达并列还是偏正关系

★ **批判性思维**
　辨析"区域"和"地区"

调查研究方法
1. 查证方法：difference between
2. 查英文释义
3. 通过背景材料澄清结构歧义

理解

★ **补充知识**
1. regional organizations
2. reference
3. zero draft
4. *Journal of the United Nations*
5. Open-ended Working Group
6. models of disability
7. 联合国的地理区划

★ **理解语言**
1. 区分input、output、outcome、impact
2. 区分programme和agenda
3. 区分goal和target
4. 理解文字背后的含义
5. 注意修饰关系

表达

★ **意思准确**
1. 表达含糊是因为理解含糊
2. overarching issues
3. 注意表达的细微差异
4. 注意言外之意
5. 根据语境确定译法

★ **符合形式**
1. 注意搭配
2. 语言简洁
3. 变换视角
4. 语域适当
5. 顺句驱动
6. 外国人名的译法
7. 简要记录中不翻译人名
8. 迁就官方译本的小瑕疵
9. 联合国中文处标点符号使用规则
10. and译为分号
11. 避免包孕结构
12. 句子结构紧凑
13. 尊重约定译法
14. "残疾人"与"残障人"

变通
1. 尽量贴近原文
2. 根据情景使用更具体的词
3. as appropriate：尽量不省略
4. 尽量抄录官方译文
5. 适度灵活
6. 调整英文记录的时态
7. 重要概念不可省译

背景说明

本单元选自 2014 年 6 月 10 日至 12 日在联合国总部纽约召开的第七届残疾人权利公约缔约国大会第 3 次会议的简要记录（文号: CSP/2014/SR.3）。《残疾人权利公约》及其《任择议定书》（文号: A/RES/61/106）于 2006 年 12 月 13 日在联合国大会通过, 2007 年 3 月 30 日开放签署, 是 21 世纪国际社会通过的第一个综合性人权公约, 也是开放给区域一体化组织签署的第一个公约。该公约于 2008 年 5 月 3 日生效。

练习和讲解

▶ 原文

26. With regard to *the second question, the adoption of sustainable development goals*[1] would create *a mobilizing force*[2] for implementation of the Convention, as the practical steps and solutions *being proposed*[3] would *actively involve*[4] persons with disabilities in the post-2015 agenda. The *overarching issues*[5] of economic growth and poverty eradication also affected persons with disabilities *and the shift from the MDG logic was important*[6a] since the sustainable goals considered persons with disabilities from a development *perspective*[7]: they were *assets and resources*[8] for inclusive development, no longer *seen solely in terms of what they needed*[6b], but how they could contribute to sustainable development. However, national implementation would be necessary *and it would be up to State and civil society organizations for persons with disabilities to ensure that, once adopted, the post-2015 framework was faithfully reflected in national development agendas*[9].

✎ 原译

26. 关于第二个问题，可持续发展目标一旦通过就会为落实《公约》集中力量，因为尚在酝酿的实际措施和解决方法意味着将残疾人纳入实现2015年后的议程。经济增长和消除贫困这样影响面广的问题也影响着残疾人群，重要的是跳出了千年发展目标的思路，因为可持续发展目标是以发展的眼光看待残疾人：他们是包容性发展的资本，不再单单被看成需要外界给予的群体，而是看他们怎么能为可持续发展贡献力量。然而，国内层面的执行很重要，2015年后的框架会不会重视体现在国内发展规划中，取决于政府与残疾人权利组织的合作。

✎ 改译

26. 关于第二个问题，可持续发展目标通过后，就会为落实《公约》创造推动力量，因为本次会议提出的切实措施和解决方案将使残疾人积极参与2015年后议程。经济增长和消除贫困这两个全局性问题也影响残疾人群。跳出千年发展目标的逻辑很重要，因为可持续发展目标是以发展的视角看待残疾人，把残疾人视为包容性发展的资产和资源，而不是等待满足需求的对象。残疾人是能够为可持续发展作出贡献的力量。然而，国内层面的执行很重要，国家与民间社会创办的残疾人组织需要努力确保2015年后的框架一旦获得通过，就能忠实地体现在国内发展议程上。

⊛ 解 析

1 【关注部分在整体中的位置】Act local, think global. 在做任何翻译练习或进行翻译实践时，即使仅仅负责其中一部分，也要浏览整个文件，了解文件和作者的背景，以及本部分在整个文件中的位置。在翻译过程中，遇到与前文有关的内容（比如此处的 the second question），也要查阅前文相关部分。

这次练习摘自《残疾人权利公约》缔约国会议的一次会议记录，查看全文，可知会议的主题是 Matters related to the implementation of the Convention (continued)（与执行《公约》有关的事项（续）），下设两个议题（联合国称"议程项目"），即 General debate (continued)（一般性辩论（续））和 Round table 1: Incorporating the provisions of the Convention on the Rights of Persons with Disabilities in the post-2015 development agenda（圆桌会议 1：将《残疾人权利公约》的各项规定纳入 2015 年后发展议程）。

【《联合国日刊》】注意：翻译联合国会议的议题时，要查找《联合国日刊》（journal. un.org）中已经提供的译法，不要另起炉灶。《联合国日刊》刊载联合国各机构每天的会议安排，包括开会的机构、时间、会议室、议题等信息（参见下图）。2018 年之前，只有联大重要会议期间以六种语文提供，其余时间只有英文和法文。自 2018 年 1 月 2 日起，根据大会第 70/305 号和第 71/323 号决议，新的《联合国日刊》以六种官方语言发布。

No. 2014/111

Wednesday, 11 June 2014

Journal
of the United Nations

Programme of meetings and agenda

✉ 🐦 📘

Official meetings

Wednesday, 11 June 2014

General Assembly
Sixty-eighth session
**Interactive Dialogue on "Addressing Conditions
Conducive to the Spread of Terrorism"**[1] 📹 [webcast]

Opening
Statements by the President of the General
Assembly and the Secretary-General of the
United Nations
10:00   Trusteeship Council
Chamber

Pillar I dialogue
"Countering the Appeal of Terrorism and
Interactive Dialogue"
11:10   Trusteeship Council
Chamber

Closing
12:50   Trusteeship Council
Chamber

Security Council

09:30   7196th meeting   Security Council
Chamber

📹 [webcast]

1. Adoption of the agenda

2. United Nations peacekeeping operations[1]

New trends

Letter dated 1 June 2014 from the
Permanent Representative of the Russian
Federation to the United Nations addressed
to the Secretary-General (S/2014/384)

【区分 programme 和 agenda】《联合国日刊》中的 programme of meetings and agenda 长期以来一直译为"会议日程和议程",但"日程"和"议程"不易区分。agenda 的英文解释是:a list of matters to be discussed at a meeting (collinsdictionary.com),来自拉丁语 *agere*("to do"),所以翻译为"议题"更准确。把 programme of meetings and agenda 翻译为"会议日程和议题",两个概念的对比就比较清楚。但原有译法已经存在几十年,修改起来并不容易。以下是本次会议的日程安排:

Convention on the Rights of Persons with Disabilities

Conference of States Parties
Seventh session

10:00 to 13:00	3rd meeting ▸◀ [webcast]	Conference Room 4 (NLB)
	Matters related to the implementation of the Convention [item 5]	
	(b) Round table 1: Incorporating the provisions of the Convention on the Rights of Persons with Disabilities in the post-2015 development agenda	
15:00 to 18:00	4th meeting ▸◀ [webcast]	Conference Room 4 (NLB)
	Matters related to the implementation of the Convention [item 5]	
	(c) Round table 2: National implementation and monitoring	

[To check the list of side events please *click here*.

The Conference of State Parties will be a PaperSmart session. All documentation and statements will be available for downloading electronically through PaperSmart Portal *(click here)*. Delegations planning to deliver statements at the session are requested to submit electronic versions of their statements to papersmart@un.org, *at least two hours* in advance of the delivery.

For further information concerning the Conference of States Parties, please contact Mr. Guozhong Zhang, Secretariat for the Convention on the Rights of Persons with Disabilities, Division for Social Policy and Development, Department of Economic and Social Affairs (DESA) (e-mail zhangg@un.org); or visit United Nations Enable website: www.un.org/disabilities *(click here)*.]

【关注上下文的联系】查看摘要记录全文可知,本段及后面几段选自圆桌会议 1。会议一开始,主席向与会专家提出了三个问题供讨论:

- What specific entry points currently existed for including disability in the post-2015 agenda?

- How could a new framework best address the inequalities faced by persons with disabilities in relation to relevant emerging goals concerning poverty eradication, health and education?

- How could the inclusion of disability in the post-2015 agenda be monitored and evaluated?

练习中所说的 with regard to the second question,就是指其中的第二个问题。之所以提出这些问题,是因为即将结束的千年发展目标(MDGs, Millennium Development Goals)没有关注残疾问题,借此制定可持续发展目标(SDGs, Sustainable Development Goals)之际,各弱势群体纷纷采取行动,将本群体的诉求纳入可持续发展目标。残疾群体就是其中一个。2015 年 9 月 25 日联合国大会第七十届会议通过了第 70/1 号决议《变革我们的世界:2030 年可持续发展议程》,决议中公布了 17 个可持续发展目标和 169 个具体目标。

【关注文件形成的年代】这里需要提醒一下,翻译历史文件时,必须关注文件形成的年代,以当年的视角理解文本。本次练习中涉及的会议是 2014 年 6 月召开的,当时正在商讨制定《2030 年可持续发展议程》(2030 Agenda for Sustainable Development)(其中包含若干可持续发展目标），接续 2015 年到期的千年发展目标。上述三个问题中提到的 post-2015 agenda、new framework、emerging goals 就是指《2030 年可持续发展议程》及其包含的可持续发展目标。了解这些背景，就可以断定 adoption 是指将来的通过，而不是已经通过。单从语法上看，无法判断 adoption 发生的时间（尽管可能不影响翻译）。这是用宏观思维解决微观问题的一个典型例子。

【区分 goal 和 target】顺便指出：goal 和 target 在汉语中都翻译为"目标"，但在 MDGs/SDGs 中，goal 是个大概念，每个 goal 之下设有很多二级目标。鉴于联合国翻译不轻易添加词语的传统，选择把 goal 翻译为"目标"，为了区分，不得已把 target 翻译为"具体目标"。我们按此译法翻译即可。但这不意味着在其他场合，不能把 goal 翻译为"大目标 / 一级目标"，把 target 翻译为"小目标 / 二级目标"。

2 【理解文字背后的含义】Mobilize means to marshal, bring together, prepare (power, wealth, etc.) for action, especially of a vigorous nature (dictionary.com)，可以译为"集中""动员""调动"等词。之所以说 SDGs 可以成为 a mobilizing force，是因为一旦把残疾事业定为目标，就可以为此筹措资源。世界上有超过 10 亿的残疾人，然而，残疾问题却没有被包含进任何一个千年发展目标（goal）、具体目标（target）或监测指标（indicator），发展残疾事业师出无名，现在制定 SDGs 要避免这种情况。

【注意搭配】原译"为落实《公约》集中力量"可以接受，但似乎力度不够。改译最初是"为落实《公约》创造动员力"，但这个搭配不正确，故再改为"为落实《公约》创造推动力量"。

3 【用宏观思维解决微观问题】propose 意为"提出"。原译将 being proposed 译为"尚在酝酿"，不够准确。"尚在"隐含不成熟，原文无此意。本次圆桌会议的主题是"将《残疾人权利公约》的各项规定纳入 2015 年后发展议程"（Think global!），目的就是听取各位专家的意见，看如何在 2015 年后发展议程中体现公约规定。因此，being proposed 指圆桌会议提出的各种建议。

4 【变换视角】Involve means to include someone in something, or to make them take part in or feel part of it (dictionary.cambridge.org)，意为"使某人参与其中"。原译为"纳入"，意味着残疾人是被动参与的，与原文 actively involve 的主动含义相悖。如果按照顺句驱动的方式翻译，意思恐怕不够明确，不妨变换视角，把"残疾人"变为主语，这样更能表示残疾人的积极主动性。

5 【语言简洁】Overarching means including or influencing every part of something or encompassing (thefreedictionary.com)，原译为"影响面广的"，可以接受；根据英文解释译为"全局性

（的）"更简洁一些。overarching issues 在联合国文件中出现多种译法，除了"全局性问题"外，还有两大类：一类是"首要问题""重大问题""最重要的问题""中心问题"等；另一类是"普遍存在的问题""普遍性问题""贯穿各事项的问题""跨部门问题""跨越性问题""总体问题""总括性问题""全盘性问题"等。从上下文看，第二类表达意思比较准确。

6【区分 and 表达并列还是偏正关系】...and the shift from the MDG logic was important（6a）：本句话与上句是并列关系，原译将其译为递进关系，造成意思偏差。除此之外，本句可以不改。改译只是采用更加贴近原文的说法。

【发现衔接关系】另外，根据逻辑，the MDG logic（千年发展目标的思路 / 逻辑）就是指 6b: seen solely in terms of what they needed（把残疾人视为等待满足需求者）。

【补充知识】这里涉及对待残疾人模式的转变。过去把残疾人看作病人（叫作"医疗模式"），需要康复、照顾；现在把残疾看作社会造成的（叫作"社会模式"），只要提供必要的社会条件（如修盲道、提供盲文、消除障碍等），残疾人同样能发挥作用。有篇文章（Models of Disability: A Brief Overview）介绍了对待残疾的九种模式，可以搜索阅读。

7【语域适当】perspective 不是专有名词，所以可以灵活翻译，比如，译为"眼光"或"视角"。"视角"比"眼光"更正式一些。

8【尽量贴近原文】翻译联合国文件时尽量把每个实词都翻译出来，原译将 assets and resources 合并译为一个词"资本"，可能会被审校改过来。

9【表达含糊是因为理解含糊】原译"……会不会重视体现在国内发展规划中，取决于政府与残疾人权利组织的合作"意思含糊不清，原因是理解不到位。这句话的意思是，国际法规定再好，还要靠国内来执行。因此，政府和非政府组织要努力把将来通过的可持续发展目标转化为国内发展政策。

【尽量贴近原文】State and civil society organizations for persons with disabilities 意思是国家设立的残疾人组织和民间的残疾人组织；简而言之，就是政府和非政府残疾人组织。但联合国文件要求很严谨，译文要尽量照顾原文措辞，因此改为"国家与民间社会创办的残疾人组织"。

【"残疾人"与"残障人"】persons with disabilities 译为"残疾人"还是"残障人"存在很大争议。大陆地区最早使用"残废人"，后来改为"残疾人"，沿用至今；港澳台地区则同时使用"残疾人""残障人""伤残者""身心障碍者""失能者"。鉴于《残疾人权利公约》是从医学模式转向社会模式，很多人认为"残疾人"的说法不妥当（"残疾"明显含有疾病色彩），但既然公约的中文本已经用了"残疾人"，后来的译者也无法改变。实际上，disability 的本义是"失能"，译为"失能者"最准确。

▶ 原文

27. *On the issue of monitoring*[1], it was only possible to manage what could be measured. The collection of *disaggregated data*[2] was important, *and the added value*[3] of the post-2015 agenda was that it would encourage Member States to start collecting such data, which, in turn, would increase the focus on vulnerable groups. While the high-level political forum on sustainable development would be the main body to monitor and evaluate progress, the Committee on the Rights of Persons with Disabilities also had an important role to play in that regard.

✎ 原译

27. 关于监督的问题，只有可量化的才便于管理。汇总分列数据是重要的，而且2015年后议程的另一个好处是鼓励缔约国汇总这类数据，从而增加对弱势群体的关注度。尽管可持续发展高级别论坛将是负责监督和评估进展的主要机构，残疾人权利委员会也可以在这方面发挥重要作用。

✎ 改译

27. 关于监测的问题，只有量化，才便于管理。收集分列的数据很重要；2015年后议程的附带好处是鼓励缔约国收集分列数据，从而增加对弱势群体的关注。尽管可持续发展高级别政治论坛是负责监测和评估进展的主要机构，但残疾人权利委员会也可以在这方面发挥重要作用。

★ 解 析

1 【关注上下文的联系】这是在回答主席提出的第三个问题，即"How could the inclusion of disability in the post-2015 agenda be monitored and evaluated?"。意思是：可持续发展议程中纳入了残疾人方面的目标后，如何监测（"监督"的宾语是人）目标的落实？此处的回答是：只有量化，才能监测（It was only possible to manage what could be measured）。量化的方法是分类收集数据（即分别收集男女残疾人的受教育水平、健康状况等数据，而不是笼统收集国民的教育和健康数据等）。

2 【尊重约定译法】disaggregated data 联合国翻译为"分列数据"，意思是分别列出的数据，相对于 aggregated data（汇总数据）而言。disaggregation of data 联合国翻译为"数据的分列"。译者需要遵循先例。但在联合国文件之外，大家也可以使用"分类"或"分解"。

3 【and 译为分号】and 不必每次都翻译出来。此处省略不译，把逗号改为分号，两句话之间的逻辑关系会更清楚一些。

【注意言外之意】added value 即"附加值""附带好处"。原译"另一个好处"，给人以还有其他好处之感，而前文并未探讨其他好处，故译为"附带好处"更妥。

▶ 原文

28. *Mr. Seth*[1] (Department of Economic and Social Affairs) said that *the promise of a life of respect and dignity for all and sustainable development*[2] would be empty if the needs of the one billion persons with disabilities were not met. *Inclusive development and societies*[3] required *serious actions*[4] to guarantee the rights of persons with disabilities and ensure that they were among the main beneficiaries of and contributors to development. *Such actions could only be provided by caring societies and Governments and must be the responsibility of all stakeholders*[5], including the private sector. *There was no shortage of legislative frameworks, but the main deficit was in implementation and in translating outcomes into concrete steps—particularly at national level*[6]*—*that improved the quality of life of persons with disabilities everywhere and included them in development processes.

✎ 原译

28. 塞思先生（经济和社会事务部）表示，如果10亿残疾人的需要无法得到满足，给予全世界人民以有尊严和体面的生活和可持续发展就会沦为一纸空谈。实现包容性发展和社会意味着要采取庄严的行动，保障残疾人的权利，确保他们既是国家发展的主要受益者，也是贡献者。这样的行动，只有一个懂得关爱他人的社会和政府才会践行，同时必须成为所有利益攸关方的责任，包括私营企业。要实现这样的目标，不缺制度，缺的是落实和——尤其是在国内层面——将成果变为实实在在的行动，从而改善各地残疾人的生活质量并将他们纳入发展进程。

✎ 改译

28. Seth先生（经济和社会事务部）表示，如果10亿残疾人的需要无法得到满足，确保所有人在生活中获得尊重和享受尊严的承诺以及可持续发展就会沦为空谈。为实现包容性发展、建设包容性社会，必须认真采取行动，保障残疾人的权利，确保他们既是国家发展的主要受益者，也是贡献者。这样的行动，只有懂得关爱他人的社会和政府才会组织实施；这样的行动必须成为所有利益攸关方，包括私营企业的责任。现在不缺法律框架，缺的主要是落实以及把立法成果变为具体行动——尤其是在国家层面——从而改善世界各地残疾人的生活质量，并将他们纳入发展进程。

⊛ 解 析

1 【简要记录中不翻译人名】Seth 本来已经译出，改译又改回英文。这是因为联合国中文处规定，"除封面页以及中国代表的姓名外，人名一律不译，即使主席或报告员以本国代表身份发言时也不例外"。

【外国人名的译法】这样规定是出于效率。因为要给一个外国人定名，通常需要先查新华社的人名翻译词典；如果没有，再按照读音逐个音节翻译。按照名从主人的原则，还要知道此人的名字在当地语言中怎么读，十分麻烦，特别是一些阿拉伯名字，写出来恨不得占一行，按照音节翻译出来很别扭。这一规定省去了很多麻烦。顺便提一下，大多数情况下，还是需要把人名翻译为汉字的，具体可参照新华社编写的《世界人名翻译大辞典》。翻译地名时可参照周定国主编的《世界地名翻译大词典》。

2 【避免包孕结构】原译 "给予全世界人民以有尊严和体面的生活和可持续发展" 结构不完整。可以去掉 "以"，或者改为 "让全世界人民以有尊严和体面的方式生活"。但无论如何改，都略显冗长。改译换了个说法，避免了包孕结构（"给予" 和 "生活" 之间插入内容过多）。

3 【注意搭配】原译 "实现……社会" 的搭配不常见，改译增加了一个与 "社会" 搭配的词 "建设"。

4 【注意搭配】serious actions 原译为 "采取庄严的行动"，也是搭配不当。"庄严" 一般同 "承诺" 搭配使用。serious 有 "严肃的，严重的，重要的，认真的" 之意，可以改为 "采取认真的行动" 或 "认真采取行动"。

5 【句子结构紧凑】actions 是 societies、Governments 和 stakeholders 的共同主语，但距离 stakeholders 比较远，改译重复 "这样的行动"，使句子结构更加紧凑。原译略显自由。

6 【重要概念不可省译】首先，legislative frameworks（法律框架）被简译为 "制度" 不合适。联合国文件中，重要的概念都要翻译出来。其次，不必添加 "要实现这样的目标"。

【注意修饰关系】第三，at national level 修饰 implementation 与 translating outcomes into concrete steps 两处，但原译变为仅修饰 concrete steps，改变了原文的意思，改译予以纠正，并通过增加一个逗号，让句子更便于阅读。

【适度灵活】另外，本句中的 outcome 如果直接翻译为 "成果"，意思不明确；最初改译为 "会议成果"，但后来发现这个 outcome 就是指 legislative framework。所以，改为 "立法成果" 应该比较贴切。

【区分 input、output、outcome、impact】这里顺带解释一下与 outcome 相关的系列用词。在项目设计和评估时，经常用到一组词：inputs、activities、outputs、outcome、impact。

inputs 译为"投入",是指人、财、物的投入。activities 翻译为"活动",是指与实现项目目标(goals)相关的行动;比如,在艾滋病防治项目中,开展的活动包括宣传教育、在热点地区安装安全套分发器、定期收集监测数据等。

outputs 译为"产出",是指项目的初级结果(results)、直接结果或短期结果;比如,某艾滋病预防项目的产出可以是开展宣传活动的次数、安装安全套分发器的数量、接受抗逆转录病毒治疗的感染者数量等。

outcome 译为"成果",是指项目的二级结果或中期结果;比如,一个安全饮用水项目的成果可以是使用消毒饮用水的居民户数、患腹泻儿童的数量下降等。

impact 译为"影响",是指项目的长期影响;比如,饮用水项目的成果是腹泻儿童减少了,项目的影响可能是儿童死亡率降低了。长期影响较难衡量,因为可能是不同项目共同作用的结果。比如,儿童死亡率降低,还可能得益于其他项目,如补充营养项目。

不同的项目可能使用不同的术语,但理念是相同的,即把项目结果分成不同的层次。有的项目用 results 代替 impacts,给翻译带来了挑战。因为在中文里,"成果"(outcome)和"结果"(result)很难区分(其实英文里也不好区分)。笔者在一次项目设计培训中,曾建议改用"一级成果""二级成果""三级成果"(Level 1/2/3 results)的说法,发言者认为是很好的建议。在不要求逐字对应的情境下,为便于读者理解,并征得用户同意,不妨采用更加灵活的翻译方法。

【查证方法】如果希望了解某些词之间的区别,可以用谷歌搜索 difference between (A, B and C)。

▶ 原文

34. Mr. Halatau (Pacific Disability Forum), speaking on behalf of the International Disability Alliance, *a network of global and regional organizations*[1] *of persons with disabilities and their families*[2], said that the Alliance *should be included*[3] in the consultative processes leading up to the elaboration of the post-2015 development agenda. The Alliance *promoted the effective and full implementation of the United Nations Convention on the Rights of Persons with Disabilities as well as compliance with the Convention within the United Nations system and represented one billion people worldwide*[4]. For the Alliance, the entry point for the discussion on the inclusion of persons with disabilities in the post-2015 development agenda was article 4.3 of the Convention, which stipulated that, *in the development and implementation of legislation and policies for implementation of the Convention, and in other decision-making processes concerning issues relating to persons with disabilities, States Parties should closely consult with and actively involve persons with disabilities, including children with disabilities, through their representative organizations*[5].

联合国文件翻译 译·注·评

⊘ 原译

34. Halatau先生（太平洋残疾人论坛）代表全球和地方残疾人及其家庭组织的网络——国际残疾人联盟发言，他说该联盟应该加入拟定2015年后发展议程的协商进程。该联盟推进了《残疾人权利公约》以及在联合国体系内遵守该公约的有效和充分的执行，该联盟代表了世界10亿人民。对于该联盟来说，关于将残疾人纳入2015年后发展议程的讨论出发点是《公约》的第四条第三款，即在制定和执行履行《公约》的立法和政策时，以及在其他与残疾人相关的决策进程中，缔约国应该通过残疾人的代表组织同残疾人（包括残疾儿童）紧密协商并积极地使他们参与进来。

⊘ 改译

34. Halatau先生（太平洋残疾人论坛）代表国际残疾人联盟发言，该组织是全球性和区域性残疾人和残疾人家庭组织组建的一个网络。他说，该联盟应该被纳入拟定2015年后发展议程的协商进程。该联盟作为世界10亿人的代表，致力于推进《残疾人权利公约》的充分有效执行以及联合国系统本身对《公约》的遵守。该联盟认为，讨论将残疾人纳入2015年后发展议程的出发点是《公约》的第四条第三款，即缔约国应当在为实施本公约而拟定和施行立法和政策时以及在涉及残疾人问题的其他决策过程中，通过代表残疾人的组织，与残疾人，包括残疾儿童，密切协商，使他们积极参与。

★ 解 析

1【补充知识】关于 regional organizations 的解释，请看如下资料：

Regional organizations, also known as ROs, are, in a sense, international organizations (IOs), as they incorporate international membership and encompass geopolitical entities that operationally transcend a single nation state. However, their membership is characterized by boundaries and demarcations characteristic to a defined and unique geography, such as continents, or geopolitics, such as economic blocs. (Wikipedia: regional organizations)

【联合国的地理区划】联合国译为"区域性组织"，其成员范围超越单个国家，但限定在一定地理区域（如亚太地区、拉美地区）。联合国将世界划分为几个级别：global、regional、(sub-regional)、national、(sub-national)、local。region 是在国家之上的大区（非洲、美洲、亚洲、欧洲、大洋洲等），联合国翻译为"区域"；regional 之下分为若干"次区域"(sub-regions)，比如，亚洲分为"东亚""中亚""东南亚""南亚""西亚"；national 指国家一级；sub-national 译为"国家之下"一级，相当于我国省、自治区、直辖市和特别行政区的级别；local 是一国之内的局部地区，联合国翻译为"地方"（如 local 与"外地"相对，则译为"当地"）。注意：region 也用来指国内的区域，其上为 national，其下为 local，相当于全球语境下的 sub-national。

【辨析"区域"和"地区"】另外，鉴于联合国文件把 region 统一译为"区域"，Asia-Pacific Region 就是"亚太区域"。但中国的媒体和政府文件却一律用"亚太地区"的说法，是因为"亚太区域"的说法不符合语言规律。"区域"一词为并列结构，"区""域"为同义词，就好比"乡镇"。比如，我们可以说"魏公村"或"魏公庄"，但不能说"魏公村庄"；同理，我们可以说"区域性机构"，但不能说"亚太区域"。话虽如此，如果大家给联合国翻译文件，不妨按照联合国的规则来做。也许将来会改过来。

2 【顺句驱动】原译将同位语 a network of...and their families 前置，略显冗长，改译按照原文信息出现的顺序翻译，读起来从容一些。注意句子断开后使用句号。

3 【注意表达的细微差异】should be included 原译"应该加入"，改译"应该被纳入"。原译语言更顺，但意思不够准确：不是该组织不想加入，而是没有被允许加入。

4 【调整英文记录的时态】promoted 看似过去时，但发言时其实用的是现在时。英文记录的习惯是把时态统一往前提一个时段，即一般现在时变为一般过去时，现在完成时变为过去完成时。翻译为汉语时，依照汉语的叙述习惯，恢复讲话时的时态。因此，promoted 不能译为"推进了"，而要改为"推进"或"旨在推进""致力于推进"。据联合国同事调查，法语的记录稿直接采用讲话者使用的时态。

【联合国中文处标点符号使用规则】United Nations Convention on the Rights of Persons with Disabilities 为专有名词，且为公约名称，要加书名号。但是，如果公约名称是机构名称的一部分，则不加书名号。如 Secretariat to convention on the rights of persons with disabilities 译为"残疾人权利公约秘书处"。作为标题时也不加。根据联合国中文处规定，书名号使用的规则如下：

（1）加书名号

宪章、规约、章程、行动纲领/方案/计划、成果文件、宣言、声明、议程、指南、议事规则、政策指示、手册、软件名。

（2）不加书名号

第一，培训课程、课题、商标、奖状、会议、活动不加。

第二，按照中文处的惯例，联合国的报告、决议、决定不加。

第三，非正式称谓或未正式通过的文本（英文常用小写）不加。

【在理解的基础上翻译】as well as 连接两个并列成分，即 the effective and full implementation of the United Nations Convention on the Rights of Persons with Disabilities 和 compliance with the Convention within the United Nations system。后者的意思是，联合国系统要带头遵守《公约》，多雇用一些残疾人。原译可能没有理解这层意思，导致前后两项杂糅，意思不明。represented one billion people worldwide 如果置于原处，与上句话的关联性不强；将其前置比较符合汉语习惯。

5 【尽量抄录官方译文】如果文件引用《公约》，译者必须去查找《公约》的中文译文，尽量抄录官方译文。如果官方译文确有错误，直接抄录导致逻辑不通，译者可以纠正。原译引用《公约》部分意思正确，但没有抄录官方译文，所以改译。

▶ 原文

35. Another key element of the Convention was *article 32*[1], in which States Parties recognized the importance of *international cooperation and its promotion*[2], in support of *national*[3] efforts for the realization of the purpose and objectives of the Convention, and agreed to undertake appropriate and effective measures in that regard, *between and among States*[4] and, *as appropriate*[5], *in partnership with*[6] relevant international and regional organizations and civil society, *in particular organizations of persons with disabilities*[7].

✎ 原译

35.《公约》另外一个关键要素在于第32条，即缔约国意识到国际合作和促进对于支持国家层面的努力来实现《公约》的宗旨和目标是十分重要的，并且同意国家间或各国在该领域采取合适有效的措施，如果合适的话，并同相关国际和地区组织和民间社会搭建伙伴关系，尤其是残疾人组织。

✎ 改译

35.《公约》另外一个关键要素是第三十二条。根据该条，缔约国确认需要通过开展和促进国际合作，支持国家为实现本公约的宗旨和目的作出的努力；同意为此在双边和多边的范围内采取适当和有效的措施，并酌情与相关国际和区域组织及民间社会，特别是残疾人组织合作采取这些措施。

★ 解析

1 【尽量抄录官方译文】一提及具体条款，就要引起警觉。本段还是涉及引用公约，因此需要抄录公约的官方译文，避免另起炉灶。注意条款编号使用汉字还是阿拉伯数字，取决于官方译文的用法。

2 【适度灵活】its 指代的是 international cooperation，即"促进国际合作"。原译"国际合作和促进"不通顺。《公约》灵活翻译为"开展和促进国际合作"。

3 【适度灵活】national 本来是形容词，但此处转为名词 nation 翻译，作为 effort 的主语，比直译为"为实现《公约》宗旨作出的国家努力"更通顺。

4 【适度灵活】between and among States 直译为"在两个和多个国家之间"，《公约》灵活处理为"双边和多边"，明显优于原译"国家间或各国"。

5 【尽量不省略】as appropriate 意为"视情况而定"或"酌情"，在联合国文件中经常使用，堪比汉语中的"依法"，有时翻译出来觉得十分多余，但不敢轻易省略。

6 【语言简洁】in partnership with 原译为"搭建伙伴关系"，这一表达不常见。最常见的说法是"建立伙伴关系"或"打造伙伴关系"。官方译文采用了更简洁的处理方式。

7 【适度灵活】in particular organizations of persons with disabilities 对前文的 organizations 进行补充说明，应尽量置于被补充的成分之后，但有时不得已也会采用原译的表达方式。

▷ 原文

47. Ms. Nigussie (Ethiopian Centre for Disability and Development), responding to questions *from the floor*[1], said that the earthquake disaster in Japan, like other disasters around the world, had shown that the interests of persons with disabilities were hardly taken into account in the development of early warning systems and other disaster reduction instruments. Yet, States should be reminded of their obligations under article 11 of the Convention, *where they agreed to take all necessary measures to ensure the protection and safety of persons with disabilities in situations of risk, including situations of armed conflict, humanitarian emergencies and the occurrence of natural disasters*[2]. With respect to the lack of indicators to measure progress in promoting the rights of persons with disabilities, *any national-level indicators that had been accepted by persons with disabilities could be submitted as examples and even best practices for consideration by the Open Working Group*[3]. She urged *participants*[4] to *keep track of developments*[5] in their respective countries and to continue putting pressure on *officials*[6] to ensure that the *references to disability*[7] in the *zero draft*[8] of the *proposed sustainable development goals*[9] and targets were not *watered down*[10] in the final document.

📖 原译

47. Nigussie女士（埃塞俄比亚残疾和发展中心）回应了听众席的问题，表示如同世界上的其他灾难，日本的地震灾难显示在建立预警系统和其他减少灾难的机制时残疾人的利益几乎没有被考虑在内。但是，各国必须牢记《公约》第11条规定的各国义务，即各国同意采取所有必要的措施在包括武装冲突、人道主义紧急情况以及自然灾难的发生的危险情况中保护残疾人并确保他们的安全。在缺乏指标来衡量促进残疾人权利的进展方面，任何得到残疾人认可的国家一级的指标都可以由开放工作组作为实例甚至供考虑的最佳做法提出。她敦促所有参与者在他们各自的国家去记录发展，并继续向官方施压，从而确保提议的可持续发展目标和具体目标的预稿中提及残疾人的内容不会在最后的文件中被删减。

📖 改译

47. Nigussie女士（埃塞俄比亚残疾和发展中心）回应了听众的问题，表示如同世界上的其他灾难，日本的震灾显示，在建立预警系统和其他减灾机制时几乎没有考虑过残疾人的利益。但是，各国必须牢记其根据《公约》第11条承担的义务，即缔约国应当采取一切必要措施，确保在危难情况下，包括在发生武装冲突、人道主义紧急情况和自然灾害时，残疾人获得保护和安全。关于缺乏指标来衡量残疾人权利方面的进展问题，任何得到残疾人认可的国家级指标都可以作为实例甚至最佳做法提交给开放工作组，供其参考。她敦促所有与会者跟踪本国动态，继续向官员施压，确保最后文件不会弱化可持续发展目标和具体目标提案预稿中提及残疾人的内容。

⊛ 解 析

1 【查英文释义】From the floor means (of a speech or question) delivered by an individual member at a meeting, not by a representative on the platform; for example, questions from the floor. (learnersdictionary.com) 原译"听众席"没错，可以简化为"听众"，也可以说"与会者"。

2 【尽量抄录官方译文】这一段又是引用《公约》的内容，应确保与官方译本一致。

【迁就官方译本的小瑕疵】官方译本"残疾人获得保护和安全"有一点搭配问题："获得安全"似应改为"获得安全保障"，但那样的话，就多出一个原文没有的"保障"。原译文"保护残疾人并确保他们的安全"解决了搭配问题。但因为官方译本意思没有错，通常情况下不会因为这一点小瑕疵而在引用时修改。

3 【通过背景材料澄清结构歧义】这句话结构上有歧义：by the Open Working Group 是修饰 submitted 还是修饰 consideration? 单靠语法知识无法判断。查 Open Working Group SDGs 得知："The Rio+20 outcome document, the future we want, inter alia, set out a mandate to establish an Open Working Group to develop a set of sustainable development goals for consideration and appropriate action by the General Assembly at its 68th session." (ulibrary.

org)。看来这个工作组是负责起草 SDGs 的，完成后交给联大通过。但工作组负责起草 SDGs，也不会凭空编造，一定是听取各方意见；谁有好的建议，都可以提交给它。因此，the Open Working Group 一定是修饰 consideration。原译理解有误。

另外，查联合国术语库，得知这个工作组的全称叫作 Open Working Group of the General Assembly on Sustainable Development Goals（大会可持续发展目标开放工作组）。联合国还有一些 open-ended working group，译为"不限成员名额的工作组"，比如 Open-ended Working Group on Ageing（不限成员名额的老龄化问题工作组）和 Ad Hoc Open-ended Working Group（不限成员名额特设工作组）。

4【根据情景使用更具体的词】此处 participants 是指本次圆桌会议的代表"与会者"，原译"参与者"意思不明确。

5【根据语境确定译法】Keep track means to be aware or keep informed (dictionary.com)，意为"了解""悉知"。development 除了常见的表示"发展"的意思之外，还指 a recent event that is the latest in a series of related events; for example, an important development in the fuel crisis (dictionary.cambridge.org)，意为"进展""动态"。

6【尊重约定译法】official 此处为名词，意为 a person appointed or elected to an office or charged with certain duties (dictionary.com)，即"官员"。尽管译为"官方"（the authority 或 the official）意思上没有什么区别，但联合国文件倾向于尽量采用原文的说法。

7【补充知识】references to disability 原译没有问题，这里只是强调一下何谓 reference。《2030年可持续发展议程》共 11 次提及残疾，比如：

All people, irrespective of sex, age, race or ethnicity, and persons with disabilities, migrants, indigenous peoples, children and youth, especially those in vulnerable situations, should have access to life-long learning opportunities that help them to acquire the knowledge and skills needed to exploit opportunities and to participate fully in society.（所有人，特别是处境困难者，无论性别、年龄、种族、民族为何，无论是残疾人、移民还是土著居民，无论是儿童还是青年，都应有机会终身获得教育，掌握必要知识和技能，充分融入社会。）

按理说 all people 已经包括所有人了，后面不用再分别提及各类人群。但因为各类人群的代表机构都希望发出自己的声音，所以这个单子会越列越长。

8【补充知识】Zero draft means a draft of a document prepared prior to a first draft and with less polish. It's a way of indicating the very rough or provisional status of a document. 联合国的术语库中译为"预稿"，没有问题。

【尊重约定译法】zero draft 是一个形象说法。我们通常说某个事物的 1.0 版、2.0 版，zero draft 是在 1.0 版之前的版本，即仍然非常粗糙的草稿。为保持这一形象，笔者认为可以译为 0.0 版。但既然联合国文件中已经确定译为"预稿"，为统一起见，还是翻译为"预稿"。

9 【语域适当】鉴于联合国文件中 proposal 经常翻译为"提案"，不妨换个说法，把原译的"提议的可持续发展目标"改为"可持续发展目标提案"，听起来更加正式。

10 【根据语境确定译法】Water down means to modify or adulterate, especially so as to omit anything harsh, unpleasant, or offensive; for example, to water down the truth. (dictionary.com) 所以，可以译为"淡化""弱化""掺假"等；"删减"也可以，缺点是不够委婉。

第 ⑥ 单元　秘书长关于白化病患者面临的社会发展挑战的报告

📖 学习要点

思维方法

★ **宏观思维**

　通过背景资料消除疑问

★ **逻辑思维**

　1. 发现内在逻辑

　2. 根据概率判断修饰关系

★ **批判性思维**

　1. 辩证看待词汇表

　2. 原译不当可以修改

　3. 纠正原文笔误

调查研究方法

　1. 查英文释义

　2. 根据注释顺藤摸瓜

　3. 利用Wikipedia

理解

★ **补充知识**

　1. multiple discrimination

　2. disaggregated national statistics

　3. albinism

　4. mainstreaming

　5. 区分goals和targets

　6. 能用自己的话解释才算理解

★ **理解语言**

　定语从句不能跨越谓语修饰主语

表达

★ **意思准确**

　1. 词性转换

　2. 谨慎添加括号

　3. 根据语境确定译法

　4. address译为"关注"

　5. 重要信息后置

　6. 注意词义褒贬

★ **符合形式**

　1. 尊重约定译法

　2. 拆分长句

　3. 区分及物和不及物动词

　4. 多用逗号

　5. body parts的译法

　6. 使用平行结构

　7. 警惕便装术语

　8. 确保信息层层推进

　9. 确保译法统一

　10. 转换视角

　11. 抄录他人译文不多不少

　12. access: 根据宾语决定动词

　13. 避免歧义

变通

　1. 理解是灵活的基础

　2. 慎重补充隐含内容

　3. 慎重解释原文

　4. 一个词译为四个字

背景说明

本单元选自"Report of the Secretary-General on the Social Development Challenges Faced by Persons with Albinism"（《秘书长关于白化病患者面临的社会发展挑战的报告》），文号为 A/72/169。白化病患者又被称为"月亮的孩子"，他们所经受的痛苦不仅仅来自疾病本身，还包括不同程度的歧视与不公正对待，甚至迫害与屠杀。本报告揭示了白化病患者所面临的社会发展挑战，并提出相应政策消除歧视，"不让任何人掉队"。

练习和讲解

▶ 原文

Summary: This report presents the main social development challenges faced by persons with albinism, taking into consideration the *specific*[1] challenges faced by women and children, and primarily focusing on the barriers in accessing health, education, employment and in participating in political, social, civic and cultural life. *Drawing upon the collective promise of the 2030 Agenda for Sustainable Development to "leave no one behind"*[2], it provides a framework for conceptualizing and removing barriers to social inclusion faced by this population and identifies existing policy responses. It *subsequently*[3] provides recommendations to Member States, the international community, civil society organizations and the private sector.

✐ 原译

摘要：本报告介绍了白化病患者面临的主要社会发展挑战，包括妇女儿童面临的具体挑战，侧重在获得医疗、教育、就业权和参与政治、社会、民间和文化生活方面的障碍。本报告以"不让任何人掉队"的《2030年可持续发展议程》的集体承诺为基础，提供了一个认识该群体在融入社会方面的障碍和消除障碍的框架，同时介绍了现有的政策反应。基于此，本报告为各会员国、国际社会、民间社会组织和私营部门提供了若干建议。

✐ 改译

摘要：本报告介绍了白化病患者面临的主要社会发展挑战，包括白化病妇女和儿童面临的特别挑战，重点关注该群体获得医疗、教育、就业以及参与政治、社会、民间和文化生活方面的障碍。本报告以《2030年可持续发展议程》集体作出的"不让任何一个人掉队"的承诺为基础，提供了一个认识和消除该群体融入社会方面所面临障碍和消除障碍的框架，同时介绍了现有的政策回应。接下来，本报告为各会员国、国际社会、民间社会组织和私营部门提供了若干建议。

✦ 解 析

1 【根据语境确定译法】specific 翻译为"特别"好一些，而不是"具体"。这里是指弱势群体（妇女、儿童、少数者群体等）因为白化病和特定身份而面临的多重歧视，即除了自己身为女性、儿童、少数民族等受到歧视外，作为白化病患者还遭受歧视。

【补充知识】"多重歧视"可译为 multiple discrimination 或 cumulative discrimination。

2 【发现内在逻辑】原译定语过长，且表达不符合汉语的习惯。究其原因，是对原文理解不透彻。"不让任何一个人掉队"是世界各国在《2030 年可持续发展议程》中提出的，意思是谋求共同发展，不让任何弱势群体掉队。

【辩证看待词汇表】leave no one behind 是一个重要口号，经常出现，需要一个统一的译法，联合国的词汇表中，译为"不让任何一个人掉队"，因此改译增加了"一个"。虽然这两个字多余，但为了统一，也不宜修改，毕竟这样说也没有错误。如果词汇表中的译法错误，译者可以通知词汇专员讨论修改。有时，词汇表中的术语来自另一个语境，不一定符合需要，也不必照搬。

3 【查英文释义】词义拿不准时，要查英英词典。subsequently 在词典中的定义是 following in time or order; succeeding (thefreedictionary.com)。此外，作为摘要，此段是依照先后顺序对全文内容作的总结，不能把 subsequently 引申翻译成"基于此"，在本语境中，它并没有承载这样的因果关系。

▶ 原文2

4. Generally, information on the social situation of persons with albinism is lacking, *notably due to the absence of disaggregated national statistics*[1]. *There is relatively more information on the human rights situation of this population in sub-Saharan Africa, given that the issue was brought to the fore in response to reports of horrendous physical attacks against persons with albinism in some countries*[2]. Despite this information gap, *testimonies*[3] gathered by the Independent Expert, academic publications and news pieces, suggest that persons with albinism face similar patterns of social exclusion and discrimination worldwide.

◢ 原译

4. 一般来说，主要是由于缺少各国的分列统计，白化病患者社会状况方面的资料比较少。撒哈拉以南非洲白化病患者的人权状况方面的信息较多，因为有报告称该地区一些国家的白化病患者受到恶性人身攻击，使这一问题受到关注。尽管缺少信息，通过独立专家、学术出版物和新闻报道采集的证据显示，全世界白化病患者所面临的社会排斥和歧视状况大同小异。

◢ 改译

4. 总的来说，关于白化病患者社会状况的资料比较匮乏，主要原因是各国缺少分列的统计数据。在撒哈拉以南非洲，关于白化病患者人权状况的信息较多，因为有报告称该地区一些国家的白化病患者受到恶性人身攻击，从而使这一问题受到关注。尽管缺少信息，但通过独立专家、学术出版物和新闻报道采集的证言显示，全世界白化病患者所面临的社会排斥和歧视状况大同小异。

✦ 解 析

1 【重要信息后置】本句是陈述事实和对造成该事实原因的解释，重点是斜体部分的解释，该部分信息后置，翻译时不需要按照因果的逻辑顺序调语序，而应继续把重要信息或者新信息后置。

【尊重约定译法】disaggregated 译为"分列"，是依照联合国的习惯。按国内习惯，应该说统计数据的"分解"或"合并"。联合国要求各国发布详细的统计数据，而不只是笼统的数据。比如，不要只给出"儿童死亡率"，而应分别统计男童和女童死亡率、少数者群体儿童死亡率、残障儿童死亡率、白化病儿童死亡率，等等。同样，不要只给出儿童辍学率，而要分别给出男女学生、少数民族、农村和城市儿童辍学率。"分列"理解为"分别列举"，也是达意的说法，既然已经长期使用，也不必改为"分解"。

2 【拆分长句】第二句是长句。原译译者在翻译时机械对译，导致汉语拖沓、缺乏节奏。翻译英文长句须注意拆分，将长句变为短句，才能充分发挥汉语的优势。

【多用逗号】将 in sub-Saharan Africa 翻译为状语，便于添加逗号，增强句子节奏感。

3 【利用 Wikipedia】在遇到一词多义时，应仔细查找并结合语境确定词义。在 Wikipedia 中搜索 testimony 一词可找到以下信息：

In the law, testimony is a form of evidence that is obtained from a witness who makes a solemn statement or declaration of fact. Testimony may be oral or written, and it is usually made by oath or affirmation under penalty of perjury.

由此可见，testimony 的基本意思是"证言"，既可指口头的证言，又可指书面的证词。

这个词的引申意思是"证据""证明"，比如 collinsdictionary.com 这样解释："If you say that one thing is testimony to another, you mean that it shows clearly that the second thing has a particular quality"。但在法律语境下，"证言"只是证据（evidence）的一种。此处是指独立专家的调查情况，顶多问问被害者或旁观者，不会像刑事侦查那样，去搜集各种证据。

▶ 原文

5. *In response to the reported attacks against persons with albinism, the Office of the High Commissioner for Human Rights and the Independent Expert have addressed human rights violations affecting persons with albinism*[1]—*including attacks, killings*[2], desecration of *graves*[3], *trafficking of body parts*[4], *displacement*[5], discrimination based on disability, color as well as challenges concerning the right to the *highest attainable standard of health*[6] and the right to education. The present report focuses on the social development challenges affecting persons with albinism.

✑ 原译

5. 作为对白化病患者受到袭击的报告作出的反应，人权事务高级专员办事处和独立专家对白化病患者遭受的侵犯人权的行为作出了处理。这些侵犯人权的行为包括袭击、杀害、亵渎陵墓、贩运身体构成部分、流离失所、残疾和肤色歧视、无法获得最高标准的健康和受教育权。本报告重点关注白化病患者的社会发展挑战。

✑ 改译

5. 针对白化病患者遭受袭击的报道，人权事务高级专员办事处和独立专家已作出回应，开始关注白化病患者遭受的侵犯人权行为，包括袭击、杀戮、亵渎坟墓、贩运人体部件、被迫离开家园、残疾和肤色歧视，以及在获得能达到的最高标准健康和教育权方面面临的挑战。本报告重点关注白化病患者的社会发展挑战。

★ 解　析

1 【拆分长句】第一句斜体部分，原译译者拘泥于原文的结构，导致出现"作为对……作出的反应，办事处和专家对……作出了处理"这样拗口的句式。遇到英文长句，可以围绕句子中的动词或名词化动词造句，然后按动作的时间顺序排列，添加必要的衔接成分，从而译出通顺的汉语。有时在句子中找不到动词的逻辑主语，需要根据上下文添加。比如，本句话隐含的动词有 attack、violate、affect、report、respond、address（按时间顺序），围绕这些动词分别造句，得到如下句子：白化病患者遭受袭击、白化病患者的权利遭受侵犯、白化病患者受到影响、媒体报道了袭击、高专办作出了回应、高专办关注白化病患者问题。把这些短句合并、调整，就是完整的意思：有报道称，白化病人遭受袭击，人权高专办和独立专家作为回应，开始关注白化病患者人权受到侵犯的问题，包括……

【address 译为"关注"】address 原译为"处理"。但人权高专办和独立专家不可能到各国去处理个案。"处理"是国家的责任。翻译为"解决"更不对；几个人解决不了问题。经查，address 的意思是：to think about and begin to deal with (an issue or problem) (en. oxforddictionaries.com)，如"A fundamental problem has still to be addressed."。再如：

- How do we begin to address the issue of vandalism?
- We need to gauge neighbourhood support and address legitimate concerns.
- Have his policies begun to seriously address the enormous problems facing our nation?
- Fortunately, recent studies have begun to address these important issues.

dictionary.cambridge.org 的解释是：to give attention to or deal with a matter or problem，如"The issue of funding has yet to be addressed."。

受此启发，此处译为"开始关注"。

2 【区分及物和不及物动词】killing 原译为"杀害"，改译为"杀戮"，是因为"杀害"需要宾语，"杀戮"不用。

3 【根据语境确定译法】grave 原译为"陵墓"，改译为"坟墓"，是因为帝王的坟墓才叫"陵墓"，这些白化病患者，都是穷苦人家，修不起"陵墓"。

4 【补充知识】大家可能不理解为什么有人会贩卖白化病患者的身体部件。遇到不理解的地方，可以先搜索本文有无解释，比如用 body parts 搜索，就发现本文有个注释：

For an example of a person with albinism living in a region where supernatural explanations prevail, see Michael Hosea, "Living with albinism": "practitioners of witchcraft hunt and kill us to use our hair, body parts and organs in charms and potions".

原来有些地方迷信，用白化病患者的身体部件制作饰物（charms）或药剂（potions），真是长见识啊！（Live and learn!）

【body parts 的译法】另外，body parts 看似简单，也不好翻译。"人体器官"是一个医学术语，英文为 organs，在人体的 79 种器官中，竟然连手指头都没有包含在内，所以翻译为"人体器官"似乎不合适。网上给出的译法包括"身体部分""身体部位"。前者比较抽象，后者是一个位置，"位置"无法贩卖。翻译为"肢体"，像是指躯干四肢，太大了，做不了挂件。如果把身体比作机器，各部分似乎可称为"部件"，这也符合注释当中把人体"部件"做成 charms 的逻辑。

【尊重约定译法】关于 traffic，联合国中文处也曾反复讨论，是翻译为"贩运""贩卖"，还是"拐卖"（人口）。最后的决定是，为统一起见，一律翻译为"贩运"。因此，阅读联合国文件会经常看到"贩运"一词。既然已经集体决定，译者就要遵守。

5 【根据语境确定译法】对于 displacement 也可能存在疑问。虽然联合国词汇表把这个词翻译为"流离失所"，但是是什么原因导致白化病患者流离失所？是被别人赶出家门吗？为什么要驱赶白化病患者？搜索本文件，找不到线索。查 albinism 和 displacement，发现一份非政府组织的报告，就叫 "Children with Albinism: Violence & Displacement"，其中提到：

There are hundreds of displaced persons with albinism in Tanzania. Due to the fact that most victims of attacks are children, those who fled their homes are also mostly children.

看来这些孩子是被迫逃离家园。把"流离失所"归为"侵犯人权行为"，不太符合逻辑，因为"流离失所"至少表面上看，是一种主动选择，不存在"侵犯者"。改为"被迫离开家园"更符合逻辑。

6 【警惕便装术语】the highest attainable standard of health 是一个不加引号、没有大写的便装术语，有固定译法："能达到的最高标准健康"，意思是在当地条件下可以达到的最高标准，不是全世界最高的标准。

▶ 原文

7. *Social development*[1a] is closely related to *social inclusion*[1b], which is *the ability of all individuals to participate fully*[2] in economic, social, political and cultural life. Discrimination and the lack of access to services and material resources are the main barriers to social inclusion. Promoting social inclusion requires both removing barriers to people's participation and taking active *inclusionary steps*[3] to improve the terms of participation in society for people who are excluded. The latter entails *enhancing access to opportunities (education, health and other services), access to resources (employment and income opportunities)*[4] and participation in social, political, civic and cultural life.

✎ 原译

7. 社会发展与融入社会密切相关。融入社会是指所有人充分参与经济、社会、政治和文化生活的能力。遭受歧视和得不到公共服务和物质资源是融入社会的主要障碍。促进社会包容，一方面要消除人们参与社会的各种障碍；另一方面要采取积极的促融措施，改善被排斥者参与社会的条件。后者需要改善获得各种机会（教育、卫生和其他服务）的渠道，包括获得物质条件的渠道（工作和收入来源）、参与社会、政治、民间和文化生活的渠道。

✎ 改译

7. 社会发展与社会融入密切相关。社会融入是指所有人都能够充分参与经济、社会、政治和文化生活。歧视和得不到公共服务和物质资源是融入社会的主要障碍。促进社会融入，一方面要消除人们参与社会的各种障碍；另一方面要采取积极的包容性措施，改善被排斥者参与社会的条件。后者要求提供更多的机会和资源（获得教育、卫生和其他服务以及获得工作和收入机会），使被排斥者参与社会、政治、公民和文化生活。

★ 解析

1 【使用平行结构】social development（1a）与 social inclusion（1b）在译文中是并列关系，并列成分的结构和词性最好一致。既然前者译为"社会发展"，是一个名词短语；后者也应是名词短语，所以改译为"社会融入"。

2 【词性转换】原译"所有人充分参与的能力"改为"所有人能够充分参与"，即把名词 ability 翻译为动词"能够"。

3 【确保译法统一】inclusionary steps 原译"促融措施"，笔者认为很好。但联合国翻译有一种倾向：一个萝卜一个坑。一个译者妙手偶得，把 inclusionary steps 译为"促融措施"，另一个译者不一定能够想到。即使把 inclusionary steps 列入词汇表，也不敢保证人人都去查，而把 inclusionary 译为"包容性"，译文统一的可能性会更大。

4 【转换视角】have/gain access to 是"能够获得""利用"的意思。但如何翻译，需要一事一议。此处如果使用"获得"，就要说"后者要求加强被排斥群体对机会和资源的获得"，比较拗口。被排斥群体的获得，就意味着政府提供，所以，改为"后者要求提供更多的机会和资源"也是不错的选择。

▶ 原文

14. *Discrimination is a major driver of social exclusion that continues to underpin group-based socio-economic differences worldwide*[1]. It includes "any distinction, exclusion or restriction [...] *which has the purpose or effect of impairing or nullifying the recognition, enjoyment or exercise, on an equal basis with others, of all human rights and fundamental freedoms in the political, economic, social, cultural, civil or any other field*"[2].

✍ 原译

14. 歧视仍然是世界各地不同社会经济群体互相排斥的主要驱动力。歧视包括"基于种族、肤色、世系或民族或人种的任何区别、排斥或限制[……]，其目的或效果为取消或损害政治、经济、社会、文化或公共生活任何其他方面人权及基本自由在平等地位上的承认、享受或行使"。

✍ 改译

14. 歧视仍然是社会排斥的主要原因，造成了世界各地不同群体之间的社会经济差异。歧视包括"[……]任何区别、排斥或限制，其目的或效果是妨碍或否定在政治、经济、社会、文化、公共生活或任何其他领域平等承认、享受或行使全部人权和基本自由"。

✪ 解 析

1　【定语从句不能跨越谓语修饰主语】本句的难点是理解。Discrimination is a major driver of social exclusion（歧视是社会排斥的主要原因）容易理解。that continues... 这个定语从句修饰谁？只能修饰 exclusion，因为定语从句不可能跨越谓语动词修饰主语。那么，exclusion continues to underpin group-based socio-economic differences worldwide 是什么意思？ group-based socio-economic differences 意思是不同群体之间的社会经济状况差异，比如，农村人口、残障人士和妇女普遍贫困、社会地位低。underpin 的意思是：to support (a building or other structure) from below by laying a solid foundation below ground level or by substituting stronger for weaker materials (en.oxforddictionaries.com)。这句话的字面意思是，社会排斥仍然是不同群体社会经济差异的支撑。说得更明确一些，就是社会排斥造成了不同群体间的社会经济差异。但改译没有说"歧视仍然是社会排斥的主要原因，社会排斥造成了世界各地不同群体之间的社会经济状况差异"，而是一气呵成，"社会排斥"作两部分的共同主语。这样做看起来改变了原文的修饰关系，但实际上意思相同。

【补充知识】原译"不同社会经济群体互相排斥"意思大错。通常是弱势群体想进入主流社会，但受到排挤进不去。不是相互排斥。联合国文件中经常用到的一个概念是 mainstreaming（主流化），就是把弱势群体纳入社会主流，是相对于边缘化（marginalization）来说的。

【注意词义褒贬】另外，driver 常见的用法是 a driver of economic growth，译为"经济增长的推动力（或驱动力）"。但"歧视是社会排斥的驱动力"搭配不当。因为"驱动力"是褒义词，"歧视"是贬义词。

2　【抄录他人译文不多不少】遇到引用，要查明出处。如果出处有中文版，则沿用中文版的译法。此处引用来自《消除一切形式种族歧视国际公约》，该公约有中文版，原译也是中文版的译法，但多抄了几个字："基于种族、肤色、世系或民族或人种的"，应当删除。

【原译不当可以修改】然而，在引用他人译文时，还要注意是否有误。尽管总的原则是尊重原译，但如果原译不当，还是可以修改的。仔细对照原译和原文，发现原译的确不尽如人意，至少 others 和 all 没有翻译出来。省略"其他"还情有可原，因为"在平等地位上"隐含了"其他"，但省略 all 则不可取，因为 all 强调全部人权，而非部分人权；impairing or nullifying 翻译为"取消或损害"，次序反了，虽然不是大问题，但通常不要改变并列项目的顺序。另外，句子结构也很复杂，不易理解。这种情况下，译者可以选择"多一事不如少一事"，原译照搬；也可以本着对读者负责的态度，稍加改进。笔者采用了后一种做法，对原译稍作改动："其目的或效果是妨碍或否定在政治、经济、社会、文化、公共生活或任何其他领域平等承认、享受或行使全部人权和基本自由。"鉴于 others

翻译出来很困难，改译也没有翻译。

【能用自己的话解释才算理解】这句话是在给"歧视"下定义，但因为内容太多，不易理解。笔者的解释为（非权威）：所谓歧视，就是一些人区别对待、排斥或限制另一些人，并妨碍国家承认另一些人和自己享有平等的权利；如果国家承认一些人的权利，另一些人就去阻挠这些人平等地享受和行使这些权利。但这样的解释不算翻译，联合国文件（尤其是法律文件）必须紧扣字面意思。

【慎重解释原文】这句话很难翻译，经过反复修改，才确定下来。原因是"承认、享受或行使"三个动词的逻辑主语不一致："承认"的主体是国家，"享受"和"行使"的主体是公民。要改为简明易懂的汉语，可能需要对原文作较大改动。比如："[……]任何区别、排斥或限制，其目的或效果是妨碍或否定一些人在与他人平等的基础上获得、享受或行使政治、经济、社会、文化、公共生活或任何其他领域的全部人权及基本自由"。其中增加了"一些人"，并换个角度，把国家承认（recognize）一项权利，理解为个人"获得"一项权利，从而把三个动词的视角统一为公民。但如果说增加"一些人"还有可能被接受的话，把关键词 recognize 译为"获得"，很难被接受。原因很简单：将来有关机构可能会解释 recognize 一词，而所有的解释都不会脱离该词的本义，如果译为"获得"，与本义无关，译者会陷入被动。考虑再三，只能改译到这个地步。

▶ 原文

16. Persons with albinism may experience further discrimination based on gender, age, race and other status. For instance, *in countries where the society continues to be de facto divided along racial lines and skin color to be socially meaningful*[1], persons with albinism in dark skin communities are likely to experience a double marginalization: *for belonging to the dark skin community and for being different from members of their own community*[2].

✍ 原译

16. 白化病患者可能面临更多基于性别、年龄、种族和其他身份的歧视。比如，在种族仍然是实际界限并且肤色仍然在社交方面起重要作用的社会里，黑肤色群体中的白化病患者有可能遭遇双重边缘化：因为其来自黑肤色社区，加之在社区成员中与众不同。

✍ 改译

16. 白化病患者可能面临更多基于性别、年龄、种族和其他身份的歧视。比如，有些社会仍然在事实上按种族画线，肤色仍具有社会意义，这时黑肤色群体中的白化病患者有可能遭遇双重边缘化：一是因为属于黑肤色群体而受到白人歧视；二是因为与本族人肤色不同而受到本族人歧视。

⊛ 解 析

1 【理解是灵活的基础】这句话没有译好，最主要的原因还是理解不充分。理解不充分，就不敢越雷池半步，导致中文前置定语过长，行文拖沓，意思含混。改译在理解基础上，灵活分解定语从句。

2 【发现内在逻辑】这句话的主要问题也是理解不到位，导致译文表意不到位。译者虽忠实地译出了原因，但读来仍觉得没有说到重点，隔靴搔痒。仔细阅读原文，并稍加思考就会了解，黑肤色群体中的白化病患者被边缘化，一是其本身肤色较黑，不是白种人，因此在白人当权的国家，受到白种人的歧视；二是在深肤色的群体中，其肤色较白，因此受到深肤色群体的歧视。

【慎重补充隐含内容】注意，原文没有明确说明"白人"，但改译增加了"白人"一词，让意思更加明确。这样做在联合国的语境下有一定风险，因为说不定作者是有意不指名道姓。但鉴于此处仅仅是一份报告，不是公约，况且里面用了 dark skin community，其对立面明显就是 fair skin community，所以，笔者认为，灵活一些也无妨。当然，不添加"白人"，对于了解背景的读者来说，也可能会理解。

▷ 原文

27. Furthermore, the 2030 Agenda sets forth Sustainable Development *Goals and targets*[1] that are highly relevant to the situation of persons with albinism, notably the targets focusing on persons with disabilities ([2]i.e. *equal access to education (targets 4.5 and 4.A), to full and productive employment and decent work (target 8.5), to transport systems (target 11.2) and public spaces (target 11.7)*[3], empowerment and promotion of social, economic and political inclusion (target 10.2); and increase availability of high-quality, timely and reliable data *disaggregated by disability*[4] (target 17.18). Other relevant targets include the call for appropriate social protection systems (target 1.3); access to economic resources (target 1.4); *reduced vulnerability [to] and impact [of,] [and] building resilience to*[5] economic, social and environmental shocks and disasters (targets 1.5 and 11.5); ending hunger (target 2.1); access to adequate and equitable *sanitation and hygiene*[6] (target 6.2); and eliminating discrimination (targets 10.3 and 16.B) among others.

✍ 原译

27. 此外，议程确立了与白化病人高度相关的目标和具体目标，尤其是重点关注残疾人的具体目标，即享有平等的受教育机会（目标4.5和目标4.A）、充分和生产性就业和体面工作（目标8.5）、交通运输系统（目标11.2）和公共空间（目标11.7），增强权能和促进融入社会、经济和政治生活（目标10.2），以及增加按残疾情况分列的高质量并且及时可靠的数据（目标17.18）。其他相关具体目标包括呼吁确立适当的社会保障制度（目标1.3）；确保获取经济资源的机会（目标1.4）；降低对经济、社会和环境冲击和灾害的易受影响程度，进行能力建设以增强抵御能力（目标1.5和目标11.5）；消除饥饿（2.1）；确保享有适当和公平的环境卫生和个人卫生（目标6.2）；消除歧视（目标10.3和目标16.B）等。

✍ 改译

27. 此外，《2030年可持续发展议程》确立了与白化病患者高度相关的总体目标和具体目标，尤其是重点关注残疾人的具体目标，即平等获得受教育机会（目标4.5和目标4.A）、平等获得充分的生产性就业和体面工作（目标8.5）、平等利用交通运输系统（目标11.2）和公共空间（目标11.7），增强权能和促进融入社会、经济和政治生活（目标10.2），以及加强获得包括残疾人情况的高质量和及时可靠的数据（目标17.18）。其他相关具体目标包括呼吁建立适当的社会保障制度（目标1.3）；确保获取经济资源的机会（目标1.4）；面对经济、社会、环境冲击和灾害，降低脆弱性，减少影响，增强抵御能力（目标1.5和目标11.5）；消除饥饿（2.1）；确保享有适当和公平的环境卫生和个人卫生（目标6.2）；消除歧视（目标10.3和目标16.B）等。

⊞ 解 析

1 【区分 goals 和 targets】goals and targets 是同义词，字典上提供的译法都是"目标"。但如果看一下 SDG 本身，会发现 goals 是总体目标，共有 17 项，每项总体目标下面，还有很多 targets（具体目标），共有 169 项。联合国中文处译员把 goals 翻译为"目标"，把 targets 翻译为"具体目标"，对两者作了区分。另一个区分方法是分别翻译为"大目标"和"小目标"，但既然最初的翻译没有选用，译者也不必改变。这里为了更明确区分，改译增加了与"具体"相对的"总体"。

【一个词译为四个字】一个英语单词翻译为四个字的情况比较少见，但必要时也可以。比如 gender，有时为了与 sex 进行区分，就翻译为"社会性别"。

2 【纠正原文笔误】仔细查找，发现这个左括号缺少相应的右括号。鉴于下一句讲 other relevant targets 的时候并没有使用括号，翻译中删除了此括号。官方文件后来也删除了该括号。

【谨慎添加括号】联合国文件翻译中，减少括号的情况很少，但有时需要增加括号。句子太长的时候，增加括号是个便捷的手段。不过对于增加括号，中文处持非常审慎的态度，尽量不增加。

3 【access：根据宾语决定动词】英文 access to 是一个很棘手的短语，要视其宾语决定选用哪个汉语动词。此处 equal access to 后面一口气加了好几个词（组），译者需要根据每个词（组）的情况添加相应的汉语动词。

4 【避免歧义】disaggregated by disability 原译为"按残疾情况分列"。如果查一下 SDG 的中文版，发现上面确实是这么翻译的。说明原译者参照了该中文版，非常好。但问题是，SDG 中这么翻译无歧义，放在此处却产生了歧义。SDG 当中的相应段落是：

"17.18 到 2020 年，加强向发展中国家，包括最不发达国家和小岛屿发展中国家提供的能力建设支持，大幅增加获得按收入、性别、年龄、种族、民族、移徙情况、残疾情况、地理位置和各国国情有关的其他特征分类的高质量、及时和可靠的数据。"

从这一段来看，SDG 要求各国的统计数据要作好分类，数据中要包括残疾人的情况。但如果只说"按残疾情况分列的数据"，以其他分类标准作参照，有可能误解为再把"残疾情况"细分（比如分为不同级别和类别的残疾）。所以改译为"包括残疾人情况的"。

5 【纠正原文笔误】这个短语中的中括号是笔者加上的，因为原文有瑕疵。这里依据 SDG 当中的相应内容作了补充，否则无法理解。另外，vulnerability and impact 原译者处理成了"易受影响程度"，也是参照了 SDG 中文版中的措辞，但此处并非直接引用相关段落，可以灵活处理。

6 【一个词译为四个字】原译将 sanitation 和 hygiene 分别翻译为"环境卫生"和"个人卫生"，是正确的译法。请参考如下资料：

Sanitation is the effective use of tools and actions that keep our environment healthy. These include latrines or toilets to manage waste, food preparation, washing stations, effective drainage and other such mechanisms.

Hygiene is a set of personal practices that contribute to good health. It includes things like hand-washing, bathing and cutting hair/nails. Hand-washing is the single most important activity we can all do to encourage the stop of disease.

The difference is subtle but important. While both sanitation and hygiene are related, we must be taught both effective tools and effective behaviors to protect our health. Imagine how important these can be in places without a toilet or where hand-washing has never been learned! (digdeep. org)

▶ 原文

54. In sub-Saharan Africa, *children with albinism are particular targets of witchcraft-related attacks due to the belief that the innocence of the victim increases the potency of witchcraft*[1]. *Infanticides of children with albinism have also been reported in some African countries*[2].

✍ 原译

54. 在撒哈拉以南非洲，由于人们相信受害者的天真无邪可使巫术更灵验，白化病儿童是与巫术有关攻击的特定目标。白化病儿童惨遭杀戮的事件也在一些非洲国家报道过。

✍ 改译

54. 在撒哈拉以南非洲，白化病儿童特别容易受到与巫术活动相关的攻击，原因是人们相信受害者的天真可以增加巫术的法力。也有报告指出一些非洲国家存在杀死白化病婴儿的现象。

★ 解 析

[1]【重要信息后置】无论中文还是英文，都倾向于（不是绝对）把重要的信息后置，所以，原文信息的排列是有意义的，译者应尽量保留原文的信息排列顺序（除非在语法上说不通）。这句话先叙述白化病儿童成为巫术受害者的事实，然后说明原因，原因是重点，所以，改译维持了原文的信息顺序。

【通过背景资料消除疑问】为什么"天真"可以增加法力？如有疑问，可以查找资料：

Children also make up a large proportion of the victims, not least because of another traditional belief that the more innocent a victim is, the more potent his or her body parts will be for the potion. (news.un.org)

[2]【注意词义褒贬】这句话有两个地方需要关注。一是 infanticide 原译译为"惨遭杀戮"增加了感情色彩，不妥当。这个词是拉丁词源，属于科学用语，就像 homicide（杀人）、pesticide（杀虫）一样，因此翻译为"弑婴"。但这个译法难以和白化病婴儿搭配，所以改为"杀死白化病婴儿"。

【根据概率判断修饰关系】二是 in some African countries 修饰谁的问题。可能修饰 infanticide，也可能修饰 reported。如果是前者，意思是"有报道称，某些非洲国家存在杀死白化病婴儿的现象"。这个报道，可能是本国媒体的报道，也可能是外国媒体的报道。而且非常有可能是外国媒体的报道。因为如果这个现象在本国司空见惯，媒体是不会报道的。如果是修饰 reported，意思就是媒体在非洲国家报道了杀死白化病婴儿的事情，没有在国际媒体上报道。这种可能性较小。

【根据注释顺藤摸瓜】为了确认具体意思，笔者发现这句话有个注释"See A/HRC/31/63"。找到这份文件，发现这份文件的注释显示，是 UTSS 提交给联合国的报告揭露了当地的情况。UTSS 是一个关注白化病的国际非政府组织。看到这里，又发现 report 也不能翻译为"报道"，而应翻译为"报告"。

▷ 原文

66. Civil society organizations (CSOs) representing persons with albinism are present in most countries. *The type and range of activities undertaken by these organizations depend largely on the situation of persons with albinism in their respective countries and the State capacity to provide accommodation*[1]. CSOs are especially important in countries of sub- Saharan Africa. In this region, the main activities of CSOs include *awareness-raising campaigns*[2], service provision and State lobbying.

✐ 原译

66. 大多数国家都有代表白化病患者的民间社会组织（CSOs）。各国白化病患者的状况和国家提供合理便利的能力，很大程度上决定了这些组织所开展活动的类型和范围。在撒哈拉以南非洲国家，民间社会组织尤为重要。在该地区，民间社会组织的主要活动包括开展宣传项目、提供服务和对政府进行游说。

✐ 改译

66. 大多数国家都有代表白化病患者的民间社会组织。这些组织开展活动的类型和范围，很大程度上取决于各国白化病患者的状况和国家提供便利的能力。在撒哈拉以南非洲国家，民间社会组织尤为重要。在该地区，民间社会组织的主要活动包括开展提高认识运动、提供服务和游说政府。

★ 解 析

1 【确保信息层层推进】这句话仍然是信息流动性的问题，要明确旧信息和新信息交替出现，由旧信息引出新信息，层层推进。上一句谈的就是民间社会组织，这一句也应将其作为旧信息先抛出，形成自然过渡。总的原则是尽量保留原文的信息排列顺序；原文不符合信息流动规律时，可以调整为符合信息流动规律。

2 【尊重约定译法】也可以译为"宣传活动"，但联合国倾向于直译为"提高认识运动"。

第 ❶ 单元　消除对妇女歧视委员会的结论性意见（一）

📖 学习要点

思维方法

★ **宏观思维**

　1. 调查宏观背景以理解局部问题

　2. 通过调查背景澄清歧义

　3. 从整体结构看department的级别

　4. 用宏观思维解决微观问题

★ **逻辑思维**

　1. 根据意思判定结构

　2. 了解文字背后的逻辑

★ **批判性思维**

　1. bill、act与"法"的译法辨析

　2. 通过调查背景纠正原文的表述瑕疵

　3. 根据逻辑推断纠正原文的表述瑕疵

　4. 尊重原文观点

调查研究方法

　查英文释义

理解

★ **补充知识**

　1. legal capacity

　2. passive legal capacity

　3. active legal capacity

　4. bill

　5. act

　6. private bill

　7. public bill

　8. presentation

　9. Laws of Lerotholi

　10. line of succession

　11. Constitutional Court

　12. 法律文件的编号

　13. 调查适可而止

★ **理解语言**

　1. 区分inheritance和succession

　2. 理解句子结构

　3. 根据语境确定词义

表达

★ **意思准确**

　1. 准确表达

　2. 尊重约定译法

　3. 区分相似概念

　4. "夫妻共同财产"的说法

　5. access to justice译法探讨

　6. 避免表达歧义

　7. 用词准确

★ **符合形式**

　1. 外国名字的译法

　2. 遵循先例

　3. 语域适当

　4. 通过调整顺序使结构紧凑

　5. 用词对称

　6. 仁智之见

　7. 根据语境确定译法

　8. 拆分长句

　9. 比照翻译Chieftainship

　10. 语言简洁

　11. 分号的用法

<table>
<tr><td>12. 注意细微之处</td><td>2. 译为上义词</td></tr>
<tr><td>13. 符合汉语习惯</td><td>3. 基于内心确信的灵活翻译</td></tr>
<tr><td>14. 咬文嚼字</td><td>4. 比喻的处理</td></tr>
<tr><td>**变通**</td><td>5. 适度灵活</td></tr>
<tr><td>1. 顺接可以省略关联词</td><td></td></tr>
</table>

背景说明

本单元选自消除对妇女歧视委员会《关于莱索托初次至第四次合并定期报告的结论意见（增编）》（CEDAW/C/LSO/CO/1-4/Add.1，可在网上下载全文）。

消除对妇女歧视委员会（Committee on the Elimination of Discrimination Against Women, 简称 CEDAW Committee）是根据《消除对妇女一切形式歧视公约》（The Convention on the Elimination of All Forms of Discrimination Against Women, CEDAW）第十七条设立的"条约机构"（treaty body），负责监督公约的实施。公约缔约国每四年向委员会提交一份报告，说明公约实施情况，供委员会审议并提出建议。关于消除对妇女歧视委员会在联合国人权体系中的位置，见下面的联合国人权机制结构图。

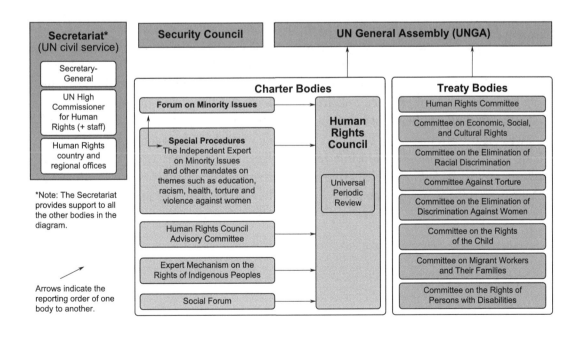

  《消除对妇女一切形式歧视公约》是一个有关妇女权益的国际公约，是联合国为消除对妇女的歧视、争取性别平等制定的一份重要国际人权文书。该公约于 1979 年 12 月 18 日在联合国大会第三十四届会议上获得通过，并于 1981 年 9 月生效。多年来，公约在全世界为越来越多的政府与公众，特别是妇女组织和妇女所熟知，越来越广泛地发挥着保障妇女人权、提高妇女地位的重要作用（中国人权网）。

  公约中文的正式简称为《消除对妇女歧视公约》，国内学者进一步简化为《消歧公约》，但联合国还有一个《消除一切形式种族歧视国际公约》，所以《消歧公约》这个说法可能会引起误解。《消除对妇女歧视公约》被国际社会称为 International Bill of Rights for Women（《国际妇女权利法案》），俗称 Women's Convention（《妇女公约》）。

  莱索托于 1995 年批准了该公约，本应在一年内提交初次报告，以后每四年提交一份，但该国一直没有提交，直到 2010 年才一次性提交拖欠的四份报告。本单元所选内容是消除对妇女歧视委员会对报告审议后提出的意见，内容涉及继承权、财产权和土地权不平等以及一夫多妻制问题。

练习和讲解

▶ 原文

  7. The Ministry of Gender has proposed *harmonization*[1] of *the Laws of Lerotholi*[2] with *the Legal Capacity*[3] of Married Persons Act (LCMPA) and *the process is at a Draft Bill stage*[4] *for presentation to Parliament in its next session in August 2013*[5]. The intention of the harmonization is to repeal Section 11 of the *Laws of Lerotholi* which discriminates against women in inheritance and to put *widows*[6] in full control of their *joint estate*[7] after passing off of their husbands in line with the provisions of the LCMPA. The Law Reform Commission is currently reviewing, with the aim of developing a unified code on inheritance, the Administration of Estates *Proclamation*[8] No.19 of 1935; *Inheritance Act No. 26 of 1873*[9], Intestate Succession Proclamation No. 2 of 1953, Wills Act 1876, Marriage Act 1974 to give redress to the unequal inheritance rights.

原译

7．性别事务部已提议将《巴索托法》与《已婚人士法定身份法（LCMPA）》统一，这一进程已完成草案起草，将在2013年8月召开的议会下届会议期间提交。统一的目的是废除在继承问题上歧视妇女的《巴索托法》第11条，使寡妇在丧偶后能按照《已婚人士法定身份法》完全控制共有遗产。为了制定一部统一的继承法典，性别事务部正在审查1935年《遗产管理宣言》、1873年《继承法》、1953年《无遗嘱继承宣言》、1876年《遗嘱法》和1974年《婚姻法》，以矫正不平等的继承权问题。

改译

7．性别事务部已提议将《莱罗托利法》与《已婚人士法律能力法》相协调，目前正在起草法律草案，该草案将在2013年8月召开的下一届议会上提出。协调的目的是废除在继承问题上歧视妇女的《莱罗托利法》第11条，使丧偶妇女能按照《已婚人士法律能力法》的规定完全控制共有财产。为了制定一部统一的继承法典，法律改革委员会目前正在审查1935年第19号公告《遗产管理公告》、1873年第26号法《继承法》、1953年第2号公告《无遗嘱继承公告》、1876年《遗嘱法》和1974年《婚姻法》，以解决继承权不平等的问题。

解 析

1 【区分相似概念】harmonization of laws 和 unification of laws 是两个不同的概念，译文应有区分。前者通常译为"协调"，后者是"统一"。协调的目的是消除不同国家法律在原则上的矛盾，细节可以保留不同。"统一"则意味着实施同样的法律。有时还会遇到 harmonization 和 coordination 并列，给翻译带来挑战。也许需要把 harmonization 改为"调和"，把"协调"留给 coordination，这样才能一劳永逸地解决问题。但这是一个重大决定，实施起来会有困难。

2 【补充知识】通过查找资料，发现 Laws of Lerotholi 是一百多年前莱索托的国王 Lerotholi 把当时的习俗编纂起来形成的一部法典。原译采用的译法"巴索托法"来自 CEDAW 委员会的另一份文件，其英文版中仍然是 Laws of Lerotholi。经调查，"巴索托"（Basotho）是莱索托主体民族的称呼：

The people of Lesotho are called Basotho (plural) and Mosotho (singular). The culture is cohesive, with Basotho comprising over 99 percent of the country's population, the remainder being of Asian or European origin. (defensewiki.ibj.org)

【外国名字的译法】既然该法以国王的名字命名，汉语没有理由改为以民族名称命名。所以，还是需要按国王的名字翻译出来。新华社编写的《世界人名翻译大词典》中收录了这个名字，译为"莱罗托利"，可按此翻译。如果该词典中没有收录，则按照英文读音来翻译。各音节对应的汉字，可以按照陆谷孙主编的《英汉大词典》所附《英、法、德、俄、西班牙语译音表》确定，这两份资料都可在网上查到。

3 【补充知识】legal capacity（法律能力）可分为 passive legal capacity（消极法律能力，中国叫作"权利能力"）和 active legal capacity（积极法律能力，中国叫作"行为能力"）。

Passive legal capacity refers to the basic civil rights of any natural legal person. It arises from the moment of birth and continues until death. Active legal capacity refers to the capability of the citizen to acquire and exercise civil rights, to create civil duties and discharge them. (ifrs.rn) 权利能力是指一个人与生俱来的基本民事权利，比如财产权；而行为能力是指获得和行使这种权利的能力，比如，一个人任何年龄都可以拥有财产（权利能力），但到了18岁才能处置财产（行为能力）。

4 【准确表达】译文"这一进程已完成草案起草"不够准确：是正在形成草案。可以简化为"目前正在形成（编写）法律草案"或"目前已进入法律起草阶段。

【补充知识】立法程序中的 bill 是 a proposal for a new law, or a proposal to change an existing law that is presented for debate before Parliament (parliament.uk)，汉语中叫作"法案""法律案""法律草案"。进入议会讨论前，叫作 draft bill。Draft bills are issued for consultation before being formally introduced to Parliament. 相当于中国的法律草案"征求意见稿""讨论稿"，可以译为"法律草案""法律草稿"。在英国（莱索托是英联邦国家），根据法案适用对象的不同，bills 又分为 public bills（公共法案）和 private bills（私人法案）。前者适用于公众，通常由政府提出，叫 government bills（政府法案）；后者由私人主体提出，服务于局部公众或私人主体，如地方政府或公司。不在政府担任职务的议员提出的公共法案，叫作 private member's bills（个体议员法案）。

【补充知识】按说法律通过之前叫作 bill，通过之后应该叫作 act。但实际上，已经通过的法律，也可能继续称为 bill。最典型的例子就是经常听到的 Bill of Rights（《权利法案》），它实际上不是"法案"，而是法律。《妇女公约》早已通过，但被人称为 International Bill of Rights for Women（《国际妇女权利法案》）。

国会或议会通过之后的 bill，改称 act，按说应该翻译为"法"，如 Clean Air Act 应译为《清洁空气法》；但一些不严谨的译者也翻译为"法案"，如《清洁空气法案》，使情况更加复杂。

【遵循先例】中国的法律，比如《空气污染防治法》，按照英语的用词习惯，应该翻译为 act，即 Air Pollution Prevention and Control Act，但鉴于多年来我们已经习惯于使用 law，即 Law on the Prevention and Control of Air Pollution，也不便于改变。实际上，law 是法律的统称，单个立法用 act。

5　【补充知识】原文 for presentation to Parliament in its next session in August 2013，这一句中的 presentation 通常翻译为"提交"。但"提交"在英文中是 submit。presentation 要比 submit 复杂很多：

When a Bill is presented to the House, the Clerk announces the motion to present the bill as listed on the notice paper. The Member then stands and presents the Bill to the House, and hands a signed copy of the Bill to the Clerk, together with an explanatory memorandum. The Clerk reads out the short title of the Bill. This is known as the first reading. Copies of the Bill and the explanatory memorandum are then circulated to all Members. At this point the Bill becomes a public document. (naurugov.nr)

由此可见，presentation 实际上是向议会介绍法律草案、陈述草案内容，就像我们在会议上做 presentation 那样。这个词一直没有贴切的译法。动词 present 的本意是"呈现""介绍""提出""报告"（to bring or introduce into the presence of someone, especially of superior rank or status），不妨按此思路翻译。

6　【语域适当】widows 译为"寡妇"，不符合本文的语域。

7　【根据语境确定词义】estate 虽然有"遗产"的意思（everything that a person owns when he dies），但 joint estate 的意思是 an estate owned by two or more people with the same rights of possession (collinsdictionary.com)，即我们所熟悉的"共同财产"。译为"共有遗产"，细想起来是"两人死后留下的共同财产"，恐怕不符合事实。

这里是几个相关的英文说法：

婚姻财产制：the matrimonial property regime；夫妻共同财产：joint estate, common property, joint property, community of property。

8　【根据语境确定词义】proclamation 原译"宣言"是联合国术语库提供的译法。术语库译为"宣言"，是指联合国通过的宣言，而此处是一个国家发布的国内规范，语境不同，译法可能不同。根据资料：

A proclamation is an official declaration issued by a person of authority to make certain announcements known. Proclamations are currently used within the governing framework of some nations and are usually issued in the name of the head of state. (Wikipedia: proclamation)

从这里的解释看，译为"公告"比较合适。

9 【法律文件的编号】Inheritance Act No. 26 of 1873：原译省略了"第……号法"，可能是不清楚法律名称中几个要素之间的关系。据调查，该短语的意思并不是"1873 年通过的第 26 号《继承法》"（隐含另外还通过 25 部《继承法》），而是 1873 年通过的第 26 号法，该法的名字叫《继承法》。更符合逻辑的表述方式是：Inheritance Act, 1873 (Act 26 of 1873)（经查，正式说法是：The Law of Inheritance Amendment Act, 1873 (Act 26 of 1873)），因此，建议译为"1873 年第 26 号法《继承法》"（增加一个"法"字）。给法律编号的目的是便于引用（可以说"1873 年第 26 号法"）。

有时还会加上通过法律（条例、公告）的具体日期，如 Sunday Observance Ordinance, 1838 (Ordinance No. 1 of 22 March 1838)，意思是 1838 年 3 月 22 日通过的 1838 年第 1 号条例《守星期日条例》。不是说 3 月 22 日通过了若干条例，此为该日第 1 号条例，另外还有几个。可以译为：1838 年《守星期日条例》（1838 年第 1 号条例，3 月 22 日通过）。英文之所以有这些不合逻辑的说法，我想主要是为了简洁。

▶ **原文**

8. Despite the Constitutional and Legislative measures, Lesotho has also established the Land Administration Authority (LAA) for efficient issuance of leases and the LAA has also assisted in effectively implementing provisions of the Legal Capacity of Married Persons Act and the Land Act 2010 which give women *the right to hold title to land*[1a] without the need *to inherit it*[1b] and *to register their rights to the said land*[1c]. This year LAA has undertaken a series of public gatherings nation-wide *to sensitize*[2a] *Basotho men and women*[3] about their rights to hold title to *land*[4a] and *registration of same*[4b] especially women who did not have the right before the enactment of the LCMPA which influenced enactment of the Land Act 2010 *and also to inform them of procedures involved therewith*[2b]. Coupled with this initiative the Government of Lesotho has also put in place Land Courts to accelerate *access to justice*[5] and promote protection of economic rights.

原译

8. 除宪法和立法措施外，莱索托还成立了土地管理局（LAA），以提高签发租约的效率。土地管理局还帮助有效地执行《已婚人士法定身份法》和2010年《土地法》的规定，这些规定允许妇女无须通过继承和登记土地所有权的方式保留土地所有权。今年，土地管理局在全国召开了一系列公众集会，向巴索托的男性和妇女宣传他们保留土地所有权的权利。《已婚人士法定身份法》的制定影响了2010年《土地法》的制定，管理局尤其为那些在此之前不具备保留土地所有权权利的妇女进行了注册，并向他们传播了这两部法律中涉及的程序。除这项举措外，莱索托政府还设立了土地法庭，以加速提供司法救济和促进保护经济权利。

改译

8. 除宪法和立法措施外，莱索托还成立了土地管理局，以提高签发租约的效率。土地管理局还协助有效执行《已婚人士法律能力法》和2010年《土地法》的规定，这些规定使妇女有权不通过继承就取得和登记土地所有权。今年，土地管理局在全国举办了一系列公众集会，向巴索托族男女宣传他们取得和登记土地所有权的权利以及登记程序。宣传对象尤其包括在《已婚人士法律能力法》制定之前不享有这项权利的妇女；该法的制定影响了2010年《土地法》的制定。除这项举措外，莱索托政府还设立了土地法庭，以加速提供司法救济，促进保护经济权利。

解析

1 【调查宏观背景以理解局部问题】因为不懂 the right to hold title to land without the need to inherit it，尤其是斜体部分（1a 和 1b），所以需要在网上查找该国土地所有制情况。调查发现，莱索托是个王国，土地名义上为国王所有。允许私人拥有土地（如宅基地、菜园），但农业用地不能继承。成年女性传统上被视为未成年人，"未嫁从父、出嫁从夫、夫死从子"。妇女在财产权方面受到很多限制，包括不能拥有、继承、处置土地。后来修改了《土地法》，男女可以同等获得土地，但《土地登记法》没有修改，不能以妇女的名义登记。再到后来，妇女也可以以自己的名义登记土地了。以下资料中介绍了莱索托按照习俗分配土地的方法：

Under customary law, women are considered minors. A woman before marriage is under the guardianship of her father; upon marriage, her husband takes over guardianship from her father and upon his death, guardianship is transferred to his heir.

Women acquire land rights through their husbands. In the event of divorce or separation, a woman loses her rights to her husband's field and is expected to reincorporate herself into her parents' production unit. Sometimes, unmarried, divorced or separated women are loaned pieces of land by their brothers or fathers to produce food. These arrangements are intended to be temporary, usually until a woman gets married or remarried. An elderly, unmarried woman may be granted a small field in her own right at the discretion of the chief or village headman to enable her to produce her own food. (fao.org)

莱索托实行长子继承制，妇女没有土地继承权：

The customary laws of Lesotho state that an heir of immovable property will be the first born male child. It goes further to indicate that in the case where there is no male child in the family, the inheritance will go to the next closest male relative in the family. Therefore, according to the customary laws, a female is not entitled to any land inheritance.

When the head of the family dies, the heir inherits all the immovable property in that household, including fields and buildings. The heir is expected to use the property to take care of all the minors and needy members of the extended family and to arrange family obligations. (helplesotho.org)

2010 年，莱索托通过《土地法》赋予妇女同等土地权：

The Government of Lesotho had also enacted the Land Act in June 2010, superseding a previous law that had discriminated against women in land ownership. The new Act provided for equal title to land for both men and women and introduced leasehold in the rural areas, thus facilitating women's access to credit using land as collateral. (CEDAW/C/SR.1007)

由此可见，男女都可以租赁土地，妇女不必通过继承来获得土地。这就是 the right to hold title to land without the need to inherit it 的意思。

【通过调查背景澄清歧义】原译此处理解错误。本来是 to hold title to land（1a）和 to register their rights to the said land（1c）并列，但原译误以为 to inherit it（1b）和 to register their rights to the said land（1c）并列。如果了解 The Lands Registry Act of 1967 specifically provides that no land shall be registered in the name of a married woman，可能就会作出正确判断。注解 4 中的 land 与 registration of same 的关系也可以帮助判断。原文的结构歧义常常需要通过调查背景来解决。

【查英文释义】hold title to 当中的 title，意思是 a legal right to the possession of property, especially real property (dictionary.com)，即持有或拥有土地权益。中国最近几年的土地确权可以用 titling 一词：

Land titling is a form of land reform in which private individuals and families are given formal property rights for land which they have previously occupied informally or used on the basis of customary land tenure. (Wikipedia: land titling)

2【通过调整顺序使结构紧凑】to sensitize（2a）和 and also to inform them of procedures involved therewith（2b）是并列成分，原译按照原文的次序，把后者也放在后面翻译；改译把 and also to inform them of procedures involved therewith 提前，意思可能更加紧凑。原译能够灵活翻译 sensitize 很好。

3　【用词对称】原译译为"男性和妇女"可以，但用"男性和女性"更对称。改译用了更简洁的"男女"。

【避免表达歧义】Basotho 是莱索托主体民族的称呼，用"巴索托族男女"意思更清楚。"巴索托的男性和妇女"会被认为是某一个地方的男女。

【了解文字背后的逻辑】LCMPA 是对 Basotho men and women 的进一步解释。联合国文件中，特别强调弱势群体，因此经常会把各种弱势群体（都有各自的代表机构）一一列举出来，比如妇女、儿童、残疾人、少数者群体、男女同性恋。

4　【根据意思判定结构】land（4a）和 registration of same（4b）是并列关系，原译理解错了，导致翻译错误。

5　【补充知识】access to justice 很难翻译。United States Institute of Peace 对它的定义如下：

Access to justice is more than improving an individual's access to courts or guaranteeing legal representation. Access to justice is defined as the ability of people to seek and obtain a remedy through formal or informal institutions of justice for grievances in compliance with human rights standards. (usip.org)

access to justice 就是有冤屈的个人通过正规和非正规司法机构获得司法救济的权利。联合国文件中有多种译法，比如"诉诸司法""诉诸法律""司法救助""获取公正""伸张正义"。鉴于"司法救助"在中国有明确定义，即"指人民法院对于民事、行政案件中有充分理由证明自己合法权益受到侵害但经济确有困难的当事人，实行诉讼费用的缓交、减交、免交"（见最高院关于司法救助的规定），而这个定义相对于 access to justice 而言明显过窄，所以不适合使用。其余几个视情况都可以使用。笔者认为作为名词，还可以翻译为"司法救济权"，或灵活处理为"诉诸法律（司法）的权利（机会）"。

> ▶ **原文3**

8. *The Department*[1] of Gender has been holding and is continuing to hold meetings with Community Councils *with a view to*[2] making sure that women do not face any *challenge*[3] about *land allocation within Community Councils*[4]. The Government of Lesotho has also put in place a Gender and Economic Rights *programmes*[5] *targeting*[6a], inter alia, *commercial banks and financial institutions*[6b] with sensitization on the rights of married women to access credit as appears *in the LCMPA using land as collateral where necessary*[7].

原译

8. 性别事务司已经且将继续与社区委员会召开会议，目的是确保妇女在社区委员会内土地分配问题上不会面临任何挑战。莱索托政府还设立了一个尤其以商业银行和金融机构为目标的性别和经济权利项目，旨在宣传已婚妇女必要时可按照《已婚人士法定身份法》，用土地作担保获取信贷的权利。

改译

8. 性别事务司已经并将继续与社区委员会举行会议，确保妇女在社区委员会分配土地时不会遇到任何困难。莱索托政府还设立了一个性别平等和经济权利计划，特别以商业银行和金融机构为目标，宣传已婚妇女有权在必要时以土地作抵押，获得《已婚人士法律能力法》中所述的信贷。

⊛ 解 析

1 【从整体结构看 department 的级别】在一些国家，department 是部级机构，有些国家是部之下的司级机构。翻译具体国家的机构时，如果不敢确定，需要查一下该国的机构设置。经查，莱索托设有 Ministry of Gender and Youth, Sports and Recreation，下设 Department of Gender。原译应当是经过核实的。

2 【顺接可以省略关联词】with a view to 等顺接手段，如果上下文意思清楚，可以省略不译。

3 【仁智之见】用"挑战"还是"困难"，并无对错之分。审校的修改，有时候仅仅是因为语言习惯稍有不同。对于此类修改，译者不必在意。

4 【通过调查背景纠正原文表述瑕疵】land allocation within Community Councils：到底谁来分配土地？我们在谷歌中输入 Lesotho Community Council，查查社区委员会的职责，可以看到其职责包括分配土地。明白了意思，就可以翻译得直截了当（把 within 理解为 by），不像原译那样绕弯子。很多情况下，译文说不清楚，根本原因还是理解不透彻。

5 【遵循先例】联合国往往将 programme 翻译为"方案""计划"；国内同样情况下往往翻译为"项目"。但实际上，一个方案可能包含很多 projects（项目）。所以，联合国的区分也是有必要的。

6 【理解句子结构】targeting（6a）和 commercial banks and financial institutions（6b）应该视为一个整体来理解，即以商业银行和金融机构为宣传对象，要求它们关注妇女权利。原译没有看透这层意思，导致句子结构搭建错误，译文意思不连贯。

7 【译为上义词】这部分除了法律名称需要修改外，其余部分不修改也可以。修改前后的意思没有什么区别，尽管句子结构有差异。collateral 的意思是：property (such as securities) pledged by a borrower to protect the interests of the lender (merriam-webster.com)，是"抵押品"的意思。尽管"担保"的概念（包括保证、抵押、质押、留置、定金）更大，但此处并非精确区分法律概念，以上义词翻译下义词是常见做法。

▶ 原文

10. The Department of Gender conducted mobile campaigns, meetings, public gatherings and *consultations*[1] in all the Districts to sensitize and get the views of the public on unequal inheritance rights and succession to Chieftainship. The outcome was that majority of both Basotho men and women agreed that the law should provide equal inheritance rights *with reservations*[2] to arable land. *Few*[3a] were of the opinion that women especially girl children could only have inheritance rights where there is no male child in a family. In relation to succession to Chieftainship *majority*[3b] of both Basotho men and women were *adamant*[4] that Chieftainship defines them as Basotho such that unmarried women whether or not born of royal blood cannot succeed to office of Chieftainship to avoid *uncertainty in the line of succession*[5]. *Fewer*[3c] agreed to *unmarried women succeeding to Chieftainship only in the event that the law was amended to force them not to marry for fear that should they marry in a non-royal family the line of succession would be distorted*[6]. *Few*[3d] understood *Chieftainship*[7] as a form of *inheritance*[8] that the laws of inheritance should be amended to provide for equal inheritance rights.

✎ 原译

10. 性别事务司在所有行政区举办流动宣传活动、会议、公众集会和磋商，向公众宣传不平等的继承权和酋长继位的问题，并获取公众的意见。结果表明，大多数巴索托族男性和女性均同意，法律应规定男女享有平等的继承权，但耕地除外。少数人认为，只有在家庭中没有男孩时，女性尤其是女孩才能拥有继承权。关于酋长继位的问题，大多数巴索托族男性和女性均坚信，酋长地位决定了他们巴索托族人的身份，因此为了避免继承序列的不确定性，未婚女性无论是否拥有王室血统均不得继承酋长职位。极少数人同意，未婚女性只有在修订法律从而强迫她们不得结婚的情况下才能继承酋长地位，原因是担心如果她们嫁入非王室家庭将扰乱继承序列。少数人将酋长地位理解为一种遗产，因此应当修订继承法，对平等继承权作出规定。

✎ 改译

10. 性别事务司在所有行政区举办流动宣传活动、会议、公众集会和咨询活动，向公众宣传继承权不平等和酋长继位问题，并听取公众意见。结果表明，大多数巴索托族男性和女性均同意，法律应规定男女享有平等的继承权，但耕地的继承除外。少数人认为，只有在家庭中没有男孩时，妇女尤其是女孩才能拥有继承权。关于酋长身份的继承问题，大多数巴索托族男性和女性均坚持认为，酋长身份决定了他们巴索托族人的身份，因此，为了避免继承序位的不确定性，未婚女性无论是否拥有王室血统均不得继承酋长身份。少数人同意，未婚女性可以继承酋长身份，但前提是通过修订法律，强制她们不得结婚，原因是担心她们嫁入非王室家庭后，将扭曲继承序位。个别人把酋长身份看作一种财产继承方式，认为应当修订财产继承法，规定平等的继承权。

★ 解 析

1 【根据语境确定译法】consultation 的含义是：the act of consulting; conference; a meeting for deliberation, discussion, or decision (the freedictionary.com)，即 "咨询" "磋商"。联合国语境下，consultation 通常是指对重大事件的商讨，所以经常翻译为 "磋商"。此处虽然是联合国文件，但内容是某国政府部门征求村民意见，所以不是磋商，而是 "咨询"。

2 【基于内心确信的灵活翻译】with reservations 字面意思是 "有保留意见"。"对耕地持保留意见" 又是什么意思？如果不敢确定，可以利用本句查相关资料。调查发现，联合国其他文件中出现过基本相同的一句话，但内容更丰富，从而有助于确定这句话的意思："The outcome was that the majority of Basotho women and men agreed that the law should provide equal inheritance rights with reservations to arable land that has to remain with the family."。这句话清楚表明，女性可以继承其他家庭财产，但不能继承耕地。所以，原译 "耕地除外" 是正确的；译者一定做了调查研究。

3 【根据逻辑推断纠正原文的表述瑕疵】这部分涉及 few（3a 和 3c）如何理解：是按正常的英文语法理解为否定性表达（"很少"），还是按逻辑推理，理解为肯定性表达（"有少数人"）？与 (the) majority（3b）相对的是 a few，所以，有理由推断 few 和 fewer（3c）都旨在表达 "有少数人"。Few understood Chieftainship 中的 few 作为与 Fewer agreed to 中 fewer 的并列成分，也应理解为肯定表达。另外，从意义上来看，如果持这种观点的人 "几乎没有"（few），便没有必要加这句话（当然，也不排除当时采用问卷调查的形式，这句话用来说明很少有人选择这个选项）。对于原文存在的语言瑕疵，译者应尽力通过各种办法克服，不用有意复制原文的瑕疵。当然，如果没有发现原文瑕疵，导致译文也存在瑕疵，译者也不承担责任。

4 【用词准确】adamant 意为 not willing to change one's opinion, purpose, or principles; unyielding (dictionary.com)，更准确的译法应是 "坚持某人的观点" "坚定认为" 等，但不能等同于 "坚信"。

5 【查英文释义】通过以下资料可以推断，line of succession 的意思是 "继承序位" "继承顺序" 或 "继承序列"：

The United States presidential line of succession is the order in which officials of the United States federal government discharge the powers and duties of the office of President of the United States if the incumbent president becomes incapacitated, dies, resigns, or is removed from office (by impeachment by the House of Representatives and subsequent conviction by the Senate) during their four-year term of office. (Wikipedia: line of succession)

至于 uncertainty，参照下一句，应该就是指 distort the line of succession，即由父系传承变为母系传承。

6 【拆分长句】这半句话原译句子较长，应想办法拆解。

7 【比照翻译 Chieftainship】根据英文的构词法，参考类似构成的词如 citizenship 和 leadership 可知，它既可指身份，又可指地位，具体取何种含义要参考上下文和词义搭配。前文说 Chieftainship 决定了身份，因此，这里将其译为"酋长身份"更合理。

8 【区分 inheritance 和 succession】上面在讲 succession，翻译为"继承"，此处突然出现一个 inheritance，词典上也翻译为"继承"。这属于修辞上的变换用词，还是不同的概念？搜索关键词查 difference between succession and inheritance，可以看到 succession 是指王位等的继承，而 inheritance 是指财产的继承。此处为了区分，有必要把后者翻译为"财产继承"：

Inheritance succession refers to the manner in which property is distributed when a person dies. In almost all cases, a person would like their estate to be distributed upon death in a very specific manner. Most persons leave their property to immediate family members, close relatives, and close friends. (legalmatch.com)

▷ **原文**

11. *The Ministry of Local Government, Chieftainship and Parliamentary Affairs has also embarked on nation-wide consultations geared towards review of the Chieftainship Act as a whole and Section 10 forms part of the Sections that will be reviewed*[1] *and this becomes a window of opportunity*[2] *to push for amendment of Section 10 which*[3] *differentiates between married women and unmarried women in succession thereby affording only married women the right to succeed to Chieftainship.*

✑ **原译**

11. 地方政府、酋长和议会事务部已着手在全国开展磋商，旨在对《酋长地位法》进行整体审查并对以第10条为代表的部分条款进行审查。借助这一机会窗口，可以推动对第10条的修订，该条在继位问题上对已婚妇女和未婚女性区别对待，从而仅给予已婚妇女继承酋长地位的权利。

✑ **改译**

11. 地方治理、酋长身份和议会事务部已着手在全国开展磋商，以便对《酋长身份法》进行整体审查，第10条是被审查的条款之一。借助这一机会，可以推动对第10条的修订；该条在继位问题上对已婚妇女和未婚妇女区别对待，仅给予已婚妇女继承酋长身份的权利。

★ 解析

1 【语言简洁】原译可以接受，但不如改译简洁。

2 【比喻的处理】a window of opportunity 是近年来流行的一种说法，若一定要保留形象，可译为"机遇之窗"。这种比喻性的说法，如果能够引进汉语，不觉得生硬，可以直译。如果中文比较生硬，宁可放弃比喻。

3 【分号的用法】这里意思明显有分层，改译此处用了分号，也可以用句号。汉语起草的文件中，往往一逗到底，层次不清，翻译也要注意这个问题。

▶ 原文

12. On the 29th August, 2012 the High Court of Lesotho *sitting as a Constitutional Court*[1] heard a *Constitutional Application in which Senate G. Masupha (the only child and daughter of the late Principal Chief Masupha and Masenate) challenged*[2] Section 10 of the Chieftainship Act for excluding *unmarried women*[3] from succession to Chieftainship on the basis that it is unconstitutional for being discriminatory on the basis of sex relying on Sections 18 (3) and 19 of the Constitution which prohibits discrimination on the basis of sex amongst others and equality before the law and equal protection of the law. The Chieftainship Act in Section 10 (4) affords *surviving wives*[4] of Chiefs the right to succession *in their own right*[5] in the event that their husbands die without any male children but denies unmarried women such a right even if they are the only daughters of late Chiefs. It is on this basis that Miss. Senate challenged the Act.

✎ 原译

12．2012年8月29日，莱索托高等法院召开宪法法庭，审理了一个关于《宪法》适用问题的案件。案中，塞内特·G. 玛苏法（已故的玛苏法大酋长与妻子玛塞纳蒂的独生女）以《酋长地位法》第10条排除未婚女性继承酋长为由挑战这一条款。理由是，基于《宪法》第18条第（3）款和第19条中禁止基于性别等理由进行歧视的规定、法律面前人人平等和平等的法律保护的原则，第10条因为基于性别的歧视而违宪。《酋长地位法》第10条第（4）款给予酋长健在的妻子在其丈夫亡故而又无任何男性

✎ 改译

12．2012年8月29日，莱索托高等法院作为宪法法院开庭，审理了一项违宪审查申请。该案中，塞纳蒂·G. 玛苏法（已故玛苏法大酋长与妻子玛塞纳蒂的独生女）对《酋长身份法》第10条不准未婚妇女继承酋长身份的规定提出质疑，理由是，基于《宪法》第18条第（3）款和第19条中禁止基于性别等理由进行歧视、法律面前人人平等和平等法律保护的规定，第10条因存在性别歧视而违宪。《酋长身份法》第10条第（4）款规定，酋长遗孀在其丈夫亡故且没有留下男性子嗣的情况下享有独立

📝 **原译**

子嗣的情况下可以自己继位的权利，但剥夺了未婚女性的这一权利，即便她们是已故酋长的独生女。基于此种理由，塞内特女士挑战了该法律。

📝 **改译**

的继承权，但剥夺了未婚女性的这一权利，即便她们是已故酋长的独生女。基于此种理由，塞纳蒂小姐对该法提出质疑。

⭐ **解 析**

1 【补充知识】sitting as a Constitutional Court，就说明 high court 本来不是宪法法院，但现在遇到了宪法问题，临时作为宪法法院审理案件。这个猜测在下面的段落中得到证实：

Lesotho does not have a Constitutional Court, but instead convenes a panel of judges from the high court when issues of constitutionality are raised. The verdict can now be appealed in the country's regular appeals court. (mg.co.za)

宪法法院是专门用来审查某项法律是否违宪的法院。"违宪审查"也叫"宪法审查"，英语是 constitutional review 或者 constitutionality review。

2 【根据语境确定词义】application 既有"申请"的意思，也有"（法律）适用"的意思。由 challenged 这个词可知，这个 application 是一个人提出来的。这个人是原告，不是法官，所以她提出来的只能是个"申请"。从网上资料可知，此人认为某项法律违宪，请求法院判断，所以 Constitutional Application 是"违宪审查申请"。

【用宏观思维解决微观问题】Masupha and Masenate 是一个人还是两个人？上网一查，前者是一个酋长，后者是他的妻子。Principal Chief 原译为"大酋长"，是否准确？会不会是"正酋长"（相对于副酋长而言）？后来笔者查到以下信息：

The chieftaincy is composed of the king, currently King Letsie III, 22 principal chiefs, and ward and village chiefs. (mg.co.za)

看来真是"大酋长"，原译者一定做了调查。

【注意细微之处】Senate 原译为"塞内特"，她的母亲 Masenate，原译为"玛塞纳蒂"。但仔细观察这两个名字，发现女儿的名字是母亲名字的一部分，译名应该体现出来。"玛塞纳蒂"是译者查出来的，女儿的名字可以直接采用后三个字。注意，Senate 是人名的一部分，不是"参议院"的意思。

本文说 the only child and daughter，但上网查询这个案件，发现新闻报道中她还有 brother：

In the case brought by Masupha, her mother was appointed "caretaker" of the Chieftainship when her father died. Then when her mother died, her brother and half-brother vied for the chief's position. Masupha then intervened, wanting to inherit the position as the chief's first-born child. (mg.co.za)

【尊重原文观点】是原文正确，还是新闻中的信息准确，在当前的翻译情境下，译者不必追究，按原文翻译即可。因为即使给翻译部门提出来，人家也不会理会。如果翻译工作中与作者沟通比较容易，可以请作者核实。

【符合汉语习惯】challenge 翻译为"挑战"也可以，但改为"质疑"，可能更符合汉语习惯。

3【咬文嚼字】unmarried women 翻译为"未婚女性""未婚妇女"都可以。但细想起来，"未婚妇女"说不通，因为汉语中"妇"字表明已经身为人妇了，因此维持原译"未婚女性"。而 women 在英语中指成年女性，unmarried women 说得通。

4【符合汉语习惯】surviving wives 翻译为"健在的妻子"意思正确，但既然有"遗孀"可以用，不妨拿来使用。

5【适度灵活】in their own right 的含义是 by reason of one's own ability, ownership, etc.; in or of oneself, as independent of others (dictionary.com)，是"凭借某人的能力""不依靠他人"的意思，原译意思不清楚。改为"本身有资格继位"或者"享有独立的继位权"可能意思比较清楚。

【调查适可而止】另外，这一段说酋长死后妻子本身就有权继承酋长身份，但其他资料说，妻子只是临时代理（caretaker）：

Customary law in Lesotho says that while wives can become "caretakers" of the Chieftainship until a male heir takes over, or if their chief husbands become ill or die, women cannot, on the basis of their sex, inherit the role or succeed to Chieftainship. (mg.co.za)

也许这份资料讲的是习惯法（customary law），Chieftainship Act 作为成文法，可能真的规定遗孀有完整继承权。译者如果感兴趣，可以进一步调查。但为了完成翻译任务，这些资料已经足够。

第 8 单元　消除对妇女歧视委员会的结论性意见(二)

学习要点

思维方法

★ 宏观思维

　　通过外部资料解决结构歧义

★ 批判性思维

　　可以与审校沟通

调查研究方法

　　查英文释义

理解

★ 补充知识

1. substantive equality
2. formal equality
3. domestic worker
4. legal order
5. kafeel
6. custody和legal guardianship
7. 联合国的地理区划

★ 理解语言

1. 根据搭配确定词义
2. 根据意义判断修饰关系
3. 根据常识判断修饰关系
4. 通过调查背景确定修饰关系

表达

★ 意思准确

1. 不强调补充性信息
2. 谨慎添加显著标点
3. 使用专业术语
4. 辨析词义：撤销、撤回、废止
5. 注意语气
6. mandate翻译辨析
7. 一句话尽量不超过两个"的"字
8. 注意说话的语气

★ 符合形式

1. 拆分长句
2. 根据中心词确定搭配
3. 一个词翻译两次
4. 令人头痛的concerned
5. 符合汉语习惯

变通

1. 保守的翻译策略
2. 补充隐含信息

131

背景说明

　　本单元选自联合国消除对妇女歧视委员会《关于卡塔尔初次报告的结论意见》（CEDAW/C/QAT/CO/1，可在网上下载全文）。《意见》指出了卡塔尔国内现存的妇女问题，并提出改进建议。

练习和讲解

▶ 原文

9. The Committee notes with appreciation that *the Supreme Council for Family Affairs, in cooperation with the National Human Rights Committee of Qatar, has undertaken certain activities to raise public awareness of women's rights*[1]. However, the Committee remains concerned that the State party has not *taken adequate measures*[2] to *promote the visibility*[3] of the Convention. *It is concerned that*[4] there is inadequate knowledge among all branches of the Government, including the judiciary, of the rights of women under the Convention, the concept of *substantive equality*[5] of women and men, and the Committee's general recommendations.

✎ 原译

　　9. 委员会赞赏地注意到，家庭事务最高委员会与卡塔尔国家人权委员会一道开展了数个旨在提高公众对妇女权利的意识的活动。然而，委员会仍然对缔约国没有动用足够资源以促进《公约》的知名度表示关切。委员会感到关切的是，包括司法机关在内的政府各机关对《公约》规定的妇女权利、男女在实质上平等的概念和委员会的一般性建议了解不足。

✎ 改译

　　9. 委员会赞赏地注意到，家庭事务最高委员会与卡塔尔国家人权委员会合作开展了一些活动，以提高公众对妇女权利的意识。然而，委员会仍然对缔约国没有采取适当措施提高《公约》知名度表示关切。委员会关切地认为，包括司法机关在内的政府各机关对《公约》规定的妇女权利、男女实质平等的概念，以及委员会的一般性建议了解不足。

★ 解 析

1　【拆分长句】原译定语过长，改译切分为两句。

2　【根据搭配确定词义】take adequate measures 译为"动用足够资源"不妥当。原译把 adequate 译为"足够"，为了便于搭配，只能把 measures 译为"资源"，这么做是顾此失彼。词典对 adequate 的定义是：as much or as good as necessary for some requirement or purpose; fully sufficient, suitable, or fit (often followed by *to* or *for*) (dictionary.com)。可见，adequate 除了"充分的""足够的"之意外，还表示"合适的""恰当的"，后者与"措施"可以搭配。在联合国文件翻译中，除非特殊情况，否则尽量照顾原文的字面意思。

顺便提一下，鉴于 adequate 既有"量"的含义，又有"质"的含义，adequate housing 在联合国公约中曾译为"适足的住房"，试图把两个含义都表达出来，但在后来的翻译实践中，又改为"适当的住房"。

3【根据中心词确定搭配】"促进知名度"搭配不当，改为"提高知名度"，也可以说"提高可见度"。

【保守的翻译策略】这句话也可以译为"然而，委员会仍然对缔约国没有采取适当措施宣传《公约》表示关切"，即把"提高知名度"改为"宣传"。但由于这是消除对妇女歧视委员会的意见，可能是字斟句酌的结果，译者最好选择不脱离原文字词翻译。

4【令人头痛的 concerned】It is concerned that 是联合国文件中常见的表达方式，不容易处理。如果 that 从句较短，可以先翻译 that 从句中的内容，然后补充"……对此表示关切"；比如，上一句 the Committee remains concerned that... 可以译为"然而，缔约国没有采取适当措施提高《公约》的知名度，委员会仍然对此表示关切"。但如果 that 从句过长，涉及内容很多（如本句），这种处理方式不一定合适。原译处理为"委员会感到关切的是"，也是一种常见的方式，但笔者感觉这种译法增加了不必要的强调。改译为"委员会关切地认为"，可能既照顾了原文的顺序，语言上也比较通顺。在无计可施的情况下，联合国文件中也会把"关切"用作及物动词，如"委员会关切，缔约国频频调整负责提高妇女地位的国家机制的报告关系和职责，使《公约》的执行不稳定且削弱了执行《公约》的能力"。

5【补充知识】substantive equality 可以直接译为"实质平等"，相对于"形式平等"（formal equality）而言。有人以右边这幅图（quora.com）说明两者的区别：formal equality 就是左侧的 equality（"平等"），即每个人在形式上是平等的（都站在同样高的凳子上），但结果却是不平等的（有的能看见，有的看不见）；substantive justice 就是右侧的 equity（"公平"），即为了达到结果平等，给弱势群体以更大的帮助。

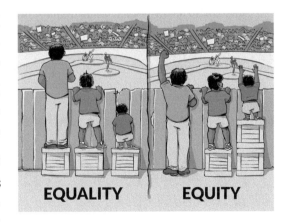

▶ 原文

10. The Committee recommends that the State party :

(a) *Enhance women's awareness of their rights and the remedies available at the national and local levels for women to claim*[1] *violations of their rights under the Convention*[2], and ensure that information on the Convention is provided to women, including *women migrant workers*[3] and in particular, *domestic workers*[4], *including in schools and tertiary education institutions*[5] and through the use of the media...

✎ 原译

10. 委员会建议缔约国：

（a）提高妇女对其在国家和地方层面上享有的各项权利、《公约》规定的妇女权利遭到侵害时可要求的救济措施的意识；确保在学校和高等教育机构等场所，利用媒体等向包括女性移徙工人、尤其是家庭佣工在内的女性提供关于《公约》的信息……

✎ 改译

10. 委员会建议缔约国：

（a）提高妇女的权利意识，告知妇女在国家和地方层面上可获得的救济措施，使妇女能够主张遭到侵犯的《公约》规定的权利；确保在学校和高等教育机构等场所，并通过媒体等手段，向女性——包括移民女工，尤其是家政工人——提供关于《公约》的信息。

★ 解 析

1 【查英文释义】关于 claim 的解释，请参阅如下资料：

A claim is something that one party owes another; someone may make a legal claim for money, or property, or for social security benefits; to demand or assert as a right; facts that combine to give rise to a legally enforceable right or judicial action; demand for relief. (*West's Encyclopedia of American Law*, 2nd ed.)

法律中经常翻译为"主张""声称"（专利文件中翻译为"要求"）。claim violations 就是"声称受到侵害"。

2 【拆分长句】长句应尽可能在理解的基础上拆分、重组，以符合汉语多短句、重节奏的行文习惯。

【一个词翻译两次】为了断句，"改译"把 awareness 翻译了两次，第一次译为"意识"，第二次改为动词"告知"。

【根据意义判断修饰关系】available at the national and local levels 只修饰 remedies，不修饰

rights。如果要修饰两个，就需要去掉 the remedies 当中的 the。况且权利也不存在国家和地方层面的区别。

【使用专业术语】remedy 在法律中的标准译法是"救济"。法律中的"救济"不是给穷人的救助，而是对权利遭到侵害的补救措施，比如金钱赔偿。联合国文件更多地把 remedy 翻译为"补救"，虽然通俗，但不够专业。

3 【符合汉语习惯】women migrant workers 直译为"女性移徙工人"，较拖沓，可变通地译为"移民女工"，简洁且有节奏感。过去，在联合国（包括劳工组织）的文件中，由于历史原因，通常把 migration 译为"移徙""迁徙"，migrant 译为"移徙者""移民"，migrant workers 译为"移徙工人"；后来在中国代表团的建议下，改为国内常用的"移民工人"。在引用历史文件特别是公约时，可以继续使用原来的译法。

4 【补充知识】关于 domestic worker，可参考以下资料：

A domestic worker, domestic helper or domestic servant, also called menial, is a person who works within the employer's household. Domestic helpers perform a variety of household services for an individual or a family, from providing care for children and elderly dependents to housekeeping, including cleaning and household maintenance. Other responsibilities may include cooking, laundry and ironing, shopping for food and other household errands. (Wikipedia: domestic worker).

中华人民共和国成立以后，有很多年不存在 domestic workers 这个职业，所以国内没有公认的说法，当时联合国文件中译为"家庭佣工""家庭工人""家庭雇工"等说法。近年来"家政工（人）"逐渐一统天下。这个说法意思明确，也没有歧视意味。

5 【根据常识判断修饰关系】单纯从语法上看，including in schools and tertiary education institutions 可以修饰四个地方，包括由近及远的三个名词（短语）：domestic workers、women migrant workers、women 和一个动词 provided。但从意思上看，前三个不合情理：学校和大学雇佣"家政工"不合常理，"学校和大学里的女移民"也不合常理；"学校和大学里的妇女"尽管意思说得通，但学校（中小学）的女生，不能被称为"妇女"。所以，including 只能修饰 provided，表示开展宣传活动的场所。另外，in schools 和 through the use of the media 是一个并列结构。

【不强调补充性信息】因此初步翻译为："确保通过学校和高等教育机构等场所，以及通过媒体等手段，向包括移民女工、尤其是家政工人在内的女性提供关于《公约》的信息。"但这个译法过于强调移民女工和家政工人，而且让人觉得她们就在学校和大学，不合常理。实际上宣传的主要对象还是普通女性，包括在校学生。在校学生通过学校组织宣传，其他女性则通过媒体。因此改为现有译法。

【谨慎添加显著标点】改译大胆添加了两个破折号，这在联合国翻译中是不鼓励的（不鼓励添加显著标点，包括括号、引号、破折号）。破折号按说可以改为两个逗号，但第一个破折号前面的内容太短，改为逗号看起来不舒服。从停顿的长短来看，似乎应当是顿号，但顿号在汉语中通常表示并列，不表示单纯的停顿。也可以把两个破折号全部删除，不用任何标点，"包括"短语前后的停顿由读者自己体会。"包括""特别是""尤其是"等补充成分前后的标点问题，是所有译员感到困扰的问题，提到的这几种办法都有人使用。但在现有标点规则下，此处用破折号可能是较好的选择。

▷ 原文

12. The Committee recommends that the State party clarify the status of the Convention in its domestic *legal order*[1], and ensure the *precedence*[2] of its provisions over national laws in cases of conflict. The Committee also recommends that the State party ensure that its *national laws*[3] are *applied*[4] and interpreted in conformity with the provisions of the Convention.

✍ 原译

12. 委员会建议，缔约国明确《公约》在其国内法律次序中的地位；并确保与国家法律发生冲突时，《公约》条款处于优先地位。委员会还建议，缔约国确保以符合《公约》条款的方式应用和解释其国家法律。

✍ 改译

12. 委员会建议，缔约国明确《公约》在其国内法律体系中的地位；并确保《公约》与国家法律发生冲突时，优先适用《公约》条款。委员会还建议，缔约国确保以符合《公约》规定的方式适用和解释国内法律。

★ 解 析

1 【补充知识】legal order 指 the set of legal norms that make up the legal system of a particular country (igi-global.com)，意思是"法律体系"。另外，legal order 还可以指法院针对当事人发布的命令，这里显然不是这个意思。

2 【查英文释义】precedence 的含义是 the condition of being dealt with before other things or of being considered more important than other things (dictionary.cambridge.org)，翻译为"优先地位"没有问题。改为"优先适用"只是换了个说法。

3 【联合国的地理区划】national laws 翻译为"国家法律"也没问题，修改为"国内法律"，意思可能更加明确。联合国把全世界分为几个层级：global、regional、sub-regional、national、sub-national、local。global 是指全球，接下来是 regional。按地理区域，全球划分为五个国家集团（regional groups），分别是 the African Group（非洲集团）、the Asia-Pacific Group（亚太集团）、the Eastern European Group（东欧集团）、the Group of Latin American and Caribbean Countries (GRULAC)（拉丁美洲和加勒比集团）、the Western European and Others Group (WEOG)（西欧和其他国家集团）。所以，联合国提到 region，就是指比国家大的地区（但在谈到国内区域均衡发展时，region 是指国内的地区）。national 是指国家一级，联合国文件中经常把这个词翻译为"国家"，但有时也根据情况翻译为"国内"，以便和"国际"形成对比。sub-national 相当于我国的省、市、自治区一级，但不能这么翻译，不得已译为"国家以下"。local 是指省级以下的地方（比如县、市），没有再往下划分。对于多数国家来说，local 已经是最低的行政级别了，但中国还有乡镇，是更加 local 的级别。

4 【使用专业术语】applied 在法律中通常译为"适用"。翻译为"应用"意思没错，但看上去比较外行。法律的适用，就是把抽象的法律规定运用到具体的案件中，解决法律纠纷。

▶ **原文**

15. While welcoming the State party's efforts to review and *repeal*[1] *or amend*[2] discriminatory legislation, including the Family Law, the Committee notes with concern the many discriminatory *provisions*[3] in laws, *such as the minimum age of marriage for girls in the Family Law, the non-permissibility for women to transmit their Qatari citizenship to their children under the Nationality Act, the Human Resources Law, the Criminal Code, which are contrary to the Convention and other international human rights instruments*[4].

✒ **原译**

15. 委员会虽然欢迎缔约国审查和撤销（或修订）《家庭法》等的歧视性立法的各项努力，但仍然关切地注意到法律中存在诸多歧视性条款。例如，《家庭法》规定了女童的最低结婚年龄；根据《国籍法》，妇女不允许将其卡塔尔国籍传给子女；这些规定和

✒ **改译1**

15. 委员会欢迎缔约国审查、废止或修订《家庭法》等歧视性立法的努力，但仍然关切地注意到法律中存在诸多歧视性规定，例如，《家庭法》中关于女童最低结婚年龄的规定，《国籍法》《人力资源法》《刑法》不允许妇女将其卡塔尔

✒ **改译2**

15. 委员会欢迎缔约国审查、废止或修订《家庭法》等歧视性立法的努力，但仍然关切地注意到法律中存在诸多歧视性规定，例如，《家庭法》中关于女子最低结婚年龄的规定，《国籍法》不允许妇女将卡塔尔国籍传给子女的规定，以及《人力资源法》和《刑

📝 **原译**

《人力资源法》《刑法》等都与《公约》和其他国际人权文书背道而驰。

📝 **改译1**

国籍传给子女的规定，都违反了《公约》和其他国际人权文书。

📝 **改译2**

法》违反《公约》和其他国际人权文书的规定。

★ **解 析**

1 【辨析词义：撤销、撤回、废止】merriam-webster.com 对 repeal 的定义是：to rescind or annul by authoritative act, especially to revoke or abrogate by legislative enactment，是"废除""废止"的意思。此外，法律撤销、撤回和废止是不同的概念。法律的撤销是指下级机关颁布的法律法规触犯上级机关颁布的法律规范时，或在没有立法权或超出立法权限而颁布法律规范时，做撤销处理。撤销的目的在于恢复原法律关系，针对的是违法或者不当的行政行为。撤回，简单地说就是收回、取消原决定。而废止是指有立法权的机关，在颁布的法律不适宜环境时进行废止；或颁布新法律时，在新法律中明文规定，自本法生效之日起，之前某某法律废止（这种是明示废止），若在法律中没有明文规定，则属默认废止。

2 【谨慎添加显著标点】or amend 指法律的修订，原译无误，但不需要放在括号内。原文没有加括号之处，译文谨慎添加，除非不得已。

3 【查英文释义】provision 的含义是 a particular requirement in a law, rule, agreement, or document; for example, the constitutional provision concerned with due process (thefreedictionary.com)，是"条款"的意思，通常译为"规定"。"条款"是"规定"的外在形式，英文可以说 clauses 或 articles。

4 【通过外部资料解决结构歧义】斜体部分（such as 短语）原译意思大致正确，只是措辞有些不当。改译 1 反倒改错了，这个短语的难点是结构。such as 后面的名词短语可以有两种断句方式。第一种是：the minimum age of marriage for girls in the Family Law, [and] ||the non-permissibility for women to transmit their Qatari citizenship to their children under the Nationality Act, |the Human Resources Law, |the Criminal Code，即 such as 后有两个并列成分，一是 age 短语，二是 non-permissibility 短语。后者又包含三个并列（《国籍法》《人力资源法》《刑法》）。这是改译 1 的理解。这个理解有两个问题：一是应该在 non-permissibility 前面加上 and，才符合英语语法；二是《人力资源法》《刑法》当中规定公民资格，不合逻辑。

经调查，发现卡塔尔《人力资源法》中确实没有关于国籍的规定，但就业上却歧视嫁给外国人的妇女所生子女（因为他们没有卡塔尔国籍）。对该法的相关介绍说：

The first priority for appointment to Government and public jobs will be given to Qatari nationals, followed by children of Qatari women married to non-Qataris, then non-Qatari spouses of Qatari citizens, then citizens of GCC countries and Arab expats and lastly nationals of all the other countries. (the-wau.com)

由此可以推断，改译 1 的理解方式不正确。应当断为：the minimum age of marriage for girls in the Family Law, || the non-permissibility for women to transmit their Qatari citizenship to their children under the Nationality Act, || [the discriminatory provisions in] the Human Resources Law, || [and the discriminatory provisions in] the Criminal Code, 即 such as 后有四个并列成分。方括号添加了原文表述不完整之处。随后的 which are contrary...当中的 which，是指 the discriminatory provisions。

按此理解，应该翻译为"《家庭法》中关于女子最低结婚年龄的规定，《国籍法》不允许妇女将卡塔尔国籍传给子女的规定，以及《人力资源法》《刑法》中的歧视性规定，都违反了《公约》和其他国际人权文书"（改译 2）。

【注意说话的语气】原译中 "《人力资源法》《刑法》等都与《公约》和其他国际人权文书背道而驰"，话说得有点重。与《公约》和国际文书相悖的只是某些规定，不是全部法律。再者，委员会的作用是提出建设性意见，不是指责一个国家的政府。

这个例子说明：原文的语法不一定站得住脚，不能纯粹基于语法来理解原文；当原文出现结构歧义时，要通过调查研究，从意义上判断修饰关系；翻译是不断完善的过程，任何人都可能出错，即使已经发布的译文也不例外。

▶ **原文**

17. The Committee notes that the Supreme Council for Family Affairs is responsible for the advancement of women and the formulation of policies on women and family affairs. However, it is concerned about its limited *mandate*[1], *authority*[2] and capacity to ensure that gender equality legislation and policies are properly developed and fully implemented in the work of all Ministries and Government offices. Furthermore, the Committee is concerned about the absence of a *centralized government unit coordinating the national machinery*[3] *on women's empowerment*[4].

⊘ 原译

17. 委员会注意到，家庭事务最高委员会负责提高女性地位，制定关于妇女和家庭事务的政策。然而，委员会关切的是，其授权、权力和能力有限，无法确保关于性别平等的法律能恰当制定，且在所有部委和政府机构的工作中能完全执行。此外，缺乏协调女性赋权国家机构的一个中央统一的政府单位，委员会对此表示担忧。

⊘ 改译

17. 委员会注意到，家庭事务最高委员会负责提高女性地位，制定关于妇女和家庭事务的政策。然而，令委员会关切的是，该最高委员会的权限、权威和能力有限，无法确保适当制定并在所有部委和政府机构的工作中充分实施关于性别平等的法律。此外，缔约国缺乏一个中央层面的机构，负责协调全国的女性赋权系统，委员会对此表示关切。

✪ 解 析

1 【mandate 翻译辨析】根据 dictionary.cambridge.org 的解释，mandate 的意思是：

> ★ **the authority given to an elected group of people, such as a government, to perform an action or govern a country:**
>
> *At the forthcoming elections, the government will be seeking a fresh mandate from the people.*
>
> [+ to infinitive] *The president secured the Congressional mandate to go to war by three votes.*

由此看来，mandate 相当于汉语的"受权"。根据《现代汉语词典》第 6 版，"受权"是"接受委托行使做某事的权力，如外交部受权发布声明"。但遗憾的是，在联合国文件中"受权"使用不多，而是更多使用"任务""任务授权"。

mandate 确实是他人交办的任务，所以使用"任务"没错。但也不一定拘泥于这个译法。根据情况可以译为"职责""职权""权限"。"任务授权"的说法有点逻辑问题。因为 mandate 实质上是"授予任务"，不是"授予权力"。"任务"和"权"之间，意思有矛盾。

另外，"授权"和"受权"不同：从赋予权力的一方来看，是"授权"；从得到权力的一方来看，是"受权"。如果合适，不妨翻译为"受权"。虽然这项权力实质上是从事某项活动的职责。

2 【查英文释义】关于 authority，请参阅如下资料：

Authority is a concept used to indicate the foundational right to exercise power, which can be formalized by the State and exercised by way of judges, monarchs, rulers, police officers or other appointed executives of government, or the ecclesiastical or priestly appointed representatives of a higher spiritual power (God or other deities). (Wikipedia: authority)

由此可见，authority 本身的含义不是权力（power）或权利（right），而是能够行使权力的一种权利，即权威。

3　【查英文释义】Machinery refers to the means or system by which something is kept in action or a desired result is obtained; for example, the machinery of government. (merriam-webster.com) 所以，不是一个单一机构，而是一个系统。

4　【一句话尽量不超过两个"的"字】centralized 译为"中央统一"没有什么错。这句话的主要问题是出现两个"的"字，导致定语过长。改译调整了句子结构，去掉一个"的"字。"中央层面的机构"也可以改为"中央统一的机构"。

▷ 原文

37. The Committee is deeply concerned about reports of various forms of exploitation and abuses of women migrant workers, including forced labour, *physical and sexual violence*[1], inhuman or degrading treatment, unpaid wages, excessive working hours, confiscation of passports, restrictions on freedom of movement and communication *in particular under the sponsorship system (kafeel)*[2]. The Committee is also concerned that:...

✐ 原译

37. 委员会对移徙女工遭受多种形式的剥削和虐待的报告深表关切，包括强迫劳动、肢体暴力和性暴力、不人道和侮辱人格的待遇、不付工资、超长工作时间、没收护照，尤其是按照赞助体系（卡费尔）限制行动和通信自由。委员会还关切的是：……

✐ 改译

37. 有报告称移民女工遭受多种形式的剥削和虐待，包括强迫劳动、身体暴力和性暴力、不人道和有辱人格的待遇、不付工资、工作时间过长、没收护照、限制行动和通信自由等，尤其是在赞助（卡费尔）制度之下；委员会对此表示关切。委员会还感到关切的是：……

✦ 解析

1　【与审校沟通】physical 的定义是：relating to the body as opposed to the mind; involving bodily contact or activity (en.oxforddictionaries.com)。

关于 physical violence，参见如下资料：

Physical violence occurs when someone uses a part of their body or an object to control a person's actions. Physical violence includes, but is not limited to:

- Using physical force which results in pain, discomfort or injury;

- Hitting, pinching, hair-pulling, arm-twisting, strangling, burning, stabbing, punching, pushing, slapping, beating, shoving, kicking, choking, biting, force-feeding, or any other rough treatment;

- Assault with a weapon or other objects;

- Threats with a weapon or object;

- Deliberate exposure to severe weather or inappropriate room temperatures; and,

- Murder. (gov.nl.ca)

汉语使用"肢体暴力""身体暴力""人身暴力"都可以。审校改为"身体暴力",不是否定"肢体暴力",是两个人的表达习惯不同。如果发现审校有意思错误,要及时与审校沟通。译者和审校共同承担责任。

2 【补充知识】关于 kafeel 制度,以下是 Wikipedia 的解释:

The kafala system (also spelled "kefala system", meaning "sponsorship system") is a system used to monitor migrant labourers, working primarily in the construction and domestic sectors, in Bahrain, Iraq, Jordan, Kuwait, Oman, Qatar, Saudi Arabia, and the UAE. The system requires all unskilled labourers to have an in-country sponsor, usually their employer, who is responsible for their visa and legal status. This practice has been criticized by human rights organizations for creating easy opportunities for the exploitation of workers, as many employers take away passports and abuse their workers with little chance of legal repercussions. (Wikipedia: kafala system)

【通过调查背景确定修饰关系】由此可见,本段所述的各种侵权行为,都可能是赞助制度造成的,所以,尽管 in particular 前面没有逗号,看似只修饰一个名词短语,实则修饰所有短语。改译单独译出,置于句子末尾,缺点是中文有些欧化。也可以前置,译为:"委员会对移民女工遭受多种形式的剥削和虐待的报告深表关切,特别是赞助制度带来的……",省略"包括",因为"包括特别是……"也有点别扭。

▶ 原文

41. (b) *The permissibility of polygamy and unequal and/or limited rights for women related to divorce, inheritance, custody and legal guardianship of children*[1]; and women's loss of child *custody*[2] upon remarriage;...

📝 **原译**

41.（b）允许一夫多妻，妇女享有的与离婚、继承、对子女的管养和法定监护权等权利不平等且（或）受到限制，妇女一旦再婚即丧失对孩子的管养；……

📝 **改译**

41.（b）允许一夫多妻，在离婚、继承、对子女的抚养权和法定监护权等方面，妇女享有的权利与男子不平等且（或）受到限制，妇女一旦再婚即丧失对孩子的抚养权；……

⭐ **解 析**

1 【补充隐含信息】首先，斜体部分的译文定语过多、过长。其次，"与离婚、继承……等权利"表述不完整，至少应改成"等相关权利"。第三，unequal 译成了"不平等"，语义正确，但不知道与谁相比不平等。结合上下文，妇女权利不平等指群体间不平等，即相对于男性而言的不平等。改译增补"男子"。

2 【custody 和 legal guardianship】custody 和 legal guardianship 有何区别？英汉词典给出的可能都是"监护"。查中国法律，发现有"抚养权"和"监护权"之分。夫妻离异，双方的监护权不受影响，但会争夺抚养权。美国法律则有 custody 和 guardianship 之分。两相对照，中国的抚养权大致相当于美国的 physical custody；中国的监护权可能相当于美国的 legal guardianship。再查卡塔尔的法律：

Qatari law applies the Sharia law concept of a sharp division between the physical custody of a child and the legal guardianship of a child. The mother is given an express statutory preference for physical custody, up to a certain age of the children. The father is given an express statutory preference for guardianship. It is extremely rare for that right to be taken away from him. It is deemed the "natural right" of the father to assert such rights to the exclusion of the mother. Guardianship is akin to legal custody. It provides the father with the exclusive right to make decisions concerning the child. (international-divorce.com)

从这一段描述中，我们也可以看到"抚养权"和"监护权"的区别。据查，原译"管养"是香港法律的用法。但既然内地法律体系中有现成说法，不妨采用。

第 9 单元　普遍定期审议工作组的报告

学习要点

思维方法

★ **宏观思维**

　　1. 通过背景理解从属关系

　　2. 用宏观思维解决理解问题

★ **逻辑思维**

　　合理推断

理解

★ **补充知识**

　　1. Universal Periodic Review (UPR)

　　2. restorative justice

　　3. retributive justice

　　4. pretrial detention

　　5. special procedure mandate holders

★ **理解语言**

　　正确判断修饰关系

表达

★ **意思准确**

　　用词准确

★ **符合形式**

　　1. 语言简洁

　　2. 统一专有名词的译法

　　3. 不改变补充信息的地位

　　4. 与其他文件保持一致

　　5. 符合习惯译法

　　6. 调整句子结构

　　7. 避免意思弱化

变通

　　1. 调整英文会议记录的时态

　　2. 适度灵活

背景说明

　　联合国人权理事会由联合国大会选出来的 47 个会员国组成, 定期审议各国的人权状况。全世界 192 个国家, 4.5 年普查一遍, 因此叫 "普遍定期审议" (Universal Periodic Review, UPR)。审议由人权理事会下设的普遍定期审议工作组完成。工作组由人权理事会全部成员组成, 每年召开 3 期会议, 每期 2 周, 审议 14 个国家, 每个国家分配 3.5 小时。

　　对各国的审议基于三份材料: 国家提交的报告(20 页)、人权高专办汇编的各人权条约机构最近对该审议的情况(10 页)、人权高专办汇编的其他材料(10 页, 来自各国人权机构、非政府组织等)。这些材料提前 6 周放在人权高专办的网站上。在 3.5 小时的审议过程中, 被审议国家用 70 分钟介绍情况, 联合国其他会员国有 140 分钟的提问时间。

审议每个国家之前，都会组成一个"三国小组"（troika），作为报告员，负责在审议前接收联合国会员国针对被审议国家的书面提问，并在审议结束后起草审议报告。审议报告包括审议过程总结、联合国会员国提出的建议、结论和被审议国家的自愿承诺。

这份报告交给工作组在同一会期晚些时候通过（程序性的，每个国家半小时）。通过之后，转给人权理事会，在人权理事会下个会期的全会上审议通过。这次审议持续 1 小时，只有这次会议允许非政府组织向政府发言提问。人权理事会也是每年召开 3 期会议，但每期 3 周，与 UPR 工作组的会期不重合。

本单元练习选自 UPR 工作组关于秘鲁的报告，文号为 A/HRC/37/8，是工作组 2017 年 11 月 10 日通过的，安排在人权理事会于 2018 年 2 月 26 日至 3 月 23 日举行的第三十七届会议（时间上最接近的一次会议）期间审议通过。实际审议发生在 3 月 15 日，见日程截图：

15 March	
9.00 – 10.00	**General debate on ITEM 5** (cont'd)
10.00 – 12.00	**ITEM 6 UPR outcomes** Czechia, Argentina
12.00 – 15.00	**UPR outcomes** Gabon, Ghana, Peru
15.00 – 18.00	**UPR outcomes** Guatemala, Switzerland, Republic of Korea

练习和讲解

▶ 原文

5. The head of the delegation noted that Peru was a country that in recent years had developed important efforts to guarantee to its citizens *the widest and most effective enjoyment of their fundamental human rights*[1] *and recognized the political and ethical need to continue to deepen and improve those efforts to overcome the differences and social gaps that still existed in the country*[2].

✎ 原译

5. 代表团团长指出，秘鲁近年来已经作出重大努力，确保公民享有最广泛和最有效的基本人权，并为克服国内仍存在的分歧和社会差距而继续深化和改善这些努力的政治和道德需要。

✎ 改译

5. 代表团团长指出，秘鲁近年来已经作出重大努力，确保公民最广泛和最有效地享受基本人权，并确认在政治和道德层面有必要继续深化和扩大这些努力，以克服国内仍存在的分歧和社会差距。

⊛ 解 析

1 【正确判断修饰关系】原译对 the widest and most effective enjoyment of their fundamental human rights 的修饰关系理解错误。"最广泛和最有效"修饰的是"享受"而非"基本人权"。

2 【调整句子结构】如果按照原文结构翻译会导致译文不通顺，可以打破原文结构。原译"为克服国内仍存在的分歧和社会差距而继续深化和改善这些努力的政治和道德需要"太长，以至于译者忘记了前后搭配，导致句子语法结构不完整。改为"并认识到为克服国内仍存在的分歧和社会差距而继续深化和改善这些努力的政治和道德需要"语法上完整了，但定语太长，不符合汉语习惯。改译将 the political and ethical need 灵活处理，顺应原文词序，搭建开放性句子结构，有效化解了定语过长带来的阅读困难。

▶ 原文

6. The human rights policy of Peru was a State policy that transcended *the temporal scope of its Governments*[1]. He noted that the Government of President Pedro Pablo Kuczynski, which had taken office in July 2016, *had*[2] focused on giving continuity to those *policies that had been working*[3] and improving policies or formulating new ones where necessary.

✍ 原译

6. 秘鲁的人权政策是一项超越政府当政时间范围的国家政策。他指出，2016年7月就任的佩德罗·巴勃罗·库琴斯基总统所领导的政府已着重继续贯彻有效政策，并在必要时进行改进或制定新的政策。

✍ 改译

6. 秘鲁的人权政策是一项超越政府任期的国家政策。他指出，2016年7月就任的佩德罗·巴勃罗·库琴斯基总统所领导的政府继续执行行之有效的政策，并在必要时改进现有政策或制定新政策。

⊛ 解 析

1 【语言简洁】temporal scope of its Governments 译为"政府当政时间范围"有些费解。其实"政府当政时间范围"可以用"任期"二字来概括。

2 【调整英文会议记录的时态】原译把 had focused 的过去完成时也体现出来，处理不当。联合国在做会议记录时会把发言者使用的一般现在时变为一般过去时；把一般将来时变为过去将来时；把过去时和现在完成时变为过去完成时。翻译时需要还原为发言者当时使用的时态，这样才符合汉语的表达习惯。据了解，法语的摘要记录文件就没有改变发言者使用的时态。

3 【避免意思弱化】policies that had been working 是指行之有效的政策，简化为"有效政策"意思弱化，还可能引起误解。

▶ 原文

6. Footnote 1. *At the 25th meeting of the Human Rights Council, held on 22 September 2017, during the thirty-sixth session*[1], under agenda item 6 entitled "Universal periodic review", the President of the Council asked the Council to consider the agreement reached by the Plurinational State of Bolivia, Peru, Sri Lanka and the Bolivarian Republic of Venezuela, *as outlined in a letter*[2] from the Plurinational State of Bolivia dated 20 September 2017, that the Plurinational State of Bolivia and the Bolivarian Republic of Venezuela would exchange places in *their respective troikas*[3]. The Council approved the change in the composition of the troikas of Peru and Sri Lanka, which had initially been selected at the organizational meeting of the Council, held on 13 February 2017.

✍ 原译

6. 脚注1. 在2017年9月22日举行的人权理事会第25次会议第三十六届会议上，理事会主席在题为"普遍定期审议"的议程项目6下要求理事会审议多民族玻利维亚国、秘鲁、斯里兰卡和委内瑞拉玻利瓦尔共和国之间达成的协议。协议内容在多民族玻利维亚国2017年9月20日的一封信中有所概述，即多民族玻利维亚国和委内瑞拉玻利瓦尔共和国将在各自的三国小组中互换位置。理事会批准了秘鲁和斯里兰卡三国小组结构的变化，其成员最初是在2017年2月13日举行的理事会组织会议上选定的。

✍ 改译

6. 脚注1. 在人权理事会第三十六届会议期间于2017年9月22日举行的第25次会议上，理事会主席在题为"普遍定期审议"的议程项目6下要求理事会审议多民族玻利维亚国、秘鲁、斯里兰卡和委内瑞拉玻利瓦尔共和国之间达成的协议，协议内容见多民族玻利维亚国2017年9月20日的来信，信中提出多民族玻利维亚国和委内瑞拉玻利瓦尔共和国在分别参与的三国小组中互换位置。理事会批准了秘鲁和斯里兰卡各自所在三国小组构成的变化。原成员是2017年2月13日举行的理事会组织会议选定的。

★ 解 析

1 【通过背景理解从属关系】第一句前半部分，由于译者缺乏背景知识，又未充分查证，造成误译。session 是指一个会期，联合国通常翻译为"届会"；一个会期之内，会开很多次会议（meetings）。所以，正确的理解为，在人权理事会第三十六届会议期间举行的第 25 次会议。凡是遇到修饰关系不清的，要去看上下文或查找背景资料。其实所谓修饰关系不清，仅仅是对于译者而言，作者认为很清楚。我们应当努力达到作者的理解水平，而不是根据个人的理解来翻译。

2 【适度灵活】第一句后半部分，as outlined in a letter 译为"在信中有所概述"，不够准确。汉语的"有所"是指"有一点点"，比如，"有所提高"是提高不大的意思。此处不是"概述"，而是"说明""指出""提出"。

【拆分长句】本句很长，主句中还有插入语和定语从句，句式复杂，翻译时应注意译文用词简洁、逻辑清晰。虽然翻译联合国文件准确第一，但准确不等同于按结构转换。准确是指意思正确，尽量照顾到原文的用词。不必照搬原文结构。

3 【合理推断】their respective troikas 应当是指两个国家分别参加的三国小组。玻利维亚和委内瑞拉原来分别参加了秘鲁和斯里兰卡的三国小组，现在玻、委两国对调一下。

▶ 原文

8. eru was finalizing the third *National Human Rights Plan (2017–2021)*[1], *taking into account the views of public entities and civil society*[2] and considering 13 social groups that required special protection. It stated that, for the first time, Peru had planned to adopt public policies for groups that had previously been neglected, such as lesbian, gay, bisexual, transgender and intersex persons and domestic workers. The plan also aimed to implement international standards on *business*[3] and human rights.

✎ 原译

8. 虑及公共实体和民间社会的意见与要求特别保护的13个社会团体，秘鲁正在最后确定《2017—2021年第三个国家人权行动计划》。秘鲁表示，这是该国首次计划为此前被忽视的群体（如男女同性恋、双性恋、跨性别者和双性者以及家政工人等）制定公共政策。该计划还旨在实施国际商业标准和人权标准。

✎ 改译

8. 秘鲁正在最后确定第三个《国家人权计划（2017—2021年）》，其中考虑到公共实体和民间社会的意见与需要特别保护的13个社会群体。秘鲁表示，这是该国首次计划为此前被忽视的群体（如男女同性恋、双性恋、跨性别者和双性者以及家政工人等）制定公共政策。该计划还旨在实施国际工商企业与人权标准。

★ 解析

1【统一专有名词的译法】联合国有专门的词汇专员，负责统一术语的翻译。遇到不确定的专有名词，可以查找联合国的术语库。National Human Rights Plan 在词汇表中没有，但有 National Human Rights Action Plan（国家人权行动计划），可以比照翻译（去掉"行动"）。注意把时间跨度置于末尾，如"'十三五'规划（2016—2020 年）"。

2【不改变补充信息的地位】taking into account...属于补充信息，不宜前置成为背景信息。按照原文顺序翻译，也便于和下一句衔接。下一句就专门讲民间社会。

3【与其他文件保持一致】联合国人权理事会 2011 年 6 月 16 日通过第 17/4 号决议，核可（联合国把 approve 翻译为"核可"）了联合国秘书长人权与跨国公司和其他工商企业问题特别代表编写的 "Guiding Principles on Business and Human Rights: Implementing the United Nations 'Protect, Respect and Remedy' Framework"（《工商企业与人权：实施联合国"保护、尊重和补救"框架指导原则》）。这份文件没有把 business 翻译为"商业"，而是翻译为"工商企业"。为了保持各文件之间的一致性，此处也需要译为"工商企业"。

▶ 原文

31. Portugal welcomed the adoption of legislation that prohibited corporal punishment of children and criminalized forced labour. It *requested*[1] information on the measures being implemented to enable victims of forced sterilization to have access to *restorative justice*[2].

✐ 原译

31. 葡萄牙欢迎秘鲁通过禁止体罚儿童和将强迫劳动定为犯罪的立法。葡萄牙请求秘鲁提供令强迫绝育受害者获得恢复性正义的当前措施相关信息。

✐ 改译

31. 葡萄牙欢迎秘鲁通过禁止体罚儿童和将强迫劳动入罪的立法。葡萄牙请秘鲁提供帮助强迫绝育受害者获得恢复性正义的措施。

⊛ 解 析

1 【用词准确】第二句中，requested 被译为"请求"，虽"请求"与"请"都包含希望对方做某事的含义，但前者暗含下级对上级之意，而后者则是敬辞。葡萄牙与秘鲁两国平起平坐，不存在下对上的关系，用"请"字即可。此外，原译中的"令"字隐含命令的意思，而此处 enable 是赋予能力，不是命令。

2 【补充知识】restorative justice（恢复性正义／修复式正义）就是旨在修复被破坏的社会关系的正义实现形式：

Restorative justice is an approach to justice in which the response to a crime is to organize a meeting between the victim and the offender, and sometimes with representatives of the wider community as well. The goal is for them to share their experience of what happened, to discuss who was harmed by the crime and how, and to create a consensus for what the offender can do to repair the harm from the offence. This may include a payment of money given from the offender to the victim, apologies and other amends, and other actions to make things as right as possible for those affected and to prevent the offender from causing future harm. (Wikipedia: retributive justice)

"恢复性正义"是相对于以惩罚为目的的"报复性正义"（retributive justice）而言的：

Retributive justice is a theory of justice that considers punishment, if proportionate, to be a morally acceptable response to crime, by providing satisfaction and psychological benefits to the victim, the offender and society. (kintera.org)

▷ 原文

32. The Republic of Korea commended Peru for the establishment of the *National Commission Against Discrimination*[1] and the "Racism Warning" platform. It welcomed *the Act and National Plan on the search for disappeared persons and the national mechanism for the prevention of torture in the Office of the Ombudsman*[2].

✑ 原译

32. 大韩民国赞扬秘鲁设立全国反歧视委员会和"警惕种族主义"平台。大韩民国欢迎监察员办公室关于寻找失踪人员的法案和国家计划以及国家预防酷刑机制。

✑ 改译

32. 大韩民国赞扬秘鲁设立国家消除歧视委员会和"警惕种族主义"平台。大韩民国欢迎秘鲁关于寻找失踪人员的立法和国家计划以及监察员办公室成立国家预防酷刑机制。

⊛ 解 析

1 【丰富词汇表】National Commission Against Discrimination 在词汇表中没有出现，译者可以自由翻译，也可向词汇专员提出将这个说法纳入词汇表。原译也可以。

2 【正确判断修饰关系】in the Office of the Ombudsman 修饰的仅是 the national mechanism for the prevention of torture，而不是 the Act and National Plan on the search for disappeared persons。经查证，菲律宾、澳大利亚等国家均设有 Office of the Ombudsman，其主要职责是调查针对政府部门和事业单位等的投诉，是政府及其相关部门的监督机构，不具有立法权。另一个查找思路是，把 Office of the Ombudsman Peru 输入谷歌，查一下相关情况。翻译时最主要的是提高警惕，时刻当心结构歧义。只有注意到结构歧义，才可能去查证。

▶ 原文

45. The delegation stated that there were 55 indigenous *peoples*[1] and 47 indigenous languages in Peru, which represented around 4 million indigenous peoples. Pursuant to the law on the right to prior consultation of indigenous peoples, between 2014 and 2017, 36 prior consultation processes involving 43 indigenous peoples *had been*[2] carried out and, in all the consultation processes carried out, agreements had been reached. It also stated that there were indigenous people in isolation and initial contact in Peru and that, in 2016, it had categorized three reserves for their protection. In 2016, the intercultural health sectoral policy had been approved and, in 2017, a working group to promote the rights of indigenous women had been created.

✐ 原译

45. 代表团称，秘鲁有55个土著民族和47种土著语言，土著人口总数约400万。根据关于土著人民事先协商权的法律，2014至2017年间，已经进行了36次共涉及43名土著人民的事先协商程序，并且在所有协商进程中都达成了协议。代表团还指出，秘鲁国内存在与世隔绝和初步与外界接触的土著人民，为了对其进行保护，秘鲁于2016年划分了三个保护区。2016年通过了跨文化的卫生部门政策，2017年成立了促进土著妇女权利工作组。

✐ 改译

45. 代表团称，秘鲁有55个土著民族和47种土著语言，土著人口总数约400万。根据土著人事先协商权相关立法，2014至2017年间，共启动了36个涉及43个土著民族的事先协商进程，并且在所有协商进程中都达成了协议。代表团还指出，秘鲁国内存在与世隔绝和刚刚与外界接触的土著，为了保护这些人，秘鲁于2016年划定了三个保护区。2016年通过了跨文化的卫生部门政策，2017年成立了促进土著妇女权利工作组。

★ 解 析

1 【符合习惯译法】明确词义。people 表示"人，人民"，而 peoples 则为"民族"之意。但在联合国文件中，有时出于特别考虑，也可能把 peoples 翻译为"人民"。译者拿不准时，需要查找联合国的术语库。

2 【语言简洁】"已经"与"了"均是表完成的时间副词，表示动作或变化的结束，用其一即可。同样，"成为"也是表示完成的动作，不需要说"成为了"。

▶ 原文

68. Costa Rica highlighted the progress made in legislation policies on human rights. However, *it was concerned that*[1] *the death penalty had not yet been abolished and the legal capacity of persons with disabilities had been limited, and at the excessive use of the policing during social protests.*[2]

✏ 原译

68. 斯达黎加高度赞扬秘鲁在人权立法政策方面取得的进展。但是，令哥斯达黎加感到关切的是，秘鲁尚未废除死刑，残疾人的法律能力有限，社会抗议活动中过度使用警力。

✏ 改译

68. 哥斯达黎加赞扬秘鲁在人权立法政策方面取得的进展，但关注秘鲁尚未废除死刑、限制残疾人的法律能力，以及对社会抗议活动过度使用警力问题。

★ 解 析

1 【适度灵活】be concerned 很难翻译，视情况可以翻译为"关心""关切""关注"。如果 concerned that 后面很长，尽量不采用"对……表示关切"的说法。原译将 it was concerned that 直译为"令哥斯达黎加感到关切的是"，这一表达形式在汉语中比较少见，而且冗长。改译将被动语态变为主动语态，灵活译为"关注"。

2 【统一主语】改译统一了本句三个并列短语的逻辑主语（统一为"秘鲁"）。

▶ 原文

85. France noted the adoption of the law on the search for disappeared persons during the period of violence from 1980 to 2000, the law on the right of indigenous peoples to prior consultation, *the implementation of which should be encouraged*[1], and the *ongoing development of the new National Human Rights Plan (2017–2021)*[2].

原译

85. 法国注意到，秘鲁通过了关于寻找1980至2000年暴力时期失踪人员的法律、应鼓励实施的关于土著人民事先协商权的法律，以及新《国家人权计划（2017—2021年）》取得持续进展。

改译

85. 法国注意到，秘鲁通过了关于寻找1980至2000年暴力时期失踪人员的法律、关于土著人事先协商权的法律，认为该国应当鼓励这些法律的落实；还注意到该国不断完善新的《国家人权计划（2017—2021年）》。

解　析

1 【正确判断修饰关系】the implementation of which should be encouraged 针对前述两项法律，即"寻找 1980 至 2000 年暴力时期失踪人员的法律"与"关于土著人事先协商权的法律"。从逻辑上讲，所有法律都应鼓励落实。

2 【用宏观思维解决理解问题】该句中的 development 与 the new National Human Rights Plan 搭配，应当是"制定"的意思。但看看这份文件的日期，是 2018 年 2 月通过的，而人权计划是 2017 年开始的，所以，应当已经制定通过，而后不断修订完善。

原文

88. Ghana welcomed the establishment of a national preventive mechanism within the Office of the Ombudsman. It expressed concern over the high number of detainees in *pretrial detention*[1], representing 55 percent of the prison population. It noted the measures taken regarding *the use of pretrial detention and the establishment of pretrial detention hearings by courts of second instance*[2].

原译

88. 加纳欢迎秘鲁在监察员办公室下设国家预防机制。令加纳表示关切的是，审前拘留期间被拘留者众多，占监狱人口的55%。加纳注意到秘鲁对二审法院实施审前拘留和设立审前拘留听讯制度采取了措施。

改译

88. 加纳欢迎秘鲁在监察员办公室设立国家预防机制。加纳感到关切的是，审前羁押数量过大，占在押人口的55%。加纳注意到秘鲁针对审前羁押采取的措施以及二审法院建立的审前羁押听证制度。

⊛ 解 析

1 【补充知识】pretrial detention 译为"审前拘留"（这也可能是很多文件中的译法），其实不太准确。"拘留"与"羁押"在法律上是两个不同的概念。在中国法律体系下，"拘留是在未批准逮捕以前，在法定的条件下，对需要进行侦查的人采取的一种紧急措施，而且只有公安机关才能进行拘留。羁押则是在人民法院决定逮捕或者人民检察院批准逮捕，并且实施逮捕以后把人犯关押起来。执行逮捕的机关，即人民法院、人民检察院和公安机关，都可以在逮捕人犯后实施羁押"。（华律网）从上下文看，此处讲的是"审前羁押"，不是逮捕之前的短时间拘留（custody）。这句背后隐含的问题，是秘鲁的取保候审适用率太低，太多的人在审前被关押。虽然 custody（拘留）也是一种 detention，但拘留一般很短，不是争议的焦点。翻译法律文件（或任何专业领域的文件）需要具备相关知识，否则就要做很多调查，有时查不胜查。最好完成后有专家帮忙修改。

原译"监狱人口"的说法也不妥当。监狱是关押已判决犯人的场所。审前羁押在看守所。无论是审前羁押，还是在监狱服刑，都可以说是"关押"。所以，用"在押人口"可以表示两种情形下的关押。

2 【正确判断修饰关系】译者对原文的修饰关系分析不到位造成错译。by courts of second instance 从语法上看，可以修饰两个成分，但实际上仅修饰 the establishment of pretrial detention hearings。the use of pretrial detention by courts of second instance 意思说不通。审前羁押发生在一审之前，二审法院不存在审前羁押。在中国，审前羁押是检察院决定的。该国原来可能是一审法院决定的，现在改为二审法院。如果无法通过译者的背景知识解决，可以查阅相关资料：

In recent years, the State of Peru has undertaken many efforts to adopt measures related to the use of pretrial detention. These include the following: **modifying the maximum duration for pretrial detention**, through Legislative Decree No. 1307 of January 2017; **establishing that pretrial detention hearings are handled by courts of second instance**, through Legislative Decree No. 1206 of September 2015; expanding the scope of implementation of expedited or summary proceedings, through Legislative Decree No. 1194 of November 2015; approving guidelines for the use of videoconferencing in criminal cases; expanding the list of alternative measures available; regulating electronic monitoring mechanisms; and promoting training programs on the New Code of Criminal Procedure that cover the exceptional use of pretrial detention and alternative measures. (oas.org)

这段话似乎可以证实笔者的猜测。

▶ 原文

106. *Morocco congratulated Peru for its ongoing commitment to human rights, manifested in the ratification of many international conventions*[1]. It welcomes its cooperation with the human rights mechanisms and *special procedure mandate holders*[2], in particular the Working Group on Enforced or Involuntary Disappearances. It noted with satisfaction the efforts to realize human rights commitments.

☑ 原译

106. 摩洛哥祝贺秘鲁对人权作出的持续贡献，这些贡献表现为批准诸多国际公约。摩洛哥欢迎秘鲁与人权机制和特别程序任务负责人，特别是与被强迫或非自愿失踪问题工作组的合作。摩洛哥满意地注意到秘鲁为实现人权承诺所作的努力。

☑ 改译

106. 摩洛哥祝贺秘鲁批准诸多国际公约，以此展现对人权的持续承诺。摩洛哥欢迎秘鲁与人权机制和特别程序负责人，特别是与被强迫或非自愿失踪问题工作组的合作。摩洛哥满意地注意到秘鲁为实现人权承诺所作的努力。

★ 解 析

1 【语言简洁】这句话仍然有翻译痕迹。可以按照"先发生的先说、后发生的后说"的规则，重新组织译文。

2 【补充知识】special procedure mandate holders 联合国多数文件翻译为"特别程序任务负责人"，比较烦琐。也有文件翻译为"特别程序负责人"，比较简洁，改译采用这个译法。mandate 的意思是"职责"，mandate holder 指"担当职责的人"，就是"负责人"。以下是一些关于"特别程序"（special procedure）的资料：

The Special Procedures of the Human Rights Council are independent human rights experts with mandates to report and advise on human rights from a thematic or country-specific perspective.

...

Special Procedures are either an individual (called "Special Rapporteur" or "Independent Expert") or a working group composed of five members, one from each of the five United Nations regional groupings: Africa, Asia, Latin America and the Caribbean, Eastern Europe and the Western Europe and others. The Special Rapporteurs, Independent Experts and members of the Working Groups are appointed by the Human Rights Council and serve in their personal capacities. They undertake to uphold independence, efficiency, competence and integrity through probity, impartiality, honesty and good faith. They are not United Nations staff members and do not receive financial remuneration. The independent status of the mandate holders is crucial for them to be able to fulfil their functions in all impartiality. A mandate holder's tenure in a given function, whether it is a thematic or country mandate, is limited to a maximum of six years.

With the support of the Office of the United Nations High Commissioner for Human Rights (OHCHR), Special Procedures undertake country visits; act on individual cases of alleged violations and concerns of a broader, structural nature by sending communications to States; conduct thematic studies and convene expert consultations, contributing to the development of international human rights standards; engage in advocacy and raise public awareness; and provide advice for technical cooperation. Special Procedures report annually to the Human Rights Council and the majority of the mandates also report to the General Assembly.

As of 1 August 2017, there are 44 thematic and 12 country mandates. (ohchr.org)

这里是几个特别程序：

- Special Rapporteur on the human right to safe drinking water and sanitation

- Special Rapporteur on the situation of human rights in Belarus

- Independent Expert on the situation of human rights in Somalia

- Working Group of experts on people of African descent

- Working Group on the issue of human rights and transnational corporations and other business enterprises

完整名单见 ohchr.org。

第 ⑩ 单元　作为缔约国报告组成部分的共同核心文件

学习要点

思维方法

★ **宏观思维**

　　根据宏观背景确定词义

★ **逻辑思维**

　　以邻取义

★ **批判性思维**

　　1. 纠正原文瑕疵

　　2. 通过调查消除疑问

调查研究方法

　　查英文释义

理解

★ **补充知识**

　　1. national government

　　2. encumbrance

　　3. excise duty

　　4. value-added tax

　　5. social protection和social security

　　6. social welfare

　　7. police prefectures

　　8. supreme不一定最高

　　9. prosecutor's office

　　10. "中央税"和"地方税"

　　11. "国会"和"议会"的区别

　　12. "提起公诉"和"支持公诉"

　　13. 理解文字背后的含义

　　14. 养老保障体系"三大支柱"

★ **理解语言**

　　1. 根据下文判断词义

　　2. 根据词源确定词义

　　3. 确定指代关系

　　4. 理解结构

　　5. 正确判断修饰关系

表达

★ **意思准确**

　　1. 根据语境确定译法

　　2. freedom of conscience译法辨析

　　3. 词义辨析:"税"和"税收"

　　4. 慎用"有人"

　　5. "法院"和"法庭"

　　6. 译文顾名思义

　　7. "可以"和"必须"

　　8. 避免歧义

★ **符合形式**

　　1. 注意节奏

　　2. 通过网络确认译法

　　3. 名词尽量直译

　　4. 语言简洁

　　5. 注意搭配

　　6. 尊重约定译法

　　7. 避免漏译

　　8. 拆分长句

　　9. 使用平行结构

　　10. 专有名词的翻译

　　11. 避免欧化表达

变通

　　1. 避免过度翻译

　　2. 适度灵活

背景说明

本单元选自爱沙尼亚向联合国人权高级专员办事处提交的"共同核心文件"（文号为 HRI/CORE/EST/2015），高专办会把这份文件分享给监测爱沙尼亚条约落实情况的所有条约机构。关于共同核心文件和联合国人权条约监测机构报告机制的变化，见以下说明：

The New Structure of Reports to United Nations Human Rights Treaty Monitoring Bodies: Governments that have ratified United Nations human rights treaties (States parties) are required to submit written reports for review by the treaty monitoring bodies. A State party report to any treaty monitoring body is composed of two documents. The first, the core document, containing an overview of the State party's demographic, economic, legal and political structure, is submitted to the Office of the High Commissioner for Human Rights to be used by all treaty monitoring bodies in all their reviews of that State party. Until 2006, this "core document" submission was voluntary, and therefore inconsistent. The second part of States parties' reports, which historically have been the focus of attention by both the treaty bodies and NGOs, is the treaty-specific document, addressing the implementation of a particular treaty the State has ratified.

In 2006, after considerable discussion by the treaty bodies, the Chairpersons of the Human Rights Treaty Bodies endorsed a new set of guidelines for the core document that significantly expands its content and importance. The core document, now known as the Common Core Document (CCD), is intended to be a significant part of the State party's review. Governments are to provide information in the CCD. (hrlibrary.umn.edu)

这份文件从地理、历史、人口、经济、文化、法律、人权保护等多方面介绍了爱沙尼亚的情况，本单元涉及其中的教育、社会保障、税收、法律等方面。

练习和讲解

▶ 原文

19. *Everyone has the right*[1] to education. Basic education is compulsory for children between 7 to 17 years and is free of charge in general schools established by the national government and by local authorities. In order to *make education accessible*[2], the national government and local authorities maintain a requisite number of educational institutions. Other educational institutions, including private schools, may also be established and maintained pursuant to the law. Parents have the deciding say in the choice of education for their children. The provision of education is overseen by the *national government*[3]. *Everyone has the right to be taught in Estonian*[4]. The language of teaching in national minority *educational institutions*[5] is chosen by the educational institution.

🖉 原译

19. 每个人有受教育的权利。7至17岁的儿童有义务接受基础教育，并且可以入读国家和地方政府设立的普通学校。为了实现普遍教育，国家和地方政府开办了一定数量的教育机构。可依法开办私立学校等其他教育机构。家长有为自己子女选择教育方式的权利。教育活动的开展受到国家政府的监督。每个人都必须以爱沙尼亚语接受教育。少数民族学校可以确定自己的教学语言。

🖉 改译

19. 人人享有受教育的权利。7至17岁的儿童有义务接受基础教育，可以免费入读中央和地方政府设立的普通学校。为了普及教育，中央和地方政府按要求开办了一定数量的教育机构。国家允许依法开办私立学校等其他教育机构。家长有权决定子女的教育方式。教育活动受中央政府监督。人人有权以爱沙尼亚语接受教育。少数民族教育机构可以确定自己的教学语言。

★ 解 析

1 【注意节奏】"每个人有"和"人人享有"虽然意思相同，但后者为两个双音节词，节奏感更强。

2 【通过网络确认译法】"实现普遍教育"这一说法比较可疑，需要查证。将"普遍教育"输入百度搜索，只搜到"普通教育"这一相似的词条。"普通教育"是与"成人教育"相对的概念。前者针对的是青少年，采用全日制教学形式；后者针对的是成人，一般实行非全日制教育，因此并非本段表达的意思。

【适度灵活】此时，译者需要回归原文。原文是 make education accessible，accessible 的含

义是 easy to approach, enter, use, or understand (collinsdictionary.com)，即"容易接近、进入、使用或理解"。下面一句的意思是，政府保有一定数量的学校，让学生有学可上。因此，为了便于叙述，可以译为"为了方便就学"或者"为了普及教育"（让所有人都获得教育机会）。

3 【补充知识】在 Wikipedia 中搜索 national government 得到以下三种基本含义：

- central government in a unitary state, or a country that does not give significant power to regional divisions;

- federal government in a federal state, or a country that gives significant power to regional divisions;

- national unity government, an all-party coalition government, usually formed during a time of war or other national emergencies.

【根据语境确定译法】考虑到本文的探讨对象是爱沙尼亚，因此，再次在 Wikipedia 中搜索爱沙尼亚，得知爱沙尼亚是单一制国家：省是爱沙尼亚最大的行政区，爱沙尼亚共有 15 个省（county），每个省又分为市（municipality），市又分为镇（town）和村（parish）。每个市都有自己的政府，有自己的代表和行政机构。由此可见，此处的 national government 应取第一个含义，即中央政府。如果爱沙尼亚是联邦制国家，可以把 national government 翻译为"联邦政府"，相对于"州政府"。联合国不少文件中，直接把 national government 翻译为"国家政府"（意思是"国家级政府"），虽然汉语中不常见，但也是一种方便的处理方法。另外，相对于 international 时，national 也可以译为"国内"。

4 【根据下文判断词义】原译将 the right to 译为"必须"，意思正好相反。"人人有权以爱沙尼亚语接受教育"，意思是人人可以选择（也可以不选择）或有权要求以爱沙尼亚语为教育的媒介语（授课语言），这才有下一句：少数民族教育机构可以选用少数民族语言作为媒介语。

5 【名词尽量直译】educational institutions 实际上就是指"学校"，但既然可以直译为"教育机构"，就不必改为"学校"。

▶ 原文

21. *At the beginning of the academic year 2014/2015*[1], there were 222,966 persons enrolled in formal education. 142,515 of them were *enrolled in general education*[2], 25,237 in vocational education and 55,214 in higher education.

⊘ 原译

21. 2014年至2015学年初，爱沙尼亚正规教育入学人数为222,966人。其中142,515人就读普通教育，25,237人就读职业教育，55,214人就读高等教育。

⊘ 改译

21. 2014—2015学年，爱沙尼亚正规教育入学人数为222,966人。其中142,515人就读普通中小学，25,237人就读职业学校，55,214人就读高等学校。

★ 解 析

1 【语言简洁】原译把 at the beginning of the academic year 翻译为"学年初"，意思正确，但如果此处说"初"，就意味着后面要介绍"学期中"或"学期末"。但后面并无此类信息。另外，"学年初"和"入学"语义重复。"入学"肯定是在"学年初"。所以，改译干脆删除了"初"字，语言更加通顺，意思也不变。如果省略一个字意思不变，就可以省略。

2 【注意搭配】原译搭配不当。"就读"无法与"教育"搭配，要么说"就读……学校"，要么说"接受……教育"。具体选择哪种搭配，取决于句中的 enroll。enroll 的含义是 to enter or register in a roll, list, or record (collinsdictionary.com)，更符合"就读……学校"的含义。

【以邻取义】另外，general education 有两层含义：一个是 secondary education；另一个是 a basic coursework program for post-secondary schools, i.e. university, college, etc. (Wikipedia: general education)。第一个意思即"中等教育"，第二个意思是高等教育机构的"通识教育"。鉴于原文 general education 与 higher education 并列，根据逻辑，应理解为"普通中小学教育"。增加了"小学"，是因为按逻辑，不应把"小学"排除在普通正规教育之外。本句采用的理解方式叫作"以邻取义"，即以临近的词确定一个词的含义。

▷ 原文

22. Estonian public sector relies *extensively*[1a] on information systems and electronic services. All public sector offices have *had Internet access*[1b] since the end of 1990s. Since 2000, all government meetings have been paperless with a web-based document and session management system called e-Cabinet. No paper documents are exchanged between the agencies during *legislative drafting and consultations*, *consultation with the public*[2] also takes place online. Estonian legal acts are published online only, in electronic official gazette (*Riigi Teataja*, www.riigiteataja.ee).

📝 原译

22. 爱沙尼亚公共部门的信息化平台和电子服务十分发达。自20世纪90年代以来，所有的政府部门都建立了网站。自2000年以来，所有的政府会议都实现了无纸化办公和会议文件的电子化，建立起了会议管理系统"电子内阁"。在法律的起草和讨论阶段，各部门不再交换纸质文件，公众意见的征询也通过互联网进行。爱沙尼亚的法律文件仅以电子公报的形式在线发布（《国家公报》：www.riigiteataja.ee）。

📝 改译

22. 爱沙尼亚公共部门广泛使用信息化系统和电子服务。自20世纪90年代末以来，所有的政府部门都已联网。2000年以来，所有的政府会议都实现了无纸化，建立了基于网络的文件和会议管理系统——"电子内阁"。在法律的起草和磋商阶段，各部门不再交换纸质文件；征求公众意见也通过互联网进行。爱沙尼亚的法律文件仅以官方电子公报的形式在线发布（《国家公报》：www.riigiteataja.ee）。

⭐ 解 析

1 【避免过度翻译】原译对 extensively（1a）和 had Internet access（1b）都有过度翻译的倾向。柯林斯词典对 extensively 的解释是 on a large scale。由此可见，extensively 只是一个程度副词，没有价值判断（"发达"还是"落后"）。同理，Internet access 按字面译为"接入互联网"或"联网"已可达意，便不必改变说法，译为"建立了自己的网站"。

2 【查英文释义】consultation 的含义是：

- the act of consulting or conference;
- a meeting for deliberation or discussion;
- a meeting of physicians to evaluate a patient's case and treatment.

legislative consultation 取第二种含义，consultation with the public 取第一种含义。

【避免欧化表达】"公共意见的征询"将动词名词化，是欧化汉语的体现，可以简单说"征求公众意见"。此外，"征询"的意思是"征求询问"，多用于面对面的情形，故此处用"征求"更为合理。

▶ 原文

38. The Constitution *provides guarantees for the protection of the rights and freedoms associated with conscience, religion and thought*[1]. Everyone has *freedom of conscience*[2], religion and thought. *Everyone may freely belong to churches and religious societies. There is no state church*[3]. Everyone has the freedom to exercise his or her religion, *both alone and in community with others, in public or in private*[4], unless this is detrimental to public order, health or morals (Section 40 of the Constitution). Everyone has the right to remain faithful to his or her opinions and beliefs. No one shall be compelled to change *them*[5] (Section 41 of the Constitution).

✎ 原译

38. 《爱沙尼亚宪法》规定良心自由、宗教自由和思想自由受到保护。每个人都享有这三种自由。除非对公共秩序、公众健康和公共道德有害，每个人都有在公共场所或在私下单独或集体的宗教自由（《宪法》第40条）。每个人都有权坚持自己的意见和信仰。不得强迫个人在上述方面作出改变。（《宪法》第41条）

✎ 改译

38. 《爱沙尼亚宪法》保障与良心、宗教和思想相关的权利和自由。人人享有良心、宗教和思想自由。人人可自由参加教会和宗教团体。没有国教。除非对公共秩序、公众健康和公共道德有害，人人都可以单独或集体、公开或秘密地行使宗教信仰自由（《宪法》第40条）。人人有权坚持自己的意见和信仰。不得强迫任何人改变自己的意见或信仰。（《宪法》第41条）

★ 解　析

1 【纠正原文瑕疵】provides guarantees for the protection of 直译为"提供关于保护……的保证"，意思含混不清。

查看出处（《爱沙尼亚宪法》第40条），发现本段直接摘自宪法条文："40. Everyone is entitled to freedom of conscience, freedom of religion and freedom of thought..."。这条规定中并没有 guarantee 这个词。出现 guarantee 一词的是第14条："14. It is the duty of the legislature, the executive, the judiciary, and of local authorities, to guarantee the rights and freedoms provided in the Constitution."。因此，此处可以不译 guarantee，直接按宪法条文翻译为"《爱沙尼亚宪法》保护与良心、宗教和思想相关的权利和自由"。当然，也可以把"保护"改为"保障"，反映原文的用词。但不必把 guarantee 和 protection 都翻译出来，因为都翻译出来弊大于利。

2【译法辨析】freedom of conscience 联合国术语库翻译为"良心自由"。作为该短语出处的《公民权利和政治权利国际公约》第 18 条第 1 款也是这么翻译的：

原文：Everyone shall have the right to freedom of thought, conscience and religion. This right shall include freedom to have or to adopt a religion or belief of his choice, and freedom, either individually or in community with others and in public or private, to manifest his religion or belief in worship, observance, practice and teaching.

译文：人人有权享受思想、良心和宗教自由。此项权利包括维持或改变他的宗教或信仰的自由，以及单独或集体、公开或秘密地以礼拜、戒律、实践和教义来表明他的宗教或信仰的自由。

联合国文件中，也有人尝试其他办法，比如译为"良知自由""信仰自由"。单从汉语来看，"信仰自由"是有意义的。"良心自由"和"良知自由"似乎不好理解。freedom of conscience 的定义如下：the right to follow one's own beliefs in matters of religion and morality (en.oxforddictionaries.com)。

有些网站的内容也支持这一点：

Freedom of conscience—sometimes called "freedom of worship" or "religious freedom"—means simply the freedom to worship in one's own way, including the right not to worship. (findingrogerwilliams.com)

由此可见，freedom of conscience 译为"信仰自由"是正确的。但如果译为"信仰自由"，就占用了 freedom of belief 的译文，遇到人权事务委员会下面的话，就会陷入尴尬境地：

The right to freedom of thought, **conscience** and religion (which includes **the freedom to hold beliefs**) in Article 18.1 is far-reaching and profound; it encompasses freedom of thought on all matters, personal conviction and the commitment to religion or belief, whether manifested individually or in community with others. The Committee draws the attention of States parties to the fact that the freedom of thought and the freedom of conscience are protected equally with the freedom of religion and belief.

【根据词源确定词义】看来还是有必要为 freedom of conscience 找到独特的翻译方法。考察 conscience 本身的意思：a person's moral sense of right and wrong, viewed as a guide to one's behaviour (en.oxforddictionaries.com)，可以译为"是非观念"。因此，freedom of conscience 也许可以翻译为"观念自由"。

【尊重约定译法】鉴于"良心自由"的译法已经被广泛接受，现在更改，恐怕会带来更多混乱。我们可以继续用"良心自由"，但要知道这个词的意思是"思想观念的自由""判断是非的自由"。

3 【避免漏译】这两句话原译遗漏。手工翻译很容易漏词、漏行甚至整段遗漏，所以完成初稿后需要逐字检查。在使用机器辅助翻译的情况下，这个问题可能会得到缓解。

4 【尊重约定译法】这句话来自《公民权利和政治权利国际公约》。公约已经有中文本，译者尽量遵从中文本的译法。除非中文本译法错误或在语法上无法嵌入。

5 【确定指代关系】最后一句中的 them 指代上一句中的 opinions and beliefs；原译文"上述方面"指代不清，不如还原为所指代的名词译出。

▶ 原文

46. *National taxes*[1a], *encumbrances*[2], fees, fines and compulsory insurance payments are established by law. *State taxes*[1b] include personal income tax, corporate income tax, social tax, land tax, value added tax, gambling tax, various *excise duties*[3], heavy goods vehicle tax. The procedure for possession, use and dispositions of public assets is provided by law. Local taxes are imposed according to the Local Taxes Act, available in English at https://www.riigiteataja.ee/en/eli/506112013012/consolide/current.

✎ 原译

46. 爱沙尼亚政府根据法律收取各项国家税收、抵押权税、罚款和强制性保险费。国家税收包括个人所得税、企业所得税、社会税、土地税、增值税、博彩税、各项增值税和重型机动车税。法律对公共资产的占有、使用和处置的程序作出了规定。地方税收根据《地方税法》（英文版见https://www.riigiteataja.ee/en/eli/506112013012/consolide/current）。

✎ 改译

46. 中央税、各种产权负担、收费、罚款和强制性保险费依法确定。中央税包括个人所得税、企业所得税、社会税、土地税、增值税、博彩税、各项消费税和重型机动车税。公共财产的占有、使用和处置程序由法律作出规定。地方税根据《地方税法》（英文版见https://www.riigiteataja.ee/en/eli/506112013012/consolide/current）征收。

★ 解　析

1 【"税"和"税收"】"税"和"税收"是两个完全不同的概念。税收指"国家为了向社会提供公共产品、满足社会共同需要，按照法律的规定，参与社会产品的分配，强制、无偿取得财政收入的一种规范形式"。（百度百科：税收）税收的本质是收入，对应的英文是 tax revenue。而税指政府为了维持其运转以及为社会提供公共服务，对个人和法人强制和无偿征收实物或货币的总称（百度百科：税），对应的英文应是 tax。

【补充知识】national tax（1a）是"中央税"或"国家税"，是与 local tax（"地方税"）相对的概念。中央税是由一国中央政府征收、管理和支配的一类税。在实行中央与地方分税制的国家，通常是将一些收入充足和稳定的税种作为中央税。由于各国税收管理体制不同，中央税的划分和规模各有不同的特点。

【根据宏观背景确定词义】本段的 state tax(1b)可以有两种理解：国家（中央）税或者州税。但根据网络资料，爱沙尼亚不是联邦制国家，所以 state 不可能是州（实际上，该国中央之下的一级区划叫作 county，中国外交部网站称之为"省"）。又根据中国驻爱沙尼亚使馆的网站，"个人所得税""企业所得税"等税种属于中央税，所以，此处的 state tax 和 national tax 为同义，都可译为"中央税"。本句整体的意思是，该国各种税费采取法定原则，没有乱收费现象。

2 【补充知识】encumbrance 通常译为"产权负担"，见香港地区某法律（注意：引文中的中文为原文所有）：

Conveyancing and Property Ordinance: "encumbrance"（产权负担）includes a legal and equitable mortgage, a trust for securing money, a lien, a charge of a portion, annuity, or other capital or annual sum; and "encumbrancer"（产权负担人）has a meaning corresponding with that of "encumbrance" and includes every person entitled to the benefit of an encumbrance, or to require payment and discharge thereof. (blis.gov.hk)

3 【补充知识】excise duty 是消费税，原译者误译成了增值税（value added tax）。Excise duty refers to the tax that is levied upon production of an item and the manufacturer has to pay it when the finished good goes out of the factory. Thus it is also called as production tax or manufacture tax. (Wikipedia: excise duty) 与关税（tariff）类似，消费税的征收对象也是制造商而非消费者，但与关税不同的是，消费税是对本地生产制造的产品征收的税费，而关税是对在海外生产制造，且进入某一国销售的产品所征收的税费。消费税属于间接税，因为不是消费者直接支付，而是先由生产商支付，然后通过定价转嫁到消费者身上。

▶ 原文

49. On the *proposal*[1] of the Government of the Republic, the *Riigikogu*[2] may, during the financial year, pass a *supplementary*[3] budget. *If an amendment proposal to the national budget or to a Bill for the budget has the effect of decreasing estimated revenue or increasing expenditure or reallocating expenditure*[4], *the maker of the proposal*[5] must append to the amendment financial calculations which demonstrate the sources of revenue necessary to cover the expenditure.

📝 原译

49. 在政府的要求下，国会可以在某个财政年度内通过一个附加的预算案。如果一份国家预算的修正案或预算案会减少估算的税收或增加开支抑或对开支进行重新分配，预算案的编制人必须附上可用于该项支出的税收来源的计算。

📝 改译

49. 在政府的建议下，议会可以在财政年度内通过补充预算。如果政府提出修正国家预算或预算提案，而此修正会减少预计收入、增加开支或导致开支的重新分配，则提出修正的机关必须在修正案后附上支出所需财源的核算方法。

⭐ 解 析

1　【根据宏观背景确定词义】proposal 的意思是"建议""提案"，不是"要求"。西方国家实行三权分立，行政机关无权命令（要求）立法机关做事。中国的立法机关也是最高权力机关，政府每年向全国人大报告工作情况，接受人大监督，不会出现政府要求人大办事的情况。

2　【补充知识】Riigikogu is the unicameral parliament of Estonia (Wikipedia: riigikogu)，由此可见，Riigikogu 应为议会而非国会。在总统制国家，如美国，称为国会，在这些国家，总统由大选选出，总统作为政府首脑和国家元首，有实权；国会则通过另外的选举选出。在议会制或君主立宪制国家，如英国，则称为议会。在这些国家，通过大选选出议会席位后，由占多数席位的党派或集团组阁，确定总理或首相人选作为政府首脑。尽管中文网络资源多处把爱沙尼亚立法机关称为"国会"，包括 Wikipedia，但中国外交部网站、新华社、联合国词汇表都使用"议会"的称呼，所以改译为"议会"。

3　【根据语境确定译法】supplementary 译为"附加的"不如译为"补充"通顺。

4　【拆分长句】本处涉及长句的翻译。遇到长句，可以先找到其中的动词和名词化动词（如 proposal），然后给这些动词加上逻辑主语，这样便可以将整个句子拆分为很多短句。比如，proposal 的逻辑主语是政府（根据上句判断），便可以生成一个短句：if the government proposes amendments，依次翻译这些短句，然后重组，便可顺利化解长句的困扰。

【理解结构】本句中另一个问题是 proposal to...or to...，proposal 指向两个成分：（已经通过的）预算和（尚未通过的）预算提案（Bill for the budget）。

5　【慎用"有人"】the maker of the proposal 是指"提出修正的机关"，虽然与"预算案的编制人"可能相同。从上文看，提出和修订预算的应当是政府机关，不是个人，也不是"有人"（有时找不到动词主语时，可以用"有人"代替，但不适合此处）。

▶ 原文

59. *The Estonian social protection system is made up of two pillars—the social security system that comprises pension insurance, health insurance, child benefits and unemployment benefits; and the social welfare pillar that consists of social assistance cash benefits and social welfare services*[1]. The pension and health insurance schemes are contributory social security schemes that are financed principally by the social tax. *The Estonian social tax of 33% (comprising 20% social security contributions and 13% health insurance contributions) must be paid by employers on top of the gross salary*[2]. The unemployment insurance contributions must be paid both by the employer and the employee; the current rates are respectively 1.6% and 0.8%. Child benefits, social assistance cash benefits and social welfare services are financed from general taxes. There are also voluntary social insurance schemes in use (e.g. III *pillar of pension insurance, health insurance*[3]). Social security schemes are administered by National Social Insurance Board, Health Insurance Fund and Unemployment Insurance Fund. Social assistance and most of the social welfare services (except for rehabilitation, technical assistance, special care and substitute care) are administered at local level.

✐ 原译

59. 爱沙尼亚的社会保障系统由两部分组成，分别是养老保险、医疗保险、育儿补贴和失业补贴组成的社会保障系统；另一个部分是社会救济金和社会福利服务组成的社会保障部分。养老保险和医疗保险属于缴费型社会保障计划，主要的筹资渠道为征收社会税。爱沙尼亚的企业必须将毛收入的33%（由20%的社会保障金和13%的医疗保险金组成）用于缴纳社会税。失业保险由企业和员工共同缴纳；现行费率分别为1.6%和0.8%。育儿补贴、现金补贴和社会福利服务经费由一般性税收支付。另外，还有自愿型社会保险计划（比如养老保险和医疗保险的第三部分）。社会保障计划由国家社会保障委员会、医疗保险基金和失业保险基金管理。社会救济项目和多数社会福利服务（不包括康复、技术援助、特殊照料和替代照料）由地方政府管理。

✐ 改译

59. 爱沙尼亚的社会保护系统由两个支柱组成：第一支柱是由养老保险、医疗保险、育儿津贴和失业津贴组成的社会保障系统；第二支柱是由社会援助现金津贴和社会福利服务组成的社会福利系统。养老保险和医疗保险属于缴费型社会保障计划，主要的筹资渠道为征收社会税。爱沙尼亚的企业必须在工资毛额之外缴纳33%的社会税（由20%的社会保障缴费和13%的医疗保险缴费组成）。失业保险由企业和员工共同缴纳；现行费率分别为1.6%和0.8%。育儿津贴、社会援助现金津贴和社会福利服务由一般税收支付。另外，还有自愿型社会保险计划（如作为第三支柱的养老保险和医疗保险）。社会保障计划由国家社会保险委员会、健康保险基金和失业保险基金管理。社会援助和多数社会福利服务（不包括康复、技术援助、特殊照料和替代照料）由地方政府管理。

✪ 解 析

1 【补充知识】这句话的主干是 the social protection system is made up of two pillars—the social security system and the social welfare pillar，译文要注意区分 social protection（社会保护）和 social security（社会保障）。关于这两个概念的区别，可以上网检索《从社会保障到社会保护：社会政策理念的演进》（中国改革论坛，唐钧），其中提到 "根据国际劳工组织的划分，社会保障的范畴包括九个劳动风险方面，即疾病、生育、养老、残疾、工伤事故、职业病、失业、死亡、家庭津贴。而社会保护政策包含的内容和使用的手段更为广泛，不仅包括上述内容方面，而且包括社会救助形式的补助甚至食物，以及提供职业培训和就业服务等"。

【使用平行结构】原译的句子结构不对称："由两部分组成，分别是……另一部分是……"应改为 "分别是 A 和 B" 的结构。

pillar 可以直译为 "支柱"，这个概念在中国也经常用到，比如：我国养老保障体系共有三大支柱，第一支柱为社会基本养老保险，属政府主导，税前列支；第二支柱为企业年金，为企业及职工自愿建立，但仅对企业缴纳部分进行一定比例的税前列支，个人缴纳部分无税收优惠；第三支柱为个人商业养老保险，近年来备受关注的 "个人税收递延型养老保险"（个人收入中用于购买商业补充养老保险部分，其应缴个人所得税延期至将来提取商业养老保险金时再缴纳）即属第三支柱。

【补充知识】social welfare 应为社会福利，而非社会保障。Welfare is a government's support for the poor citizens and residents of society who do not have an income sufficient to support their basic, human needs, such as food and shelter. As social support, welfare is realized by providing poor people with a minimal level of well-being, usually either a free or a subsidized-supply of certain goods and social services, such as universal healthcare, education, and vocational training. (Wikipedia: social welfare) 因此，社会福利是为了保障人们最基本的生活而提供的，以提供服务和产品为主，与文中提及的社会福利服务和社会援助现金津贴相符。

【通过调查消除疑问】关于 social assistance cash benefits，笔者曾怀疑是否 social assistance 和 cash benefits 是两个概念，中间少了个逗号，但看到后面还有一处相同的表达，觉得原文出错的可能性不大。于是上网调查，发现经济合作与发展组织国家更常用的是 social assistance benefits in cash，强调重点在支付的形式为 cash，正好与 social welfare services 当中的 service 相对。因此，应翻译为 "社会援助现金津贴"，而非笼统的 "社会救济金"。

2 【理解文字背后的含义】原译理解不到位，造成了误译。on top of 意思是 in addition to。原文的含义是企业必须在支付工人工资之外，缴纳相当于工资总额 33% 的社会税，其中 20% 是社会保障缴费，13% 是医疗保险缴费。需要强调的是，这 33% 只是相当于工资总额的 33%，并不是从工资中支出。如果工人还需要自己缴费，工人缴纳的部分需要从自己工资中支出。

3 【补充知识】III pillar 是指第三支柱。尽管前面讲两个支柱，但其实还有商业性的养老保险、健康保险，可以称之为第三支柱。原译看来对养老保险了解不够，所查资料还不充分。

▶ 原文

89. County and city courts and administrative *courts*[1] are courts of first instance. Circuit courts are higher courts which review rulings of the courts of first instance on appeal. The Supreme Court is *the highest court of Estonia*[2] which reviews rulings of other courts pursuant to a *quashing procedure*[3]. The Supreme Court is also the court of *constitutional review*[4]. The organization of the courts and their rules of procedure *are to be*[5] established by law. *Courts Act*[6] is available in English at https://www.riigiteataja.ee/en/eli/511072014010/consolide/current.

✐ 原译

89. 县级、市级和行政法庭是一审法庭。巡回法庭是高等法庭，负责审理一审法庭的上诉案件。最高法院是爱沙尼亚的终极法庭，负责按照程序推翻其他法庭的判决。最高法院还是负责宪法审查的法院。可以通过法律规定法院的组成和议事规则。关于法院的法律英文版见https://www.riigiteataja.ee/en/eli/511072014010/consolide/current。

✐ 改译

89. 县法院、市法院和行政法院是一审法院。巡回法院是高等法院，负责审理一审法院的上诉案件。最高法院是爱沙尼亚最高级别的法院，可按照程序撤销其他法院的判决。最高法院还是负责合宪性审查的法院。法院的组织和程序规则由法律作出规定。《法院法》的英文版见https://www.riigiteataja.ee/en/eli/511072014010/consolide/current。

★ 解 析

1　【"法院"和"法庭"】courts 通常译为"法院"，不是"法庭"。在中国的语境下，"法庭"（courtroom）是审判的场所。但在国际语境下，也把 tribunal 译为"法庭"，比如，前南斯拉夫问题国际刑事法庭（International Criminal Tribunal for the Former Yugoslavia）、国际海洋法法庭（International Tribunal for the Law of the Sea）。中国法院的民事审判庭、刑事审判庭、行政审判庭是按专业划分的审判机构，英文通常翻译为 the civil division、the criminal division 和 the administrative division。在德国，不说 division，说 chamber。

2　【supreme 不一定最高】原译将 the highest court of Estonia 处理为"终极法庭"，可能是为了避免"最高法院是爱沙尼亚最高的法院"这样的废话。但这句话确实有意思。有些地方的 supreme court 名为最高法院，事实上却是一审法院，比如纽约州的"最高法院"（Supreme Court of the State of New York）。纽约州最高级别的法院叫"上诉法院"（Court of Appeals）。为了区分 supreme 和 the highest 的译文，可以把后者翻译为"最高级别的"。

3　【根据宏观背景确定词义】collinsdictionary.com 对 quashing 的解释是 to annul or put an end to (a court order, indictment, or court proceedings)，译为"撤销"可能比较准确。"推翻"也不算错。进一步调查发现："The Supreme Court of Estonia is the court of last resort in Estonia. It is both a court of cassation and a constitutional court." (Wikipedia: Supreme Court of Estonia)，其中所说的 court of cassation 是指"纠错法院""再审法院"），即对已经发生效力的判决（通常是第二审之后）进行复查，不是普通的二审复查。无论译为"撤销"还是"推翻"，都可针对生效判决。

4　【译文顾名思义】constitutional review 译为"宪法审查"没问题，但译为"合宪性审查"更便于"顾名思义"。根据 Wikipedia 的解释，Constitutional review, or constitutionality review or constitutional control, is the evaluation, in some countries, of the constitutionality of the laws (Wikipedia: constitutional review)，即法院对法律是否符合宪法规定进行审查。合宪性审查是西方概念，我国的最高法院无此功能。我国负责合宪性审查的机构是全国人大，但从来没有启动过审查程序。党的十九大报告提出："加强宪法实施和监督，推进合宪性审查工作，维护宪法权威。"这是"合宪性审查"首次出现在党的文件中。

5　【"可以"和"必须"】原译"可以通过法律规定法院的组成和议事规则"理解错误。不是可以通过法律作出规定，而是必须通过法律作出规定。are to be 应当理解为 are。

6　【专有名词的翻译】Courts Act 明显是专有名词，因此要译为"《法院法》"。

▶ 原文

94. *The Prosecutor's Office*[1], www.prokuratuur.ee, is a government agency in the area of government of the Ministry of Justice. The Prosecutor's Office is independent upon performance of its duties assigned by the law, and its actions are based on laws and on legal acts adopted on their basis. The Prosecutor's Office *directs pre-trial criminal proceedings*[2], ensuring lawfulness and effectiveness thereof; *represents public prosecution in court*[3], participates in planning *surveillance activities*[4] necessary for prevention and identification of crimes, and *performs other duties assigned to the Prosecutor's Office by the law*[5]. The text of the law is available in English at https://www.riigiteataja.ee/en/eli/ee/513112013015/consolide/current. The Prosecutor's Office is a two-tier body, consisting of the Office of the Prosecutor General as the *higher tier*[6a] and four district prosecutor's offices as the *lower tier*[6b]. The jurisdiction of the Office of the Prosecutor General is the entire Estonia; the jurisdictions of the district prosecutor's offices are identical to those of *police prefectures*[7]. The Prosecutor's Office is directed by the Prosecutor General who is appointed to office for a term of five years. A district prosecutor's office is directed by a chief prosecutor who is also appointed to office for a term of five years.

✍ 原译

94. 检察长办公室（www.prokuratuur.ee）隶属于司法部。检察长办公室依法独立履行职责，根据各项法律和根据法律制定的法规采取措施。检察长办公室负责领导刑事案件的审前程序，确保审前程序的合法性和有效性；提起公诉；为预防和侦查犯罪参与侦查活动的策划；依法执行检察长办公室的其他职责。这项法律的英文版见https://www.riigiteataja.ee/en/eli/ee/513112013015/consolide/current。检察长办公室由两级单位组成，一级单位为总检察长办公室，二级单位为4个区域检察长办公室。总检察长办公室的工作范围是爱沙尼亚全国；各区域检察长办公室与警察总局重叠。检察长办公室由总检察长领导，任期5年。区域检察长办公室由检察总监领导，任期同样是5年。

✍ 改译

94. 检察院（www.prokuratuur.ee）隶属于司法部。检察院独立履行《检察院法》赋予的职责，其行为的依据为各项法律和根据这些法律通过的立法。检察院的职责包括：指导刑事案件的审前程序，确保审前程序的合法性和有效性；出庭支持公诉；为预防和侦查犯罪参与监控活动的策划；完成法律赋予检察院的其他职责。《检察院法》的英文版见https://www.riigiteataja.ee/en/eli/ee/513112013015/consolide/current。检察院由两级单位组成，高级单位为总检察院，低级单位为4个区检察院。总检察院的管辖范围是爱沙尼亚全国；各区检察院与警务区重合。检察院由总检察长领导，总检察长任期5年。区检察院由检察长领导，检察长任期同样是5年。

★ 解 析

1 【补充知识】Prosecutor's Office 通常译为"检察官办公室",译成"检察长办公室"显然是误译。本文讲述爱沙尼亚的情况。爱沙尼亚曾经属于苏联,其司法体制应该不会完全抛弃过去的体制,所以,采用中国常用的"检察院"应该符合情理。

需要注意的是,国内对"检察院"的翻译来自苏联的 procuratorate (the office or functions of a procurator, merriam-webster.com),该词英文中很少用,也很少有人能读出来。俄罗斯的相关英文材料中已经放弃使用这个词,改用 prosecutors' office。因此,为了便于国际交往,笔者也建议译者用 prosecutors' office 翻译中国的"检察院"。如果确实希望体现中国特色,可以用更简单的 procuracy 一词。该词比较短,意思和 procuratorate 相同。

2 【注意搭配】将 direct 译为"领导"与宾语"刑事案件的审前程序"(pre-trial criminal proceedings)搭配不当;但可说领导团队、领导某人等。此处 direct 译为"指导"更合适,指的是检察院对侦查部门(警察机关)的工作有指导作用。

【拆分长句】另外,directs...represents...participates 等动词并列,但因为各部分较长,汉语无法一气呵成,故改译为"职责包括",这样可以从容叙述各个组成部分。

3 【补充知识】根据《中华人民共和国人民检察院组织法》,检察院的职责包括对于刑事案件提起公诉,支持公诉;对于人民法院的审判活动是否合法,实行监督(由检察院对法院活动进行监督,这项权力在西方国家不存在)。"提起公诉"与"支持公诉"是两个不同的概念。前者是一种起诉类型,指人民检察院对公安机关侦查终结、移送起诉的案件进行全面审查,对应当追究刑事责任的犯罪嫌疑人提交人民法院进行审判的一项诉讼活动;而后者指检察长或检察官以国家公诉人身份出席法庭,根据事实和法律,支持检察机关对刑事被告人的指控,要求对被告人处以刑罚的诉讼活动。represents public prosecution in court 说的显然是后者。

4 【补充知识】侦查是指在刑事诉讼过程中,侦查机关为查明案情,收集犯罪证据材料,证实和抓获犯罪嫌疑人,追究犯罪嫌疑人刑事责任,依法采取的一系列专门调查手段和强制措施。文中的 surveillance activities 是侦查活动的一项内容,如通过窃听等技术手段监控犯罪。

5 【正确判断修饰关系】performs other duties assigned to the Prosecutor's Office by the law,原译未能体现原文的修饰关系。

6　【避免歧义】译者将原文中的 higher tier（6a）和 lower tier（6b）分别对应为一级单位和二级单位，意思不是很明确。因为以最高的为一，还是最低的为一，汉语中并不确定。比如：一级教授高于二级教授，但联合国工作人员中的专业一级（P1）是最低的，专业 5 级（P5）是最高的。所以，不如直接译为"高级"和"低级"。

7　【补充知识】police prefectures 是"警区"或"警务区"。一个城市可以按各种标准划分区域，比如：学区、警区、消防区、行政区，各种区划可能完全重合，也可能不完全重合。

第 ⑪ 单元　第一次全球海洋综合评估技术摘要

学习要点

思维方法

★ **宏观思维**

　　根据语境确定词义

★ **调查研究方法**

　　查英语释义

理解

★ **补充知识**

　　1. balance

　　2. excess heat

　　3. greenhouse effect

　　4. heat capacity

　　5. OMZ

★ **理解语言**

　　1. 指代关系

　　2. as well as 不是简单的并列关系

表达

★ **意思准确**

　　在理解的基础上翻译

★ **符合形式**

　　1. 补充词语以更好搭配

　　2. 省略词语以照顾搭配

　　3. 拆分长句

　　4. Southern Oscillation 译法辨析

变通

　　1. lower rainfall (precipitation)

　　2. higher evaporation

　　3. 适度灵活

　　4. 适当简化

背景说明

　　本单元练习选自 "The Impacts of Climate Change and Related Changes in the Atmosphere on the Oceans: A Technical Abstract of the First Global Integrated Marine Assessment"，可通过检索此标题获取全文。本摘要的要点为: 海洋与大气层相互关联, 都无法摆脱气候变化的影响。气候变化可导致海平面上升、海洋酸化、盐度变化、海洋分层、海洋变暖等。海洋生态系统变化速度比陆地生物快 1.5~5 倍, 且这些变化不可逆转, 因此, 海洋变化的后果不容小觑。

练习和讲解

▶ 原文

9. *The ocean's large mass and high heat capacity enable it to store huge amounts of energy, more than 1,000 times that found in the atmosphere for an equivalent increase in temperature*[1]. The Earth is absorbing more heat than it is emitting back into space, and nearly all that *excess heat*[2a] is entering the ocean and being stored there. The ocean has absorbed about 93 percent of the combined *extra heat*[2b] stored by warmed air, sea, land, and melted ice between 1971 and 2010. The IPCC has reaffirmed in its Fifth Assessment Report its conclusion that global *sea surface temperatures*[3] have increased since the late nineteenth century. The temperature in the upper-ocean (down to about 700 m), and hence its heat content, varies over multiple time scales, including seasonal, inter-annual (for example, *those*[4] associated with *the El Niño-Southern Oscillation*[5]), decadal and centennial periods. Depth-averaged ocean temperature trends from 1971 to 2010 are *positive*[6] (that is, they show warming) over most of the globe. The *warming*[7] is more prominent in the northern hemisphere, especially in the North Atlantic, but is spatially very variable. *Zonally averaged upper-ocean temperature trends show warming at nearly all latitudes and depths*[8]. However, the greater volume of the ocean in the southern hemisphere increases the contribution of its warming to the global heat content.

✍ 原译

9. 海洋的巨大体积和高热容使它能储存大量能量，比同等幅度的大气升温所产生的能量高出1,000倍以上。地球吸收的热量多于反射回太空的热量，这些过多的热量几乎全被海洋吸收和存储。海洋吸收了1971年至2010年之间由变热的空气、海水、陆地和融冰存储的所有多余热量的93％。气专委在其《第五次评估报告》中重申其结论，即19世纪末以来，全球海面温度都升高了。上层海洋（海表下700米）温度及其热含量在季节性、年际（如与厄尔尼诺南方涛动有关的变化）、十年和百年等多个时间尺度上均出现变化。全球大部分地区，1971年至2010年按深度平均的海洋温度趋势呈阳性（即出现变暖趋势）。北半球气候变暖更为突出，北大西洋地区尤

✍ 改译

9. 海洋的巨大体量和高热容使它能储存大量能量，在温度升幅相当的情况下，海洋的储能能力高出大气1,000多倍。地球吸收的热量多于反射回太空的热量，这些多吸收的热量几乎全部进入海洋并存储在那里。1971年至2010年间，因空气、海水、陆地变暖和冰雪融化而存储的所有多余热量中，海洋吸收了93％。气专委在其《第五次评估报告》中重申其结论，即19世纪晚期以来，全球海表温度全面升高。上层海洋（海表下700米）温度以及相应的热含量按季节、年度（如与厄尔尼诺南方涛动有关的温度和热含量变化）、十年期和百年期等时间尺度测量均出现变化。1971年至2010年全球大部分地区按深度平均的海洋温度变化趋势为正值（即呈

⊘ **原译**

其如此，但不同地区差异很大。按区域平均的上层海洋温度趋势表明，几乎所有纬度和深度都在变暖。但是，由于南半球海洋面积更大，南半球海域变暖更增加全球热容量。

⊘ **改译**

现变暖趋势）。北半球海洋变暖更为突出，北大西洋地区尤其如此，但在空间分布上差异很大。按气候带平均的上层海洋温度变化趋势表明，几乎所有纬度和深度的海洋都在变暖。但是，由于南半球海洋体量更大，南半球海域变暖增加了其对全球热容量的贡献。

★ **解　析**

1 【补充知识】这句话是理解不到位导致翻译错误。毫无疑问，水可以存储能量（把水加热，能量便储存在水中），空气也可以存储能量，但两者的潜力不同。明白了这个简单的道理，就不会望文生义。请看 Wikipedia 的解释：Heat capacity or thermal capacity is a measurable physical quantity equal to the ratio of the heat added to (or removed from) an object to the resulting temperature change (Wikipedia: heat capacity)，翻译为"热容"很好，显然译者进行了调查。也可以译为"热容量"：海水热容量是指使 1 立方厘米海水的温度升高 1℃所需的热量。其值为海水比热与海水密度的乘积，其单位是卡 / 立方厘米·度。（《中国百科大辞典》）所谓 an equivalent increase in temperature，是指气温上升一度。that 指代 energy。mass 译为"体积"虽无大错，但用"体量"或"质量"更加准确。另外，虽然原文句子比较长，但只要理解了意思，并不难表达出来。

2 【补充知识】原译对 excess heat（2a）的理解错误。要正确翻译，首先要了解一下什么是温室效应（greenhouse effect）：

If a planet's atmosphere contains radiatively active gases (i.e., greenhouse gases), they will radiate energy in all directions. Part of this radiation is directed towards the surface, warming it. The intensity of the downward radiation—that is, the strength of the greenhouse effect—will depend on the atmosphere's temperature and on the amount of greenhouse gases that the atmosphere contains. Earth's natural greenhouse effect is critical to supporting life. Human activities, mainly the burning of fossil fuels and clearing of forests, have strengthened the greenhouse effect and caused global warming. (Wikipedia: greenhouse effect)

下面的这张图（来自 Wikipedia）直观地展现了太阳与地球间的热交换：

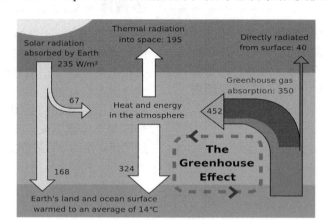

由此可见，地球变暖是因为地球吸热多，放热少。吸收的热量减去释放的热量，就是 excess heat。所以是"多吸收的热量"，而非笼统的"过多"。下一句中的 extra heat（2b）与 excess heat 是同一概念。对于任何词、句子的理解都不能脱离上下文、背景知识或者常识。

3 【补充知识】Sea surface temperature (SST) is the water temperature close to the ocean's surface. The exact meaning of surface varies according to the measurement method used, but it is between 1 millimetre and 20 metres below the sea surface. Air masses in the Earth's atmosphere are highly modified by sea surface temperatures within a short distance of the shore. (Wikipedia: sea surface temperature)

海表温度又称海温，常以℃表示。海表温度取决于海水的热量收支情况，具有明显的日变化和季节变化。（百度百科：海表温度）

4 【指代关系】严格来说，those 是指 the temperature and its heat content，但从意思来看，是指温度的变化。

5 【补充知识】南方涛动（Southern Oscillation）指发生在东南太平洋与印度洋及印尼地区之间的反相气压振动，是热带环流年际变化最突出、最重要的现象之一：

El Niño-Southern Oscillation (ENSO) is an irregularly periodic variation in winds and sea surface temperatures over the tropical eastern Pacific Ocean, affecting the climate of much of the tropics and subtropics. The warming phase of the sea temperature is known as El Niño and the cooling phase as La Niña. The Southern Oscillation is the accompanying atmospheric component, coupled with the sea temperature change: El Niño is accompanied by high air surface pressure in the tropical western Pacific and La Niña with low air surface pressure there. The two periods last several months each (typically occurring every few years) and their effects vary in intensity. (Wikipedia: El Niño-Southern Oscillation)

科学界所指的南方涛动是用塔西提岛（148°05′W，17°53′S）或复活节岛（109°30′W，29°00′S）与达尔文（130°59′E，12°20′S）两个观测站的海平面气压之差来表示的，即南方涛动指数（SOI），等于塔西提岛减去达尔文的海平面气压。SOI 的大小表示南方涛动的强弱。SOI 为负数，对应厄尔尼诺事件；SOI 为正数，则对应拉尼娜事件。SOI 变化与厄尔尼诺的发生有着很好的对应关系，二者联系密切。（百度百科：南方涛动）

【Southern Oscillation 译法辨析】Wikipedia 对 oscillation 的解释是：Oscillation is the repetitive variation, typically in time, of some measure about a central value (often a point of equilibrium) or between two or more different states. The term "vibration" is precisely used to describe mechanical oscillation. (Wikipedia: oscillation)

这个词在物理学中翻译为"振荡"（注意：不是"震荡"）：振荡是指电路中的电流（或电压）在最大值和最小值之间随时间作周期性重复变化的现象或过程。振幅恒定的振荡称"等幅振荡"；振幅随时间而递减的振荡称"阻尼振荡"或"减幅振荡"。（百度百科：振荡）

所以，也有人把 Southern Oscillation 翻译为"南方振荡"。联合国文件中多用"南方涛动"。但在汉语词典中查找"涛动"一词，均未发现该词条。"涛动"仅出现在与"南方涛动"相关的描述中，说明这个词很可能是译者在翻译 Southern Oscillation 时创造的。

笔者第一次看到"南方涛动"，感觉是大海中的波涛汹涌澎湃。但看了中英文解释后，感觉造词者的用意可能是把海平面气压和海表温度的周期性变化比作波涛的上下起伏。尽管笔者认为，如果已经有现成的词（比如"振荡"）可以借用，就不必再造新词，但既然"南方涛动"的说法已经被大众接受，而且也说得通，译者拿来使用即可。

6　【根据语境确定词义】positive 在医学领域有"阳性的"含义，在数学领域的含义是"正的"，此处讲的是海洋温度变化，纯数字的变化，显然不能译成"阳性"，可以说"正值"。

7　【宏观思维】本段都是在谈海洋储能和变暖，所以 warming 指的是海洋变暖，而不是笼统的气候变暖；如果单看 warming 还不敢确定的话，看到 in the North Atlantic 就应当引起注意。Act local, think global.

8　【补充词语以更好搭配】原译将 warming at nearly all latitudes and depths 译为"几乎所有纬度和深度都在变暖"，但纬度和深度无法变暖，应该补充上文已经出现的信息，即"所有纬度和深度的海洋都在变暖"，才更为合理。另外也要注意：上一句中的 spatially 指空间上的，应当包括气候带（zonally）和不同深度的海洋。zonally 的意思可参见 zone 的解释（dictionary. cambridge.org）：

SPECIALIZED geography , environment one of the five parts the earth is divided into according to temperature, marked by imaginary lines going around it from east to west:

temperate zones

▶ **原文**

15. Alongside broad-scale ocean warming, shifts in ocean salinity (salt content) have also occurred. Variations in the salinity of the ocean around the world result from differences in the *balance*[1] between freshwater inflows (from rivers and glacier and ice-cap melt), rainfall and evaporation, all of which are affected by natural climate phenomena *as well as*[2] by climate change. Changes in the broad scale of *patterns of rainfall*[3] will produce changes in ocean salinity, as higher rainfall will increase dilution and thus lower salinity, while *lower rainfall*[4a] will have the reverse effect. Observed changes to ocean salinity, which are calculated from a *sparse historical observing system*[5], *suggest that* areas of *lower precipitation*[4b] and *higher evaporation*[4c] such as subtropical ocean regions have become *more saline*[4d], while areas of higher precipitation and lower evaporation such as equatorial waters in the Pacific and Indian Oceans have become *less saline*[6]. Changes in salinity result in changes in the density of water, thereby driving ocean circulation. Ongoing change to ocean salinity is likely to have an effect on the circulation and stratification of seawater (Chapters 4 and 5).

✍ **原译**

15. 除大规模海洋变暖外，海洋盐度也产生了变化。世界各地海洋盐度不同，因为从河流、冰川和冰帽融化产生的淡水流入量，降雨量和蒸发量不同，而所有这一切都受自然气候现象和气候变化影响。雨量型大规模变化将导致海洋盐度变化，因为更高的降雨量将增加稀释度，从而降低盐度，而更低降雨量作用相反。根据零星的历史观测系统计算得出的盐度变化表明，亚热带海洋地区等更高降雨量和更低蒸发量的地区盐度更高，而太平洋和印度洋赤道水域等更高降雨量和更低蒸发量的地区盐度更低。盐度变化导致水体密度变化，从而驱动洋流。海洋盐度持续变化很可能影响海水环流和海洋分层（第4、5章）。

✍ **改译**

15. 除大规模海洋变暖外，海洋盐度分布也产生了变化。世界各地海洋盐度不同，是因为淡水流入（来自河流、冰川和冰帽融化）、降雨和蒸发的相对数量不同，而所有这些因素既受自然气候现象影响，又受气候变化影响。降雨规律的大规模变化将导致海洋盐度变化，因为降雨量增加会加强稀释作用，降低盐度，而降雨量减少的作用则相反。根据零星历史观测推算的海洋盐度变化表明，亚热带海洋区域等降雨量减少和蒸发量增加的区域盐度升高，而太平洋和印度洋赤道水域等降雨量增加和蒸发量减少的地区盐度降低。盐度变化导致水体密度变化，从而驱动洋流。海洋盐度持续变化很可能影响海水环流和海洋分层（第4、5章）。

⊕ 解 析

1 【补充知识】balance 除了"平衡"的意思之外，还有"两个数字之差"的意思，比如存款的"余额"（存款减去取款）就是 balance (an amount in excess especially on the credit side of an account) (merriam-webster.com)。此处意思相近：流入海洋的淡水 + 海洋上空的降水（淡水）– 海洋的蒸发（淡水）= 进入海洋的淡水数量（balance），也就是这三者相互抵销后的余量。海洋的不同区域盐度不同，是因为各区域这三者的相对数量不同。

2 【逻辑关系】as well as 不是简单的并列：

If you say that something is true of one person or thing as well as another, you are emphasizing that it is true not only of the second person or thing but also of the first one. (thefreedictionary.com)

而是强调同时受到两者影响，因此，译文使用"既……又……"结构。

3 【查英文释义】patterns of rainfall 意思是"降雨规律"；"雨量型"没有意义。误译的原因是不理解 pattern 一词的含义。en.oxforddictionaries.com 对 pattern 的解释如下：

1 A repeated decorative design.

  "a neat blue herringbone pattern."

  (+ More example sentences) (+ Synonyms)

  1.1 An arrangement or design regularly found in comparable objects.

   "The house had been built on the usual pattern."

   (+ More example sentences) (+ Synonyms)

  1.2 A regular and intelligible form or sequence discernible in the way in which something happens or is done.

   "A complicating factor is the change in working patterns."

   "The murders followed a repeated pattern."

   "The school is located a few kilometers away and is run on the pattern of other army schools."

   (+ More example sentences) (+ Synonyms)

根据 1.2 的解释，此处 pattern 的意思是"规律""模式"。对于意思不敢确定的词，可以通过查阅英英词典来澄清，不能凭猜测翻译。译者通常也不会去创造新词。

4 【适度灵活】译者将 lower rainfall（4a）、lower (precipitation)（4b）、higher evaporation（4c）、more saline（4d）等比较级分别译为"更低降雨量""更高降雨量"（意思错误）、"更低蒸发量"（意思错误）和"更高盐度"，表达较死板，削弱了中文的节奏感。可通过调整说法来增强句子的节奏感，如"降雨量减少""蒸发量增加""盐度升高"。

联合国文件翻译 译·注·评

5 【省略词语以照顾搭配】sparse historical observing system 当中，sparse 和 system 意思上无法搭配。查阅网上资料，通常的说法是 sparse historical observations（零星的历史观测）。译文省略 system。

6 【在理解的基础上翻译】suggest 这句话原译意思反了。这个问题只看译文就可以发现，因为同样是"降雨量大和蒸发量小"，怎么可能一处盐度升高，一处盐度降低？海水盐度（salinity of sea water）是指海水中全部溶解固体与海水重量之比，通常用每千克海水中所含的克数表示。人们用盐度来表示海水中盐类物质的质量分数。世界大洋的平均盐度为 35‰。海洋中发生的许多现象和过程，常与盐度的分布和变化有关。盐度分布一般受纬度、蒸发、降水、结冰、融冰和陆地径流等因素影响。在海洋，赤道一带降雨量大，盐度较低。在高纬度地区，溶解的冰降低了盐度。盐度最高的地区是蒸发量大而降雨相对较低的中纬地区。（百度百科：海水盐度）改译把 lower 和 higher 分别译为动词"减少"和"增加"。

▶ **原文**

19. The levels of dissolved oxygen in the ocean in the tropics have decreased over the past 50 years, largely as a result of ocean warming. *This has, for example, resulted in an expansion*[1] of the areas with the lowest levels of dissolved oxygen (*oxygen minimum zones—OMZs*[2]), including westward and vertical expansion of the OMZ in the eastern Pacific Ocean. Projected changes to surface temperatures and stratification are likely to result in a decreased transfer of oxygen from the atmosphere (oxygen solubility) and reduced ventilation of deeper waters, resulting in lower concentration of oxygen in the upper ocean across the tropics. Outside the tropics, current observations are not sufficient enough to determine trends, but it is expected that warming of the ocean and stratification will also result in declines in dissolved oxygen.

✎ **原译**

19. 过去50年内，主要由于海洋变暖，热带地区海洋中溶解氧水平减少。这导致的后果其中一例是溶解氧水平最低区域（氧最小层）的扩大，包括东太平洋氧最小层往西和垂直扩大。预计海表温度变化和分层很可能导致大气层转移的氧气减少（氧气溶解度），深层水域流通性降低，导致整个热带地区海洋上层氧浓度降低。热带地区以外，当前洋流观测结果不足以确定趋势，但预计海洋变暖和分层也将导致溶解氧减少。

✎ **改译**

19. 过去50年，海洋变暖、热带海洋中溶解氧水平降低的后果之一是溶解氧水平最低区域（氧最低区）扩大，包括东太平洋氧最低区往西和垂直扩大。海表温度变化和分层加强预计可能导致来自大气的氧气转移（氧气溶解度）下降，以及较深层水域供氧减少，从而导致整个热带海洋上层氧浓度降低。在热带海洋以外，当前的观察结果还不足以确定趋势，但预计海洋变暖和分层加强也将导致溶解氧减少。

⊛ 解 析

1 【适度灵活】斜体部分的译文不灵活，不符合中文的表达特点。但不可否认的是，译者对原文含义的理解是很到位的。for example 就预示着不是单一的结果，此处只举其中一例说明。但译文的表达却出现了问题：机械对译，导致译文晦涩。对照英文去检察译文，难免处于英语的"阴影"之下，不妨单独读译文，用汉语的思维去评判译文是否符合语言习惯。

2 【补充知识】"海洋含氧量最小层"又称"氧最小层"，参阅如下资料：

The oxygen minimum zone (OMZ), sometimes referred to as the shadow zone, is the zone in which oxygen saturation in seawater in the ocean is at its lowest. This zone occurs at depths of about 200 to 1,500 metres, depending on local circumstances. OMZs are found worldwide, typically along the western coast of continents, in areas where an interplay of physical and biological processes concurrently lowers the oxygen concentration (biological processes) and restricts the water from mixing with surrounding waters (physical processes), creating a "pool" of water where oxygen concentrations fall from the normal range of 4–6 mg/l to below 2 mg/l. Surface ocean waters generally have oxygen concentrations close to equilibrium with the Earth's atmosphere. In general, colder waters hold more oxygen than warmer waters. (Wikipedia: oxygen minimum zone)

大洋中溶解氧（dissolved oxygen）的垂直分布，在中层含氧量最小，出现一氧最小层，而在中层以上含氧量则升高。海洋环境中氧的消耗同有机物的氧化作用密切相关。氧化作用所消耗的溶解氧来源于大气和光合二氧最小层的作用。同时，透光层以下的水体中氧的供应完全依赖表层水体的移流和扩散作用，而表层水体则靠物理、化学和生物过程保持着高含量。（百度百科：溶解氧）

▶ 原文

24. *Shifts in primary productivity resulting from climate change will inevitably work their way up the food web*[1]. At each higher trophic layer, the effects in changes in the species composition and abundance of their food in the lower layers of the food web will make it more *(or, in some cases, less)*[2] difficult for animals to survive and to raise their progeny. How these changes in the food web will affect top predators such as marine reptiles, seabirds and marine mammals is largely unknown. Habitat changes will also affect top predators: for example, bird species living in mangroves or foraging in seagrass beds will be affected by changes in those habitats.

原译

24. 由气候变化带来的初级生产力的变化必将逐级上升影响到食物链。营养层每高一层，物种的组成和食物链中较低层级的食物丰富性发生的变化所带来的影响将会使动物更难（或者，在一些情况下，更容易）生存和抚养后代。食物链中的变化将如何影响到顶层捕食动物，比如海洋爬行动物、海鸟和海洋哺乳动物等，很大程度上还不得而知。生境的变化同样也会影响到顶层捕食动物，例如，生活在红树林中或在海草床中觅食的鸟类将会受到这些生境变化的影响。

改译

24. 由气候变化带来的初级生产能力变化必定在食物网中逐级传导。在每个较高级别的营养层，其下层食物网物种构成和食物丰度的变化都会使动物更难（有时是更容易）生存和抚养后代。食物网中的这些变化将如何影响顶层捕食动物，比如海洋爬行动物、海鸟和海洋哺乳动物等，很大程度上还不得而知。栖息地变化同样也会影响到顶层捕食动物。例如，生活在红树林或在海草床觅食的鸟类将受到栖息地变化的影响。

★ 解 析

1 【在理解的基础上翻译】本段第一句由于译者理解不充分造成了误译，扭曲了原意。理解的难点在于本句后半部分...will inevitably work their way up the food web，表层含义是这种影响将沿着食物网向上爬，换言之就是该影响将在食物网逐级传递。而原译"……必将逐级上升影响到食物链"则将重心放在了"影响食物链上"，原文意在强调该影响在食物网中的传递。

2 【在理解的基础上翻译】斜体部分机械对译，导致译文冗长，不符合中文的表达习惯。若译者能在理解的情况下翻译，或许就能减少这种错误的发生。

【适度灵活】or 和 in some cases 在句中都传达了转折的意味，且 or 略去不译毫不损失原文的含义，译者可灵活处理。

▶ 原文

30. The balance between those two changes is unclear. *A shift towards less primary production or changes in the size structure of the plankton communities would have serious implications for human food security and the support of marine biodiversity through disruption to food webs*[1]. The timing of the spring blooms of phytoplankton is also expected to change. This would also affect marine *food webs*[2], because many species synchronize spawning and larval development with phytoplankton blooms and the associated peaks in abundance of zooplankton (the microscopic animals which feed on phytoplankton and bacteria) *(Chapter 6)*.

✍ 原译

30. 这两个变化之间的平衡不甚明朗。天平倾向初级生产减少一侧或浮游生物群体结构发生变化都会使人类的粮食安全和对海洋生物多样性的支持受到严重影响。浮游植物的春季大量繁殖时机可能也会变化。这同样会影响到海洋食物链，因为很多物种的产卵和幼虫发育都会与浮游植物大量繁殖和浮游动物（靠浮游植物和细菌生存的微型动物）的相应峰值同步（第6章）。

✍ 改译

30. 这两个变化之间相互作用的结果还不清楚。如果初级生产减少，或浮游生物群体体型结构发生变化，就会因食物网的破坏而严重影响人类的食物安全、削弱海洋生物多样性的基础。浮游植物春季水华时间预计也将发生变化。这同样会影响海洋食物网，因为很多物种的产卵和幼虫发育都会与浮游植物水华和浮游动物（靠浮游植物和细菌生存的微型动物）的相应峰值同步（第6章）。

⊛ 解 析

1 【宏观思维】本句话要结合前文理解。前文讲海洋变暖可能引起初级生产增加，两种变化相抵的结果尚不清楚。这句话是说，如果最终结果是初级生产减少，将会产生什么后果，原译用"天平"作比喻，意思不明确。

2 【查英文释义】food webs 被译成了"食物链"，可能是想当然的结果。经调查，"食物链"与"食物网"是两种完全不同的概念：

A food chain is a linear network of links in a food web starting from producer organisms (such as grass or trees which use radiation from the Sun to make their food) and ending at apex predator species (like grizzly bears or killer whales), detritivores (like earthworms or woodlice), or decomposer species (such as fungi or bacteria). A food chain also shows how the organisms are related with each other by the food they eat. Each level of a food chain represents a different trophic level. (Wikipedia: food chain)

A food web (or food cycle) is a natural interconnection of food chains and a graphical representation (usually an image) of what-eats-what in an ecological community. (Wikipedia: food web).

由此可见，两者是部分与整体的关系，不能相提并论。

第 12 单元　加强水合作应对21世纪的挑战

背景说明

联合国教科文组织（UNESCO）被视为联合国的"智力"机构。教科文组织力图在各国之间建立网络，通过推进教育、跨文化交流、科研合作和保护言论自由促进世界团结。本文由教科文组织水科学司和水服务司的三位专家共同撰写，发表在 2013 年《联合国纪事》（*UN Chronicle*）上，探讨 21 世纪全球水合作的方向。《联合国纪事》是由联合国出版，在全球范围内发行的期刊，向全球报告重大国际新闻及联合国政策（网址：unchronicle. un.org）。

练习和讲解

▷ 原文

1. *The twenty-first century, part of the Anthropocene[1], will leave us with tremendous environmental changes[2]*. Unprecedented population growth, a changing climate, rapid urbanization, *expansion of infrastructure[3]*, *migration[4]*, *land conversion[5]* and pollution translate into *changes in the fluxes, pathways and stores of water[6]*—from rapidly melting glaciers to *the decline of groundwater[7]* due to overexploitation. Population density and per capita resource use have increased dramatically over the past century, and *watersheds[8]*, aquifers and the associated ecosystems have undergone significant modifications that affect the vitality, quality and *availability[9]* of the resource. Current United Nations predictions estimate that the world population will reach 9 billion in 2050. The exponential growth in population and the more intensive use of water per capita are among the leading key drivers behind hydrologic change and its impact. It is a huge challenge on an already resource-limited planet to meet the various needs of the people, *especially of those who already lack access to clean water[10]*. *The variability[11]*, vulnerability and uncertainty of global water resources will be further exacerbated *by increasingly erratic weather events[12], including droughts, floods and storms[13]*. Such disasters seriously impede efforts to meet the Millennium Development Goals. Water scarcity due to drought, land degradation and desertification already affects 1.5 billion people in the world and is closely associated with poverty, food insecurity and *malnutrition[14]*.

📖 原译

1. 作为人类世的一部分，21世纪将给我们留下诸多环境剧变。前所未有的人口增长、气候变化、快速的城市化、基础设施扩容、移徙、改变土地用途和污染改变水的流量、路径和存储：从快速消融的冰川到过度开发导致的地下水下降，都说明了这一点。过去一个世纪，人口密度和人均资源使用量显著上升，流域、含水层及与之配套的生态系统发生了巨大的改变，影响了水资源的活力、质量和可用性。联合国当前的预测估计，世界人口将在2050年达到90亿。人口呈指数级增长和人均用水量激增是造成水文变化及其影响的主要原因之一。在一个资源已经有限的星球上要满足人的多种需求是一个巨大的挑战，尤其是对那些已经缺少获得清洁水的机会的人们而言。全球水资源的多变性、脆弱性和不确定性由于天候越来越反复无常而进一步恶化，包括干旱、洪水和风暴。这些灾害严重阻碍实现千年发展目标的努力。由干旱、土地退化和荒漠化导致的缺水已经影响世界上15亿人口，并与贫困、粮食不安全和营养有密切联系。

📖 改译

1. 21世纪作为人类世的一部分，将给我们带来巨大的环境变化。前所未有的人口增长、气候变化、快速城市化、基础设施扩张、移民、土地用途转换和污染等，改变了河水流量、水流路径和水的储量。从快速消融的冰川到过度开发导致的地下水位下降，都说明了这一点。过去一个世纪，人口密度和人均资源使用量显著上升，水源地、含水层及相关生态系统发生了深刻改变，影响了水资源的活力、质量和供应。根据联合国目前的预测，世界人口将在2050年达到90亿。人口的指数级增长和人均用水量激增是造成水文变化及其影响的主要原因之一。在一个资源已经捉襟见肘的星球上，满足人的多种需求是一个巨大挑战，对那些已经无法获得清洁水的人们而言尤其如此。由于干旱、洪水和风暴等天气事件愈加反复无常，全球水资源的分布差异、脆弱性和不确定性进一步加大。这些灾害严重阻碍实现千年发展目标的努力。由干旱、土地退化和荒漠化导致的缺水已经影响世界上15亿人口，缺水问题也与贫困、缺乏粮食安全和营养不良密切关联。

★ 解 析

1 【补充知识】Anthropocene 意为"人类世"，又称"人新世"，是指地球最近的地质年代。有人认为人类活动对地球的影响足以成为一个新的地质时代，故名。anthro- 的意思是"人"，-cene 的意思是 new 或 recent。原译者显然做了调查研究。

2 【避免汉语西化】"作为"的逻辑主语是"21世纪"，但"21世纪"却出现在下一句，不符合传统语法要求，所以前置。不过，受西方语言影响，这类句子已经司空见惯，所以，不改也不算错。

3 【根据语境确定译法】expansion of infrastructure 原译为"基础设施扩容"。"扩容"意味着在原有的基础上扩大。但城市化带来的不仅是"扩容"，还包括新建基础设施，所以改为

"扩张"，意思范围更广。

4【尊重或调整既定译法】migration 译为"移徙"是联合国文件过去的译法，联合国中文处已经按照国内语言习惯修改为"移民"。如果国际公约中文本当时译为"移徙"，直接引用时可以继续使用，尽管这样做可能造成全文用词不统一。

5【land conversion 与 land development】根据 Wikipedia，land conversion 与 land development（土地开发）的区别是：

Land development puts more emphasis on the expected economic development as a result of the process; land conversion tries to focus on the general physical and biological aspects of the land use change.

逐字翻译为"土地转换"，在汉语中意思不明确。既然是土地用途的变化，不妨译为"土地用途转换"。原译"改变土地用途"意思正确。改译把"改变"改为"转换"，是希望尽量贴近原文用词。

6【补充知识】fluxes, pathways and stores of water，原译"流量、路径和存储"，不知道是否为专业说法，尤其是"改变水的存储"是什么意思？是指存储方式吗？

上网查，flux or water flux is typically expressed as volume per area per unit of time（单位时间通过单位面积的水流量）（wetpurewater.com）。根据百度百科，这个意思在汉语中的说法确实是"流量"（"流量，单位时间内通过某一过水断面的水体体积，其常用单位为每秒立方米，多用于河流、湖泊的断面的进出水量测量"）。同时可知，百度百科把"河水流量"翻译为 river discharge 是错误的。

经检验，pathway 中文里可以说"水流路径"，但"水道"更加通俗易懂。

stores 初步改译为"存储方式"。这样意思确实更清楚，但还是有疑问：土地开发造成河流路径改变可以想象，比如截弯取直；人口增加导致河水流量改变也可以想象，比如，上游用水增加，下流水量减少。问题是哪一种因素会导致储水方式改变呢？前面列举的几种因素似乎与储水方式无关。还有，如果是储水方式改变，是如何改变？是指人类建造了更多水库吗？这些问题对于专业人士来说，可能是不言而喻的，但对于没有专业背景的译者来说，就需要更多调查。正在山穷水尽之时，译者想到再查查 store 的意思。因为如果此处表示的是抽象的意义"存储"，为什么不用 storage？结果显示，store 还真有另一个意思：a large supply or stock kept for future use (merriam-webster.com)。所以，此处应当译为"水的储量"。人类活动导致可用的水储量减少，合情合理。下一句的冰川消融和地下水位下降就是储量减少的例子。

7 【批判地看待原文】the decline of groundwater 译为"地下水下降",意思不清;英文应该是 decline of groundwater levels,即"水位下降"。译文可以改善原文的表达方式。

8 【watershed、drainage basin 与 catchment】watershed 词典上常见的译文是"流域""分水岭""集水区"。请看如下资料(注意:资料中的中文是笔者添加):

A **watershed** is an area of land that drains all the streams and rainfall to a common outlet such as the outflow of a reservoir, mouth of a bay, or any point along a stream channel. The word watershed is sometimes used interchangeably with **drainage basin** (流域) or **catchment** (集水区). Ridges and hills that separate two watersheds are called the **drainage divide** (分水岭). The watershed consists of surface water—lakes, streams, reservoirs, and wetlands—and all the *underlying ground water* (地下水). Larger watersheds contain many smaller watersheds. It all depends on the outflow point; all of the land that drains water to the outflow point is the watershed for that outflow location. Watersheds are important because the streamflow and the water quality of a river are affected by things, human-induced or not, happening in the land area "above" the river-outflow point. (water.usgs.gov)

Drainage basin (流域), also called **catchment area** (集水区), or (in North America) **watershed** (集水区), is an area from which all precipitation flows to a single stream or set of streams. For example, the total area drained by the Mississippi River constitutes its drainage basin, whereas that part of the Mississippi River drained by the Ohio River is the Ohio's drainage basin. The boundary between drainage basins is a **drainage divide** (分水岭): all the precipitation on opposite sides of a drainage divide will flow into different drainage basins. (britannica.com)

watershed: drainage divide, the line that separates neighbouring drainage basins; drainage basin, in North American usage, an area of land where surface water converges. (Wikipedia: watershed)

根据资料,"流域"指由分水线(drainage divide)所包围的河流集水区(catchment area),分地面集水区和地下集水区两类。(百度百科:流域)如果地面集水区和地下集水区相重合,称为闭合流域;如果不重合,则称为非闭合流域。平时所称的流域,一般都指地面集水区。(pwsannong.com)

watershed 是为一条河流提供水源的降水区,所以可以译为"汇水区""集水区""流域"。watershed 也有"分水岭"的意思,是因为山脊两侧的水会流入不同河流。但此处说 watershed 遭受重大改变是什么意思呢?笔者没有查到直接解释,推测是指江河源头地区(水源涵养地)乱砍滥伐,导致植被减少。在缺乏植被遮挡的情况下,雨水流到山下没有缓冲时间,一下雨就形成山洪,不下雨则江河断流。改译起初改为"集水区",比"流域"意思具体一些，但还不够明确，最后改为"水源地"。

9 【根据语境确定译法】availability 原译为"可用性"，但究竟何为可用性？是从水污染角度而言，还是从总水量而言？ Available means suitable or ready for use; of use or service; at hand; readily obtainable or accessible. (dictionary.com) 在确定了词义的情况下，按照上下文灵活处理，在本段，可理解为水的可获得性，即水资源的供给。有时也翻译为"可得性"。

10 【适度灵活】especially of/that 是英文中常见的句型，用于对前文的补充说明。原译采用直译，似乎没有把话说完，改译增加了"尤其如此"，使意思完整。但并非所有 especially 句式都需要如此处理。很多情况下为了便于翻译，也采用原译的做法，稍微牺牲一点汉语的通顺。

11 【根据语境确定译法】variability 译为"多变性"意思不够清晰。经查，找到如下资料：

Variability of water and other resources in time and space is the major natural impediment for sustainable agriculture, food production... (ideas.repec.org)

此处 variability 是指水资源的时空分布不均。该词用于气候的时候，是指气候的多变性。

12 【补充知识】将 weather events 译为"天候"不妥。"天候"指在一定的时间内，某一地方的大气物理状态，如气温、气压、温度、风、降雨等，即平时所说的"天气"(《新华字典》)，就是英文的 weather，参看如下资料：

The set of atmospheric conditions prevailing at a particular time and place (whereas climate describes average conditions over a much longer term). It is the combination, experienced locally, of heat or cold, wind or calm, clear skies or cloudiness, high or low pressure, and the electrical state of the atmosphere. (*Oxford World Encyclopedia*, 1998)

weather events 可以直接译为"天气事件"。

13 【表意清晰】原译"由于天候越来越反复无常而进一步恶化，包括干旱、洪水和风暴"，其中"包括"距离"天候"太远，改译换了一种方式来表达。

14 【查英文释义】malnutrition 译为"营养"显然是失误。Malnutrition refers to faulty nutrition due to inadequate or unbalanced intake of nutrients or their impaired assimilation or utilization (merriam-webster.com)，即营养不良。

▷ 原文

2. Under these circumstances, water resources management in *river basins*[1] must be significantly more efficient in order to *ensure continued adequate water availability and environmental sustainability*[2] for present and future needs. This is certainly the most complex challenge for water professionals and managers of this century. *It is true that a great deal of effort has gone into the development of a set of indicators and policies to meet the water resource requirements of human beings and societies, but more work is still required on steps to be taken towards better water management*[3]. Furthermore, water problems extend across all dimensions from local to global, with the *adequacy of governance*[4] being one of the major imponderables.

▷ 原译

2. 在这些情况下，河流流域的水资源管理必须显著提高效率，以确保能够继续获得充足的水资源和环境的可持续性，满足当前和今后的需要。这当然是21世纪水资源专业人员和管理者最复杂的挑战。为了满足人类和社会对水资源的需求，人们确实采取了诸多努力，开发一套指标和政策；但仍须更加努力采取步骤，向更好的水资源管理迈进。此外，水问题跨越了从地方到全球的各个方面，治理的充分程度成为难以预测的主要因素之一。

▷ 改译

2. 在这些情况下，江河流域的水资源管理必须显著提高效率，以保证人类继续获得充足的水资源，确保环境的可持续性，满足当前和今后的需要。这当然是21世纪水资源专业人员和管理者最复杂的挑战。诚然，人们已经采取了诸多努力来拟定一套水资源管理的指标和政策，以满足人类和社会对水资源的需求；但仍须努力采取更多措施，向更好的水资源管理迈进。此外，水资源问题跨越了从地方到全球的各个方面，水资源管理是否得当，成为一个主要的不可预测因素。

★ 解 析

1 【适度灵活】上文用了 watershed，此处用 river basin，意思相同。A river basin (used interchangeably with drainage basin) is any area of land where precipitation collects and drains off into a common outlet, such as into a river, bay, or other body of water. (Wikipedia: river basin) 原译"河流流域"意思没有错，但因为有两个"流"字，不够优雅。river 既可以指"河"，也可以指"江"，不如改为"江河流域"。

2 【语言简洁】原译可能被误读为"获得……可持续性"，因此把句子断开，ensure 翻译两次（"保证"和"确保"，避免重复）。

3 【保持原文信息的出现次序】原译意思没有错，语言也没什么问题。改译主要是不想对原文的信息顺序作太多调整。能顺着翻译下来，尽量顺着翻译。因为改变信息出现的次序，可能造成重点发生变化。"采取步骤"和"采取措施"，意思也没有实质区别。每个人的语感会有所不同。

4 【避免汉语西化】adequacy of governance 译为"治理的充分程度"，比较西化。英语的很多抽象名词进入汉语，以"性""度""化"等形式表现出来，比如 accessibility（可及性）、availability（可得性）、affordability（可负担性），虽然听起来不太顺耳，但很多情况下绕不过去，只能听任大家使用，也算是对汉语表达方式的丰富。此处可以绕过去，不妨改为更加明白的汉语"水资源管理是否得当"。至于 governance，这些年大家都翻译为"治理"，如 corporate governance（企业治理）、social governance（社会治理），但与水资源搭配使用，还是"管理"比较通顺。

▶ **原文**

6. Against this background, *water resource challenges to attain water security*[1] are taking on a global dimension among governments, due to *an increase in water scarcity and its*[2] associated effects on people, energy, food and ecosystems. *When*[3] inadequate in quantity and quality, water can have a negative impact on poverty alleviation and economic recovery, resulting in poor health and low productivity, *food insecurity*[4], and constrained economic development. Even though the total amount of global water is sufficient to cover average global and annual water needs, *regional and temporal variations in the availability of water are causing serious challenges for many people living in severely water-stressed areas*[5]. Alongside the natural factors affecting water resources, human activities have become the primary drivers of the pressures on our planet's water resource systems. *Human development*[6] and economic growth *tripled*[7] the world's population in the twentieth century, thereby increasing pressures on *local and regional*[8] water supplies and *undermining the adequacy of water and sanitation developments*[9]. These pressures are, *in turn, affected by a range of factors such as technological growth, institutional*[10] and financial conditions and global change.

✍ **原译**

6. 在此背景下，由于缺水加大，对人口、能源、粮食和生态系统的相关影响增大，水资源对获得供水保障构成的挑战正成为一个各国政府都要面对的全球性问题。当水的数量和质量不足时，会对减贫和经济复苏造成负面影响，导致健康不佳

✍ **改译**

6. 在此背景下，由于水资源日益稀缺，加上由此对人口、能源、粮食和生态系统造成的影响，实现水安全面临的水资源挑战正成为各国政府都要面对的全球性问题。水的数量和质量问题，会对减贫和经济复苏造成负面影响，导致健康状况恶

原译

和生产率低下、粮食不安全及经济发展受到限制。即便全球水的总量足以满足全球和每年的平均水需求量，水资源在地区间和时间上的差异正在给生活在用水有严重压力的地区的许多人口构成严峻挑战。除影响水资源的自然因素外，人类活动已成为对地球水资源系统造成压力的主要原因。人类发展和经济增长使世界人口在20世纪增长了两倍，因而加大了当地和区域供水的压力，削弱了水和卫生设施的发展。这些压力又受到诸如技术增长、制度及金融条件和全球变化等因素的影响。

改译

化、生产率下降、粮食短缺，制约经济发展。即便全球水的总量足以满足全球和每年的平均水需求量，但水资源的时空分布差异正在给严重缺水地区的许多人带来严峻挑战。除了自然因素给水资源带来的影响，人类活动已成为地球水资源系统遭受压力的主要原因。人的发展和经济增长使世界人口在20世纪增长了两倍，因而加大了地方和区域供水压力，导致水和卫生设施捉襟见肘。这些压力又受到诸如技术进步、体制和经济状况以及全球形势变化等因素的影响。

解 析

1. 【语言简洁】"水资源对获得供水保障构成的挑战"前置定语略显冗长，可以说"水资源对实现水安全的挑战""水资源对供水保障带来的挑战""在保障供水方面水资源构成的挑战"或"实现水安全面临的水资源挑战"。

2. 【注意搭配】an increase in water scarcity 译为"缺水加大"，搭配不当。可以说"缺水状况日益严重""水资源日益稀缺""供水缺口日益增大"；代词 its 要翻译出来，否则关系不清楚。

3. 【适度灵活】when 不一定翻译为"当……时"，通常可以把"当"字省略。

4. 【补充知识】关于 food security，见如下资料：

Food security is a condition related to the availability of food supply to a group of people such as ethnicities, racial, cultural and religious groups as well as individuals' access to it...Food insecurity, on the other hand, is a situation of "limited or uncertain availability of nutritionally adequate and safe foods or limited or uncertain ability to acquire acceptable foods in socially acceptable ways", according to the United States Department of Agriculture (USDA). (ers.usda.gov)

"粮食不安全"是相对于"粮食安全"而言，意思没有错，但不太符合中文习惯；更通俗的说法是"粮食短缺"。

一个相关概念是 food safety（食品安全），是指食品里面是否掺假（苏丹红、三聚氰胺等），给健康带来威胁。

5　【语言简洁：少用"的"字】这句话的主要问题是太长。特别是译文中出现两个带"的"的定语。改译把"地区间和时间上的差异"浓缩为"时空分布差异"，"用水有严重压力的地区"简化为"严重缺水地区"，化解了这个问题。句子中的"的"字超过两个时，就要想办法减少"的"字的使用。

6　【补充知识】human development 是指人的身心状态的改善，比如预期寿命、教育水平、人均收入，相对于经济发展而言。联合国开发计划署（UNDP）每年出一份报告，叫作 Human Development Report，按照 Human Development Index（HDI，人类发展指数，包含预期寿命、教育、人均收入三方面的指标）给各个国家排名，2018 年，中国排名第 86 位。

经济发展不一定带来人的发展。如果经济发展成果被少数人占有或者用于发展军事，就不会带来全体国民的发展。所以，Human Development Report 应该翻译为"人的发展报告"，但可惜从一开始就翻译为"人类发展报告"，HDI 翻译为"人类发展指数"，现在已无法修改。当初这样翻译，可能是译者并不真正明白这个概念，只是从文雅的角度来看，标题中使用"人的"不如"人类"。殊不知"人类"是相对于"兽类"来说的，并非报告强调的重点。不过，报告名称不能改不代表正文不可以改。所以，此处"人类发展"改为"人的发展"。

7　【理解文字背后的含义】triple 是"成为原来的三倍"，汉语中表达为"增长了两倍"，原译正确。人的发展和经济发展会带来人口增长。比如，婴儿死亡率降低，人口当然会增长；经济发展，粮食供应充足，人口当然会增长。这句话的翻译说明，尽管我们有时能够翻译出来，但不一定明白背后的含义。译者需要随时随地提高自己的知识水平和理解能力。

8　【按相对意思确定译法】local 和 regional 在此处构成对比，前者指较小的地方，后者指较大的地方，可以分别译为"地方"和"区域"。如果 local 和"外地"构成对比，如 local residents 和 migrants 相对时，local 可以译为"当地"（站在"外地"看"当地"）或"本地"（站在"本地"看"外地"）。一个词不容易翻译的时候，找到该词的对立面，往往有助于确定词义和译法。

9　【表意清晰】undermine 的本义是（像挖矿一样）"在……下面挖"，引申为"破坏……的根基""挖墙脚""削弱"。所以，可以视情况翻译为"削弱""破坏"。但 undermining the adequacy of water and sanitation developments 翻译为"削弱了水和卫生设施的发展"可能不够准确。人多了，卫生设施跟不上，是本句话要表达的意思。改译为"导致水和卫生设施捉襟见肘"可能会体现这个意思。

10　【结合上文理解 in turn】之所以用 in turn（"依次"），需要和上文结合起来看。上文说经济发展带来人口增长，给供水带来压力；这一句说供水压力又受到经济状况的影响。technological growth 的说法不常见（中文"技术增长"也不常见）。按上下文理解，应为

"技术进步"的意思。

【根据语境确定译法】institutional 有多个意思，根据情况翻译为"制度""机构"，有时很难区分。此处的 institutional conditions 翻译为"机构条件"或"制度条件"似乎都不易理解。改为"体制状况"意思似乎明确一些。

▷ 原文

7. In the next 50 years, the world's population is expected to increase by approximately 30 percent, with most of the population expansion concentrated in urban areas. *More than 60 percent of the world's population growth between 2008 and 2100 will be in sub-Saharan Africa, comprising 32 percent and South Asia by 30 percent*[1]. Together, these regions are expected to account for half of the world's population in 2100. *These factors call for*[2] more innovative ways of managing water resources, *especially where the consideration of socio-economic systems have key importance for the development of adaptive and sustainable water management strategies to reduce human and ecological vulnerability*[3]. Furthermore, worldwide there are 276 international river basins—23 percent in Africa, 22 percent in Asia, 25 percent in Europe, 17 percent in North America and 13 percent in South America. *Overall, 148 countries have territories that include at least one shared basin*[4].

✐ 原译

7. 今后50年，世界人口预计将增长约30%，其中大部分人口增长集中在城市地区。2008至2100年间，超过60%的世界人口增长将发生在撒哈拉以南非洲和南亚，两者分别占32%和30%。2100年，这两个地区的人口总和预计将占到世界人口的一半。这些因素要求采取更加创新的方式管理水资源；在社会经济体系的考量对提出适应性和可持续的水管理战略以降低人类和生态脆弱性至关重要的领域，更是如此。此外，全世界有276个国际江河流域，23%在非洲，22%在亚洲，25%在欧洲，17%在北美洲，13%在南美洲。总体来看，148个国家的领土与别国至少共享一个流域。

✐ 改译

7. 未来50年，世界人口预计增长约30%，大部分增长将集中在城市地区。2008至2100年间，世界人口增长的60%以上将发生在撒哈拉以南非洲和南亚，分别占世界人口增长的32%和30%。2100年，这两个地区的人口总和预计将占到世界人口的一半。针对这些因素，需要采取更具有创新性的方式管理水资源，尤其是要考虑社会经济问题，这对制定有适应性和可持续的水管理战略，降低人和生态的脆弱性至关重要。此外，全世界有276个国际江河盆地，其中23%在非洲，22%在亚洲，25%在欧洲，17%在北美洲，13%在南美洲。加起来，共有148个国家的领土至少有一个共享盆地。

⊛ 解　析

1　【根据外部资料澄清歧义】原文表意不明，原译也有歧义：分别占世界人口增长的比例还是分别占 60% 的比例？鉴于 32% 加 30% 接近 60%，可能是后者，但不敢确信。经查证，International Hydrological Programme (LHP) 的报告里原句是："More than 60% of the world's population growth between 2008 and 2100 will be in sub-Saharan Africa (32%) and South Asia (30%)."。根据该资料，改译予以明确。

2　【用人作主语】将 these factors call for 译为"这些因素要求采取"，不太符合汉语表达。一般汉语中发出要求动作的是人，很少用物作为主语。改译中"需要"隐含的主语是"我们"。

3　【根据外部资料澄清含义】原文表意不明，造成译文不通顺。根据原文尾注，这句话出自 International Hydrological Programme VIII, 2014—2021 (2012), Water Security: Responses to Local, Regional and Global Challenges，但却无法在其中找到这处引用。搜索 socio-economic systems 和 water management，看到资料：

Water Resources Management and Socio-Economic Issues

The consideration of socio-economic issues in water resources management is one of the most important prerequisites for sustainable water use and to provide answers to water policy questions (McKinney et al., 1999). Social harmony and economic efficiency are the fundamental socio-economic targets at local, national and international levels.

说不定这就是报告中那句话的最原始出处，但报告中没有标明。资料中的意思是清楚的，即水的管理要考虑社会经济问题。什么是社会经济问题？社会和谐和经济效率。笔者据此修改了译文，为了简明易懂，还对句子结构作了调整。

4　【避免歧义】"与别国至少共享一个流域"有歧义，隐含着"通常与别国共享多个江河流域"。但实际意思是，有些国家虽然没有独占的江河，但至少有一条与他国共享的江河。改为"至少有一个共享盆地"可能消除这个歧义。(river) basin 可以翻译为"江河流域"或"江河盆地"。

▶原文

8. Although these challenges are global, no institution or country can face the challenges alone. International scientific cooperation is needed to bring all *players*[1] together, such as research institutions, universities, national authorities, UN agencies, non-governmental organizations and national or international associations. *The gap between science and society is profound*[2], and there is a need to scale up international collaboration on scientific research and international cooperation *to provide solutions and transformations towards water security*[3]. The great challenge for the hydrological community is to jointly identify appropriate and timely adaptation measures in a continuously changing environment.

✍原译

8. 这些挑战是全球性的，没有任何一个机构或国家可以单独面对这些挑战。需要进行国际科学合作把所有角色汇集起来，如研究机构、大学、国家机构、联合国机构、非政府组织和国家或国际协会。科学与社会间的差距巨大，需要加快国际合作和科学研究方面的国际协作，提供以实现水安全为目标的解决方案和转化。水文界的巨大挑战是如何在一个持续变化的环境中携手找到合适且及时的适应措施。

✍改译

8. 这些挑战是全球性的，没有任何一个机构或国家可以单独面对这些挑战。需要通过国际科研合作，让研究机构、大学、各国政府、联合国机构、非政府组织和国家或国际协会等所有行为主体携起手来。科学研究与社会脱节严重，需要扩大国际联合科研与国际合作，以保障供水为目标，提供解决方案和转型措施。水文界的巨大挑战是，在一个持续变化的环境中共同及时确定适当的适应措施。

★解 析

1 【根据语境确定译法】player 有多种含义，在此语境中应取以下词义：a person or body that is involved and influential in an area or activity (en.oxforddictionaries.com)，可以翻译为"行为主体"。原译将"研究机构、大学、国家机构、联合国机构、非政府组织"等概括为"角色"有些突兀，因为前面没有说明唱的哪出戏。

2 【理解文字背后的含义】"科学与社会间的差距巨大"，虽然翻译出来了，但到底是什么意思，恐怕译者也不清楚。是说科技进步还不能满足社会需要吗？在谷歌里搜索这句话，很容易找到答案：

The chasm between science and society is wide and deep…

We speculate that scientists distance themselves from society in four ways, sometimes inadvertently, sometimes intentionally. First, they tend to pursue a research agenda they are passionate about, often without thinking about how the energy devoted to a particular project serves society. Second, most scientists regard their job as finished when they report their results in a specialized research journal, adding a notch to their publication count. Third, scientists counsel that advocating for a particular societal position compromises their scientific credibility, so much so that the general credo is: "If you want to succeed as a hard scientist doing original research, you do have to be a little careful about public communications," as climate scientist James Hansen put it. And finally, many scientists feel that dealing with societal issues is some other profession's problem, something that requires too much time and for which they have little support or expertise. (blogs.nature.com)

所以，改译为"科学研究和社会脱节严重"。

3 【在理解的基础上翻译】原译"提供以实现水安全为目标的解决方案和转化"，主要问题是不知道转化什么。改用"转变"一词也行不通。transform 的字面意思其实是"转型"（form 是"型"），既然 solutions and transformations 是并列结构，都是 provide 的宾语，而 solutions 翻译为"解决方案"，即把抽象的"解决"（solution）变为具体的"解决方案"（solutions），不妨也把抽象的 transformation（单数）变为具体的"转型措施（transformations）"。改译为"转型措施"可以涵盖任何实现水安全的措施。

附录1　联合国系统（英文）

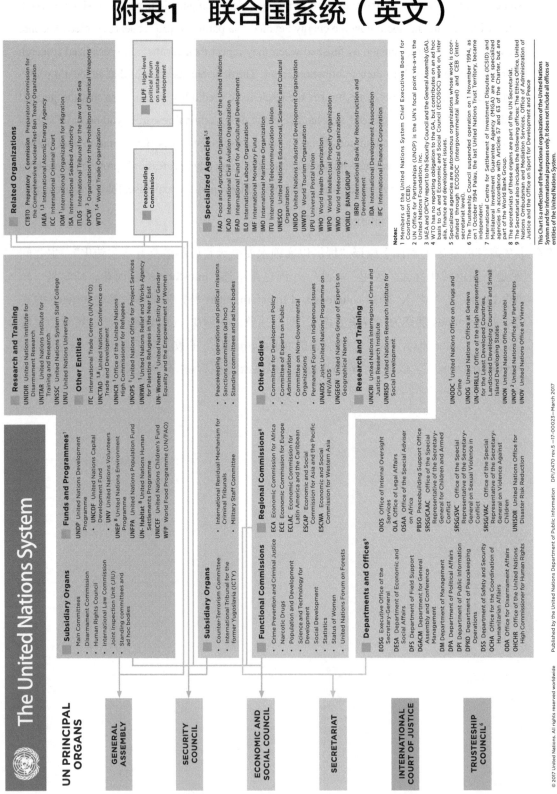

Published by the United Nations Department of Public Information   DPI/2470 rev.5 —17-00023—March 2017

附录2　联合国系统（中文）

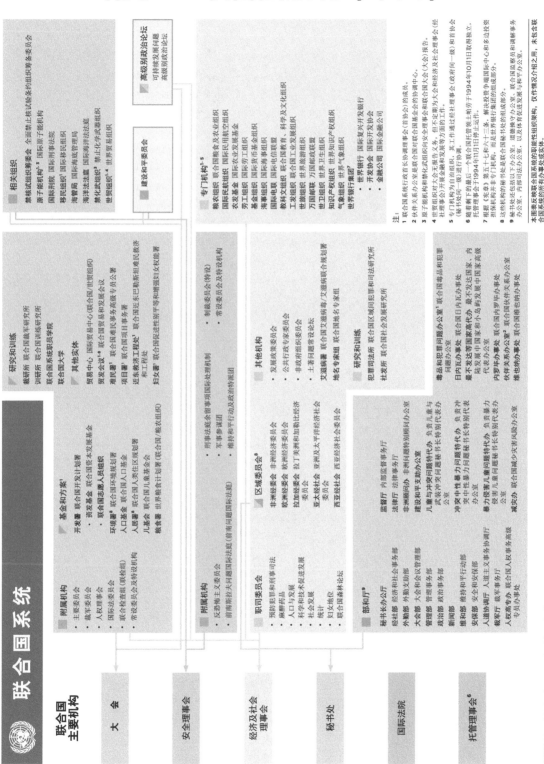